Praise for Walking the Hill

Walking The Hill: The Art of Accidental Transformation captures the value of the heart and spirit of a man-to-man relationship based on the strength, courage, truth and commitment to go the distance and dive deep. A must-read for the evolving man and will be a gift of strength and deeper presence to his woman. I highly recommend you read this book.

—John Gray, PhD, *New York Times* Bestselling Author,
Men Are from Mars, Women Are from Venus

----------o----------

Walking The Hill is for every man who is open to making the next evolutionary shift in masculinity: from human *doing* to human *being*.

The authors' choice of three facilitators—nature, exercise, and one-on-one intentional conversations with another man about the impact of formative feelings on life's decisions—is an optimal formula toward that evolutionary shift. I speak from experience as John Gray (Mars/Venus) and I have similarly taken hundreds of walks among the hills and streams of Mill Valley.

—Warren Farrell, Ph.D., Internationally Bestselling Author,
The Boy Crisis and *The Myth of Male Power*

----------o----------

Walking The Hill is a masterpiece of men's work. The seven years of walks that Gary and Mark cover in words live in the reader as experience, reminiscence, knowledge, wisdom, and an invitation for the reader to dig deep within himself for meaning.

This book is fantastic. I highly recommend it to men and women both. Its powerful insights are woven and interwoven with life and mystery and what is needed in all of us for mature love to flourish.

—Michael Gurian, *New York Times* bestselling author of *The Wonder of Boys* and *What Could He Be Thinking?*

----------o----------

Walking The Hill

Envy. Having a mountain to climb and a brother to climb it with.

Challenge. Pick a man. Pick a mountain. Climb together. Repeat.

Fear. Go towards what scares you – mountains and men are our training ground.

Love. Being acknowledged, witnessed, and lifted up by a brother – no fairy tales or happily ever-afters here.

Freedom. Brothers and mountains are waiting for you – unchain yourself from whatever is holding you back.

Legacy. Write about it.

—Dr. Robert Glover, Author of *No More Mr. Nice Guy: A Proven Plan for Getting What You Want in Love, Sex, and Life*

WALKING THE HILL

Walking The Hill
The Art of Accidental Transformation

by

Gary H. Plep, LCSW

and

Mark Yoslow, PhD

Foreword by Michael Gurian

Walking The Hill: The Art of Accidental Transformation
Copyright 2022 Gary Hal Plep, LCSW and Mark Yoslow, PhD

All rights reserved. No part of this publication may be reproduced, stored in a retrieval system, or transmitted in any form or by any means, electronic, mechanical, photocopying, recording, scanning, or otherwise, except as permitted under Section 107 or 108 of the 1976 United States Copyright Act, without the prior written permission of the publisher.

The photographs in this book are the property of Gary H. Plep and are not to be reproduced in any form without permission. Contact Gary at Transformation@WalkingTheHill.com to inquire about using or acquiring his work.

Gary and Mark are available for speaking engagements. To arrange an appearance please contact Mark at: Transformation@WalkingTheHill.com.

Photography by Gary Hal Plep
Art Direction by Mark Yoslow
Book Design by Russel Davis, Gray Dog Press

Softcover ISBN: 978-0-578-32085-4
eBook ISBN: 979-8-218-01349-3

Printed in the United States of America

It's hard to feel whole when part of you lives in another country, and has been stuck there for years.

Gary Hal Plep, LCSW
Major (CA), 129th California State Guard Support Group, Retired
A1C, USAF, 14th Air Commando Wing, Nha Trang AB RVN, HD

We suffer to be free,
and freedom transforms suffering to meaning.

Mark Yoslow, PhD

Foreword

Eleven years ago, in June of 2009, Gary and Mark organized a long weekend meeting at my property in Washington state. It was for leaders in the men's movement who were also writers and directors of programs that provide rite of passage to males. Leaders came from the United States and Canada to break bread, hike, and talk about what was next on the horizon of the men's movement. During our days together, Gary and Mark pulled me aside to discuss a book they were thinking about writing. They asked if I'd take a look at it when it was done, and I told them I would be honored to do so.

Fast forward to now. I am so glad they showed me the final product, *Walking the Hill: The Art of Accidental Transformation,* and I am honored to write this Foreword. *Walking the Hill* is a masterpiece of men's work. I came away from reading this book imagining Augustine and Aquinas as contemporaries who walked up a mountain together talking about life, time, love, and God. The seven years of walks that Gary and Mark cover live in the reader as experience, reminiscence, knowledge, and an invitation to dig deep into the self for meaning. Rather than focusing on theory, this book's bedrock is the search for a life so well lived it can be reflected back and forth in the depth of male friendship.

This is a rare concept and a rare book that combines the individual expressions of its authors with a photographic account of their journey along the path they walked together for years. The images permit us the rare gift of making the walk with them as the book peels back layers of manhood in search of the essence of a man.

I suggest reading this powerful book in short tranches—pondering what is said, applying its meaning, then moving on to the next "walk." I highly recommend *Walking the Hill* to men and women both. Its powerful insights are woven and interwoven with life and mystery and what is needed in all of us for mature love to flourish.

— Michael Gurian, New York Times best-selling author of
The Wonder of Boys and *The Invisible Presence*
December 2020

Contents

Introduction xi

The Road of Unrelenting Ascent 1
The Gate of Unknowing 19
The Leafy Path of Gentleness and Compassion 63
The Respite 85
The Quick Rise of Gentle Persuasion 93
The Field of Sage 101
The Hill of Commitment 111
The Hill of Cruelty 133
The Hill of Awareness 151
The Tree of Truth 161
The Tree of Healing 177
The Open Path 197

Epilogue 243
Endnote: The Gift (Gary) 255
Acknowledgments 259
References 263
About the Authors 270

Introduction

The following is a collection of thoughts and ideas that came to us while walking The Hill. We have put them together around particular topics that have come to us over seven years of twice-weekly and often thrice-weekly seven-mile walks above our little Silicon Valley town of Los Gatos, California. Here at the foot of the Santa Cruz Mountains we refer to the mountains collectively as "up the hill" or "on the hill." The Hill is one of these mountains.

The Hill is our secret place, often frequented by fox, coyote, deer, hawk, raccoon, bobcat, rabbit, possum, vulture, rattle snake, and mountain lion, our neighbors who leave their tracks, scat, and feathers for us to find. The way up has been carved into the face of The Hill by a raw and rutted fire road that is unrelenting in its steep elevation, with short rests that are almost flat and provide expanses and experiences of stunning, natural beauty in between the challenging ascents. The Hill tests us and always offers challenges, even though we have climbed it about eight hundred times, in every season, in scorching sun at 115°, dense fog, driving rain, freezing wind, in dust and mud. We can say that The Hill is good to us, cruel to us, rewards us, and opens our vision in both eye and spirit. We can also say that the distance we have walked is the equivalent of going from Los Gatos to New York City to Chicago on foot. The Hill lives within us.

We organized years of notes and errant thoughts and a lot of journaling by naming sections of the trail we walked. That is the table of contents we now have. It seems that sections of the trail, their beauty, or difficulty, or change with the seasons, dictated what we talked about or thought about when we arrived at that part of the walk. And Walking The Hill is in large part the like the sections of the trail. We were advised to try and keep the

chapters about the same length. That didn't feel right. The process of our experience on The Hill wasn't nice and neat and even, nor was the long-term effect of our journey. This was another truth we did not want to give up for the sake of appearances. In our experience transformation isn't nice and neat and even.

To help readers know who is speaking along the way we have placed our names in parentheses after section titles, so you will see (Gary) or (Mark) as you journey up or down The Hill with us. Our voices are different, so the writing from one section to another is different. We were given advice about this, that we should edit our work so that everything sounds the same. Somehow we felt that was not as honest as we want to be. When you speak from your heart you want your voice to ring true.

Also you will find brief sections in *italics* and these are meant for you, our readers, as suggestions and support for your spiritual development as men and women in the world. When you are moved to act on them, we suggest keeping a journal, and start each entry with the date. We keep journals for many parts of our lives, especially business and travel, and rarely for developmental and spiritual experience. It helps to keep track so you can see where you have been, where you are now, and where you are going.

For us these walks have offered a safe place, and moments of grief, inspiration, revelation, camaraderie, painful honesty, and wonder. It has been an amazing catharsis for us and we hope something will be stirred up for you. Be warned that we are sensitive sorts, so be prepared for emotions and feelings that we have often held back in the false belief they would heal on their own. The walk up The Hill has stirred up more than dust, more than a simple memory or two. Judge if you will, but also, ask yourself what have you not revealed, not to others, but to yourself? There is a whole other world available on The Hill. The physical challenge is a rite of passage that is answered by opening the heart.

The Hill (Gary)

The Hill is a place I discovered about eight years ago. Someone told me about a trail close to my home that came off a private road. I decided to explore the area and found a long, winding, uphill, blacktop mountain road that eventually came to a gated unpaved fire road with warning signs about fire truck access and mountain lions that qualified it as a trailhead.

It was pleasant to arrive at this beautiful, slightly inclined trail that seemed to lead into the trees and became level. Because it was a fire road, I could not park my truck at the trailhead, so I drove down the road to the nearest place I could legally park and walked back up the mile of very steep, winding, blacktop road from there.

The first time I introduced Mark to The Hill we walked up the blacktop to the trailhead and he asked, "So this is where the hike STARTS? You gotta be kidding!" It took only several hikes for him to adapt to the stress of the approach to the trailhead and to the challenging and constant incline of The Hill, but he had a background for that, as you'll see.

My fantasy when I first discovered The Hill was that the trail remained level after the slight incline from the trailhead, and just followed the curve of the mountain. That was a wrong assumption. It wasn't long before it started uphill again, and went on and on and up and up. I kicked myself a little for living in Los Gatos for the last twenty-six years without knowing the trail even existed. However, more importantly, I had found my sanctuary

in the mountains, complete with awesome views of the whole Bay Area. I could see south to Monterey and north to San Francisco, and the trail provided an incredible workout to boot, especially if I put some weights in my pack. I saw no one, and I had a large piece of Nature to myself. This was somewhat like the experience I had growing up in the little town of Coos Bay, Oregon, where my buddies and I would hike the logging roads. It was a blissful feeling, and a great pleasure to know I could be so far removed from the world I lived and worked in, and yet so close to my home. I should mention that I have never hiked to the end of the trail for a purpose you can only imagine.

Thus we begin the trail for this story.

The Hill (Mark)

I sometimes think to myself that we are not much more than two men who walked a lot, up and down the same mountain for years, and just kept on doing it because we liked it. I'm not sure when it became clear that we were searching for something, and that The Hill became the physical means of following a spiritual path. I can say that The Hill gave Gary and me a higher form of friendship and bonding than I had ever known. The hunger for that sense of being connected to another life and of having a shared vision of what it means to be a good man in the world is not an experience that is easy for me to describe. It is in the sharing of that vision that wisdom is defined, and I've come to believe that wisdom, especially spiritual wisdom, is the greatest gift we leave behind when we are gone. Our writing together is a step toward preserving that wisdom. Perhaps it will be of use to you.

Spiritual awakening is a challenging process for a man who feels isolated and inferior, which describes the plight of so many men because there is so much forgiveness of self that must be done just to get on the path to being awake, much less walking that path with integrity. It is not easily done alone or with a companion on the journey, but having another person who is willing to take on this challenge brings the added dimension of relationship to the process. At least, this has been my experience. Gary is the friend, the older brother, the heart-full teacher, at times the father I never had

in my youth. I have him now, and we are together in this work, and his encouragement never stops. Sometimes I think I'm able to encourage him as well.

Gary has come home to himself after being at a loss for the feeling of coming home, a loss that lasted four decades after Vietnam. I have come home after four decades of holding myself back from the risk of living within my art, the hidden cost of an abusive childhood, a loss that haunted me until I reopened the place in my heart where my love of writing was born.

The Hill has given us a second chance at the path we have permitted to become overgrown. Time after time we discovered that the path is there, beneath the bramble, which, when pulled aside, reveals the stones that lead us on, two elders who trudge this path that is unrelenting in its ascent, seeking the light within.

We are finally home.

Walking The Hill

Chapter 1

The Road of Unrelenting Ascent

How to Start a Spiritual Journey if You're Stupid (Mark)

I've learned to appreciate that moment when two men find themselves laughing their butts off in the midst of a physical challenge that is so hard that it could give either of them a heart attack and kill their ass. And in that moment the laughter makes it harder to resist the inner growth that comes from very challenging experience. The laughter opens us up like a can of tuna.

What spiritual experience comes down to is the process of taking a step beyond what we are right now. What gets in the way of that growth, in our experience at least, is that discouraging internal voice that says "No" and "You Can't" and "You Never Will."

It is really easy to resist the idea that we actually know everything we need to know in this moment to make spiritual progress. It is really tough to access that knowledge if we believe we can't do it. Resistance makes us ignorant.

Gary and I have found that the knowledge of the ancients makes sense if we accept our ignorance and enter beginner's mind. It is a precursor to deep learning. A great block to beginner's mind is to despise the mistakes we make in life, and use them as proof that we cannot learn from them. Our mistakes are the milestones that tell us about what is most important to us. Forgiving our mistakes seems to be the gift offered by the unrelenting ascent of The Hill. If I can't forgive myself for not being in perfect physical condition then getting to the top of The Hill is going to be more painful than it needs to be.

Inner Life (Gary)

I read in one of my favorite books a passage that pretty much defines me not as a therapist who is a human being, but a human being who happens

Walking The Hill

to be a therapist. "Patients are often disappointed to learn that I too wander unredeemed, that I am no better off than they are. Eventually, they may realize comfort implied in my turning out to be just another struggling human being" (Kopp, 1972, pp. 8–9). I, too, have an inner life, a history that defines me as Gary, and it is from this ground that the journey here begins.

Find Something of Greater Value (Mark)

I learned the following from Gary, and we live it in our men's group. It takes an important event to pull men together to form a community. Men need to have a sense of organization, a time in the week that becomes sacred. It needs to be at a time that is not easy to fulfill, and that is the test. Witnessing the willingness to be tested and succeed has deep meaning for a group of men. There is a longing for this experience. Once we find it we want to control it in some way. The secret knowledge that letting go of control is the fastest route to connection is not something we learn early in life. Men want to hold on to control, and the opportunity for connection slips through their fingers as sand in an hourglass. The key is what remains, and that is a choice: to be full of regret or to find something of greater value—to live life in such a way that we have no regrets.

Community (Gary)

I organized a car pool to attend the Sterling Men's Weekend in April 1983. Mark Ruskell, Barry Hayes, and I drove in my '76 VW camper to Berkeley to do this weekend together, never having known each other before. It had been the suggestion of my ex-wife and my present wife to do this weekend. Thank you, Susan and Sue. We shared the weekend experience—which was very intense and I highly recommend it for men—and a room for a few hours of sleep. Obviously it was a bonding experience, as we became lifelong friends. We then spent another three months on a team of men the organizers put together. There were twelve of us, and we were from all over the Bay Area.

Commitment (Gary)

This was to be a "commitment." We needed to pick a time and day to meet once a week, and commit to it. Wednesdays at 4:30 a.m. in Los Gatos was the only day and time that worked for everyone. That was fortunate for six of us: Mark Ruskell, Barry Hayes, Art Basham, Rick Gordon, Ed de Deo, and me, who lived in Los Gatos. Meeting at 4:30 a.m. every Wednesday wasn't easy, but it was well worth it because of the energy it generated. It was damn exciting to witness that kind of commitment from twelve men. Everyone made it happen for three months. After that we were down to the six of us. We met every week for three years at one man's home. I think that ended when we (or I) pissed off someone's wife. I was never sure. It had been a great experience, and I was sad. I subsequently talked to Mark and Barry about it. Mark and I continued to meet for lunch on occasion, and eventually the two of us, at my suggestion, recruited a new team. There were six of us again, although with some new men: Larry Atwell, Patrick Purcell, and Mike Wilson, all marriage and family therapists. They were also men who had done the Sterling Men's Weekend at various times. Mike and I had worked together as counselors in juvenile hall and both of us had become Probation Officers. I went into juvenile probation and Mike chose adult probation. We also became psychotherapists. Barry rejoined us and we added Walt Jesson, another psychologist. We met in Vasona Park at lunchtime for years.

You are probably thinking, "What a heady bunch, all in the fields of medicine and mental health." I assure you that since all of us had done the Sterling Men's Weekend we were far from heady. We were always willing to challenge one another, sometimes compassionately and sometimes not so much. It was a bonded group where it was safe to share and it was honest in its support. A rare and valued entity.

I find that having such a circle of men enriches life beyond measure. I have had some trying moments and I think all of us have had them. It's invaluable to have brothers who trust one another and provide a safe place to express and witness. No booze, BS, or sports stories required. I feel it's like an ancient sacred circle where men sat around the fire after a hunt. There is risk and reward. I challenge men to create such a circle as it has and continues to be an essential *ingredient in my life for growth and survival—survival at a much higher level than doing it alone. I tried doing it alone. Remember the song lyrics "I am a rock, I am an island" (Simon and Garfunkel, 1966)? "Universal Soldier" (Buffy Sainte-Marie, 1964) was also such a song. When I was a kid I thought that was heroic. BS. Doing it alone is not heroic, it sucks.*

If you read this you know it's true. It may feel safer but this book doesn't support doing life safely. If you want safe, read Mother Goose or something. Watching sports and drinking beer with a group of men is still doing it alone and you know it.

History Hurts (Gary)

Now I feel sad. There is so much history that I can't bring back; I have the feeling of wanting to do something about it. It just escapes from my brain and then comes back to revisit. Part of me wants to control it, to make it different. I want another chance to relive it. There are no do-overs for some things. I wish I could have had a better understanding about that in my youth. I was eager to learn, even the hard way. I guess the message to keep is to live each moment to its max. One of my values I propound is to live life in such a way that I have no regrets. No regrets as I always say.

As a man gets older he spends more time looking back than looking forward. We all have regrets but if you have a circle of men to run major life decisions by and are forthcoming, and honest about your decision-making, you'll have fewer regrets. Especially if you have men in your life who will challenge you if they feel you are off course. I don't recommend "friends" that won't challenge you when it's obvious that you might need a course correction. It especially helps if you have a few elder men in the group who are willing to share their wisdom and unashamedly share their mistakes. Find a group of men you can trust by researching men's organizations. I can certainly recommend you check out the New Warrior Training and the Sterling Men's Weekend and I am sure there are others out there as well. I don't recommend you research them on the web, as a few scared men have written adversely and also broken confidentiality and shared the content of these weekends, which really hinders the magic of what happens. Men's work is not women's work. It is neither tidy nor pretty. I am always happy to act as a conduit when I can. Call me.

Imagine a room with 150 to 250 men willing to challenge each other sixteen hours a day for two-plus days. You get down to the truth about almost everything in life. Feelings expressed all out. What an incredible life-changing experience.

A Good Suggestion (Mark)

At Gary's suggestion I did The Sterling Men's Weekend starting on March 12, 2005, during my fourth year in graduate school, just before I started writing my dissertation in the spring. Strict confidentiality regarding the weekend prevents me from describing the experience. I can say that I recommend it for any man who needs to shed constraints around his family history, relationships, friendships, and professional life.

If you research the weekend you will find lots of negative information about Sterling from people who either could not hack it and left, or who know nothing about it and wish that the tactics of insult and accusation will result in drawing more information from the founder or graduates. The weekend was a watershed experience for me. Ignore the fear mongers and naysayers. Do it.

Finding a Consistent Challenge that Has Joy and Risk in It (Gary)

We can spend so much time looking for a way to live by thinking about it. Where does the joy come in? From simple challenges? That's where The Hill comes into the picture. Mark and I walk it two or three times a week, and it is never the same, and it is never easy, because it presents a consistent physical challenge, and reveals so many emotional challenges, and provides a medium for their release.

Without these simple challenges men become stagnant. They live in their heads, and joy escapes them or even feels as if it is a threat. Mark and I have learned that stagnation enjoys itself and feeds on isolation, loneliness, and a lack of new experience.

Challenge yourself in some way on a regular basis and you will experience more aliveness. If you can drag along a witness, that is even better. Find someone who holds you accountable to him and himself to you.

Walking and unwinding up The Hill we go again and again. We don't stop until we hit our marker, the big Live Oak way up on the shoulder of the trail almost level with the mountain's top, and then it's piss and head back down. Even down can be difficult. The earth is dry and the gravel and dust combine to form a surface as slick as ice and leaves little for our shoes to grip. Sometimes we crab-walk sideways to avoid a slide. I have a scar on my left knee from such a slide. I cushioned my fall with the water bottle I held in my right hand. Perhaps it is a metaphor to always have a cushion even when you are coming down.

Looking for ways to challenge ourselves we find a deep sense of satisfaction that is visceral and accelerates the flow of blood throughout the whole body and brain. Exercise and challenge feeds the warrior within us. If you don't have any warrior energy in you go find it. Vitality flows out of exercise and challenge and replicates the world in many ways. It prepares us for when the world tests us. I challenge you to find such a challenge if you don't have one. It is emotionally and physically cathartic and enlivening. I am always pushing men to walk in their spirit, to be a spirited being. That is a gift to yourself and everyone around you. Physical and emotional challenges keep you prepared and alive—walking in your spirit. Do you have a sense of freedom to walk in your spirit, to be the man you want to be?

No Time Off (Mark)

I was with Gary on the hike when he took that bad slip going downhill. Without the water bottle in his hand to break his fall, Gary could have broken his wrist, and very badly injured his knee. I mention this because I watched him pick out blood-soaked shards of rock that were embedded in the skin on his bloody knee from the impact of the fall when we finished our decent to the road where I could legally park my car. It took a while for it to heal.

Do you think we took time off from The Hill during the next few days?

Raising the Bar (Gary)

A word or two on passion is to be shared here. This book could not have been written without feeling. It wasn't a passion to write a book. It was passion for passion's sake, the desire to feel every moment in every cell of the body while being witnessed by Nature and God if you will. Emotions were stilled, stirred, and they welled up over and over and over. The depth of experience of emotion brought laughter, anguish, and quiet contemplation. The whole of the man was evoked in every fiber of the body and every synapse of the brain.

I celebrated the beauty of that experience mixed with our verbal thrashing about as we threw out feelings and thoughts that had never been allowed the full breath of expression. It was a freedom to be totally ignited in fire that brought words by necessity to paper, not to proclaim anything but simply to express an energy that lives in the heart. Ah, what freedom there is in the full truth of expression.

When is the last time you allowed yourself to yell as loud as you can just for the sake of hearing and releasing? It is something I strongly encourage on Vision Quests where nature is your witness and Mother Earth nurtures the nature of who you are at your core. Go out in nature and yell. Somehow it doesn't work in the city. But in nature, it's good for the soul.

It gives me a great sense of pleasure while I am leading Vision Quest to leave my base camp and head down the mountain a short distance as the sun is sinking below the horizon and yell as loud as I can and hear it's slight echo off an opposing mountain in the valley, and then to wait for the yell of a man returning the call from his Vision Quest circle.

The Value of the Witness (Gary)

I believe there is great value in talking out loud to hear one's inner self. To process out loud if you will. But even better is to have someone who will simply hear you, mirror back, or challenge what you have called up while you are pushing or being pushed up The Hill. This is the value of a true friendship that supports feeling from the depths that allows no filter while pushing up The Hill. The Hill is no place for filters.

A man must risk something within himself to discover or even maintain his passion. It is not something that is static. It must remain fluid and never be allowed to stagnate. It only comes from a depth of feeling and a Commitment. This book came only out of that level of engagement. We had to master The Hill again and again, in the ever-changing circumstances of the environment and ourselves.

Many men say they don't know what their passion is, but I am betting they haven't risked feeling enough to find out. We are a nation of thinkers not feelers.

I believe a man having a passion is a necessary life force and is required to lead anything in life. And if you are not leading you are following. If you are following you must be asleep or unconscious. That is the purpose of addictions of any kind, not just to alcohol and drugs. Addictions keep men from feeling from the depth of their hearts. To feel our hearts, to have passion, to be leaders we must seek the next ridge and push ourselves to see what is on the other side.

Passion is an energy that constantly moves and transforms if you are willing to risk. Without risk there is nothing but a void. Most men choose safety and comfort, but it is out of pain and the stretch provided by a challenge that we discover valuable elements of ourselves. Freedom is not achieved without pain.

We are a culture ruled and often paralyzed by shame, so for many, the risk to feel passion is too scary. I understand that, and it is the way most parents controlled their children going back centuries. It is also the way many religions have controlled and cultivated their flock. Read John Bradshaw's *Healing the Shame that Binds You* for that one. The way out of shame for many has been the route of numbing shame through an addiction. That was part of the beauty of our conversations on The Hill—to cut through shame with truth telling. Our walks and conversations ripped us open, exposed raw emotions as we pushed our bodies up The Hill time after time. There lives the sense of freedom.

The ancient practice of shaming children to get them to conform is universal and all of us have been affected by it in some way or another. Note that I am not shaming the generations that have gone before us. They were more in survival mode than present generations. The need to control children existed for their very survival. The very opposite seems to be true now. The generation of permissiveness and entitlement now exists and feels it deserves everything without any challenge. Without taking on challenges in the world and challenges from parents we have a lost generation. Expectations of a free lunch kill the spirit of survival. Again this is why challenging yourself is so vital. Freedom requires you to challenge yourself on a regular basis. Sorry, present generation. You too will learn at some point that there really is no free lunch.

One of the challenges I strongly recommend to men is to commit to a meditation practice (as opposed to a medication practice). Usually it's terribly painful for a man to meditate because he will have to feel and quiet what I call the ego drive (safety drive) of the brain. In the quiet you may find the richness of discovering your deeper truths. Speaking them out loud is a way to hear and edit or modify by hearing a deeper truth and getting feedback from a brother or even a modification from inside yourself as you hear something you know isn't quite right. Practice talking to yourself out loud in private. It's a helpful risk. Try it with a trusted friend. I am sure you will find it revealing and clarifying.

I asked a shaman friend of mine for a practice to heal my grief from Vietnam. She offered me this practice: sit in a meditation position for twenty minutes a day for six months. She also gave me a breathing practice. I had never meditated before. I committed to do exactly that. I sat for twenty minutes a day for six months and learned to meditate. It was incredibly difficult. I started the practice by checking my watch every couple minutes. It was very uncomfortable and I would fidget around for twenty minutes continually checking my watch. I began to do that less and less and the feelings started coming up when I got quiet. I felt grief that I had never allowed. Gradually I relaxed into just being. Long periods of time would go by with my feeling nothing and out of nowhere the gasp would come and I would feel the depth of pain. I finally got so good about just being there that I forgot that there was a large mirror in front of me on the floor. I opened my eyes to see someone sitting in front of me. Scared me, too . . . until I realized it was me. I guess you could say I got quiet enough to see myself.

Accepting Acknowledgement (Gary)

I started groups in my private practice, and that felt good as a therapeutic model, but lacked what I longed for. So I got clear about my vision of a group, and put it out to the community that I wanted to create a group of heart-centered men who were willing to go deep in their personal exploration and growth. I chose the name Men of Fire due to the group's level of passion. Now, eighteen years later I was on the mountain conducting a closing ceremony for what we had created. In the final moments I received a gift from one of the men.

Acknowledgment is a difficult thing for a man to accept. It seems to be more important to ignore our accomplishments for some greater good. In my groups, I have each man acknowledge himself for something he has done during the week. He may also acknowledge others. I have included this as a part of the closing ritual, but today I too ignore my own being for the sake of others. Isn't that what I am supposed to do? It's only recently that I can say "thank you" and let the acknowledgment in.

So, in acknowledgment, I told the men in this circle that they were exceptional men. I told them that I could no longer find appropriate men to fill their places as they left—other than a few short-timers, the group only had twenty-two regulars over the course of eighteen years. I said it again as

I looked around the circle and made eye contact with each man stating that they were exceptional men. Then I was tapped by the man on my left who said I had forgotten someone.

"Who?" I asked.

"You've forgotten yourself. You, too, are an exceptional man."

I tapped myself on my bowed head a couple times with the wood talking stick and acknowledged that I too was an exceptional man. I told them that it had always been important to me to be as invisible as possible. Now today, as I reflect back on this day, and conversations in other groups, I see something I didn't see before. If you don't acknowledge yourself you become invisible. I have liked invisibility because there is less risk of being shamed. Risk acknowledgment of yourself not aggrandizement. It's another form of leadership, providing a humble lesson learned. I acknowledge my leadership and the results I have witnessed. I talk about it as a reward for brutal honesty given to another man out of love: A passion to see men grow and value their gifts.

Risk acknowledging yourself for an action you've taken if it has served a purpose and provides a lesson that others may grow and learn from.

I ask myself sometimes why Men of Fire needed to end. Perhaps Men of Fire fulfilled its mission in the darkness of my barn (garage) but needed to be brought out into the light. We had a truth stick carved for the group that is now used by four men's groups instead of one. Maybe everything does have a purpose over time.

The Trajectory of a Man's Life (Mark)

Today I said to Gary that I am often surprised by how powerful a single moment can be in a man's life, and how it can define the trajectory of his existence.

Wanting to Be in Groups with Men Is a Calling Not Only for the Leader (Gary)

Creating connection among men takes a unique form. It involves finding a meeting place that has some magic in it. It needs to be represented by symbols that define ownership of a circle containing experiences that form over time into a history. One of these symbols has great meaning for me, and it may be the foundation of my work with men.

First off, I knew I was alone in life at the age of four. I had been separated from my mother for months and was living with my aunt and uncle due to my father's affair and the obvious discord it created. Very shortly after my mother and I were reunited I approached her as she was standing in the kitchen with her back to the stove. She was crying. She looked at me and said, "You don't understand your father is dead." The message was very clear. I can't be here for you. You are on your own. There was a distinct void of affection or attention.

Mother encouraged me to roam the block in front of the building. I just remembered in this moment that I didn't want to go outside, that my mother supported me to go outside, play, and make friends. I didn't know how to do that. Her only restriction was that I didn't leave the block.

I wandered around the wood walkways in front of our apartment building not sure of what to do, and then eventually to the sidewalk that surrounded the block. I stood on the corner, and two boys appeared, and one of them said that some other boys were looking for a fight, and it was going to be only us against them. He said we would need our strength, and so he handed me a Three Musketeers candy bar. That was a big deal. A Three Musketeers cost a whole nickel in those days. We waited. No one ever showed up, and I never saw those boys again. That was my first experience of a group. Pretty funny as I look back on it, but there was something magical about the experience that I didn't realize until I started telling my story.

More than that, this experience created a formula for my life. That simple experience was an incredible gift. It gave me a sense of purpose, commitment, the power of belonging and connection. A simple bonding moment at four changed my whole life as I only now realize it has directed most everything I have ever done.

Belonging and connection are essential if men are to do heart-centered work that is focused on personal exploration and growth. An added dimension is that the group easily makes something obsolete: the void that men try to fill with excitement, fantasy, and objects. This void is the space men attempt to fill with toys, such as cars, boats, anything to stave off the feeling of emptiness. The group experience makes that feeling obsolete, fills the void, and can be so powerful and self-sustaining that it can pass through years. Life becomes real, real quick.

The Importance of the Witness in Life and Death (Gary)

A group traces and represents life. It also traces and allows a place for death to have meaning. All of the grace a man carries with him, no matter how difficult his circumstances, becomes a gift for the men who witness his presence and his passing.

Loss (Gary)

The loss of a brother, a tried and true friend, scars a man's heart forever. The loss of a true friend, someone you adventured with and with whom you shared your truth, your joys and sorrows, your longings, and your foolishness, leaves a big hole. A bond broken by death leaves one wanting forever.

Mark Ruskell came to our men's team meeting with some bad news one day. I always remember that day as he sat down at our regular bench in Vasona Park and said with tears in his eyes, "I've got cancer." No one knew how to respond. We just sat there. He had esophageal cancer, and it restricted his eating to the point where this big man became skinny and shaved his head. He started missing meetings because of doctor appointments and lack of energy. He called to say he would not be at the meeting but I had not retrieved the call, it had gone to voice mail. That was a week before he died.

I had gone to see him at home the week before he made that call. He was moving around fine, and we talked some about his options regarding further treatment. He had been watching TV; *JAG* was his favorite show. He had also been reviewing a dive trip with his girlfriend, Jay, when they watched manta rays feed. It was pretty dramatic as he reviewed the video with me. He picked up a large margarita glass he had acquired in Mexico and he made a point to say that he had no regrets about the things he had done and the fun he had in his life. Jay came home and I excused myself and left. That was the last time I saw him alive.

My wife and I went to the hospital when we found out he was there. Jay was with him but he was struggling too much for visitors. We told her to let him know we were there, and we wanted to know what support Jay might need. He died shortly after that. I spoke for our circle at his funeral. I had every man in our circle bring a single red rose to symbolize our love for him. I miss the no bullshit, straight up conversations we used to have. I could always count on Mark to speak "his" truth. I didn't want "the" truth, like my old friend Steve used to say, but "his" truth. An important distinction.

A couple years after Mark's death I began working with a contractor, David Oxley, to replace my back deck. I was basically David's helper. We worked together and joked about the usual guy things. Finally one day after swapping stories about one thing or another he said, "You have to meet Mark. You guys are so similar in attitude I think you would get along well."

Mark Yoslow was working on his PhD in clinical psychology and was looking for some mentoring. We met at lunch with David, and I began to share my feelings and aspirations with him, and he with me. A couple months later I invited him to join me on my routine hike on The Hill, and we were off and walking together. So from now on in the story it's about Mark Yoslow and me, yet Mark Ruskell lives on in my memory. Mark to Mark.

Fridays, 10:00 to 11:30 a.m. (Mark)

After our lunch with David, I asked Gary if we could meet again, as he was clearly the most knowledgeable professional I'd met on the subject of men's work, and I felt drawn to that work. He was only free on Fridays, which was the day David had introduced us. Gary invited me to meet him at Los Gatos Roasting Company on Friday at 10:00 a.m. two weeks later.

I was very excited about this meeting. Part of it was being with men such as David and Gary who were very different from the people I was raised with back in New York. They took an active interest in helping to support men and raise boys in their communities. To me they represented openhearted men who valued, embodied, and communicated a deep sense of connection. I had a really limited idea of what connection meant. I was not a west coast guy.

I was born in Brooklyn, New York. My parents knew as much about raising a boy as they knew about bomb disposal. They knew little about support, encouragement, and love. I can tell you now that, because I was raised in an emotional environment like that, true connection for me is like sticking my finger in an electric socket. Getting the chance to know someone so different from my experience, who was deeply immersed in the men's movement, not only talking about it, but doing it, held a lot of meaning for me.

I showed up at 10:00 a.m. and Gary was already seated at a table. We sat and talked about the commitment that is inherent in doing heart-centered work with men, and how it is critical to remember that the work in the circle is managed by and for the men with minimal guidance from the leader: "The critical piece in this work is that it's not about you. It's about the men."

This was the first of about seventy-five meetings with Gary over the next year and a half. Gary and I met at the Los Gatos Roasting Company every Friday morning, from 10:00 to 11:30. It was similar to showing up at church or synagogue, temple or mosque, for spiritual support, but without the religion.

These meetings with Gary had the feeling of being in a school described by G. I. Gurdjieff and his student, P. D. Ouspensky, in the 1920s and 1930s. You need to know that Gurdjieff had a split reputation between being a deep resource of ancient knowledge and an outright con man. My sense is that the people he knew he could not teach he toyed with for his own entertainment. I chose to set that negative aspect of the man aside and focus on the wisdom he offered to the few who could keep up with him. It was the wisdom that I saw in Gary, and I was honored that he considered me worthy of his time.

The principles of Gurdjieff's school focused on the notion that the ordinary man is asleep, and it is only through the practices of self-observation and self-remembering that one can awaken and live a life free of crippling fears and destructive desires. He called this the Fourth Way.

The three traditional ways or schools focused on the mind, the emotions, and the body. The Fourth Way harmonized all of these in a school of self-observation. Gurdjieff designed a series of practices and exercises and introduced his students to principles that had origins lost in time. The best source of information on these esoteric teachings is Dr. Maurice Nicoll, a noted British psychiatrist who attended Gurdjieff's school and produced a six volume series on the Fourth Way.

The subject matters Gary shared with me resonated with the principles of the Fourth Way, and yet he was unfamiliar with Gurdjieff. Gary was sharing ancient knowledge, a deep learning that he had accumulated from working with circles of men for thirty years. It seemed to me that he had hit upon knowledge that appears to be embedded in our DNA as men, and is revealed within the context of a circle focused on discovering one's inner core. For some this brought a deep sense of self, for others it meant revealing a spiritual center.

We started out with Gary being present for me, and evolved into our being present for each other. Along the way, after a couple of months of meeting together, and becoming bonded as friends, Gary invited me on his walk, "up a hill behind my house." This was a sacred place for him, and he honored me with the invitation.

Chapter 2

The Gate of Unknowing

You Begin Where You Stand (Mark)

I had a great teacher, years ago, who led a group of students in the study of self-observation and self-remembering. At the time I found myself so burdened by every aspect of my life that I could not see where to begin this work, as I had so much running through my mind I could not keep track. It was as if I needed to erase all of my involvements so I could begin with a clean surface. I voiced my concerns to the group. The teacher's response was very powerful for me: "You begin where you stand." I thought I understood what he said, and later learned that I had no idea of what he meant.

To begin a man has to take a stand on something, anything, and remain true to it no matter what. Once this state of mind is established a man can begin to self-observe and self-remember because he is doing so within a place of strength. This becomes his rock. Everything that serves his stand is held close, and negative influences are acknowledged and not chosen, and are no longer served in a way that creates the state of being overburdened.

This was my first appreciation of how little I knew about what it means to be a man in the world. There is the sense of not knowing where to start. Staying in this sense of not knowing allowed me to "un-know" so much of what I have been taught about restricting my own growth in favor of fulfilling roles that have been chosen for me, and mistaking the roles for my identity. I saw that this is how men become trapped in identifying themselves by what they do. Any other roles different from the accepted norms we know are viewed as the precursors to anarchy with a fear that is similar to that of a child being alone in the dark. It takes a while to learn that the dark is exactly that—the dark—and what I feared was a dark mirror of myself, not the dark itself.

When I encounter being a man in the world and the opportunity to define for myself what that is I enter the Gate of Unknowing with a positive step, almost gleeful for not knowing anything. That is how I received the gift of seeing how certain I was of knowing so much about what I do, and realizing I know so little about what I am in the world.

Living in the mountains helped me learn what it meant to be a man in the world, what it meant to take a stand, and how it defined who I am.

The Mountain Life (Mark)
I had lived in the Santa Cruz Mountains for ten years before I met Gary, so I knew the subtle meaning of his invitation for "a walk up a hill." There was no level ground up on the hill; it was very up or very down with some moderate grades in between, and never flat without intervention by a backhoe or a dozer. People who lived "on the hill," meaning "in the mountains," referred to people who lived in town at the foot of the mountains as "flatlanders."

Brotherhood and Firewood (Mark)

The hill had a culture and a lifestyle of its own. In winter, on a stormy night with the rain pouring down out of pitch black skies, able-bodied men would don their slicker sets and go up to the general store bringing a chainsaw, rope, grappling hooks, peaveys (a tool for rolling logs), and other gear. We would drive around to houses owned by elderly couples to see if they needed any help, and make the rounds of the storm drains, harness up and repel down into them with a short bar chainsaw, and clear the drains to prevent accumulation of water, and stop mudslides and highway collapses before they happened. If we had to drop a two-hundred-foot pine that was losing its roots, and was headed for a house, we would meet in a circle the next morning, plan strategy, identify the climber, the rope man, and the ground men, and then drop it in ten-foot logs away from people's homes before the tree could fall and crush their roofs.

Once you showed up, and took the risks with everyone else, no one forgot your name or what you did to help. You became part of a circle of men with tools and trucks who were ready to show up to save lives, homes, hillsides, and roads. And it was good to go to the general store at the end of the night, where John, the owner, would stay late to pour us a glass of bourbon whiskey, and hear about what happened. It was a sacred thing to be a part of that group. There was brotherhood on the hill, something I had longed for all of my life. I sometimes long for those days.

I'd left New York as a free-lance writer specializing in science and medicine. On my time off back in New York my passion was powerlifting. I worked long and hard to get to the point of lifting a half ton on a sled leg press, and squatting a little over four hundred pounds. At 5-foot 9-inches I weighed 215 pounds, and I was in okay shape for someone forty years old. I met my wife in the gym, and we both had the dream of moving to California. I had a friend who lived in the hills above Los Gatos. Before we were married, we went to visit him at his house on the hill deep in a redwood forest. I had been there before and she fell in love with the big trees and all the life in the woods. I took her for a drive up to the top of Bear Creek Road to see the expanse of misty mountains in the golden light of the late afternoon, and said to her, "This is where I make my stand." We were

married on August 12, and on August 13 we flew out from New York. Two weeks later we rented a house up on the hill in the Santa Cruz Mountains.

When I arrived in California I was hoping for freelance work in medical advertising, my profession for the last twelve years, but the local economy was in recession, so I took any work I could get where strength was a requirement. During the time we lived on the hill I worked as a mason tying steel for foundations and pouring concrete and doing brick laying for fireplaces and houses and cinder block construction for retaining walls. I was a ditch digger setting up 4x6x5-foot French drains filled by shovel with two-inch rock. I did poison oak and brush removal, and worked as a ground man for tree work.

After living on the hill for a while I learned that supplying firewood could be a good business to support my writing habit. Through a friend at the local water company I obtained permission from the owner of a sixty-five-acre property to maintain his land by taking out all of the dead trees and branches I could find, and my payment was the firewood. That took me into the forest on the hill, into the tall pines, the big oaks, and the enormous madrones. There were standing dead trees, and downed tree trunks, and dead branches on live trees, and all of that was waiting to be harvested. At one point I was delivering five mixed cords a week, and I split all of it by hand. It was hard work, and I was in heaven. I hired local men to work with me who knew me from the hard days and nights in winter, and I was part of a crew I had created. When we were invited out by the members of that crew, I knew that the money on the table came from the hard work we did together, and it had meaning.

After the summer, autumn, and winter seasons and the sale of the cords we harvested, the members of my crew moved on to other jobs, and I was in the forest on my own with my firewood harvesting gear and my 1963 Chevy One Ton with its 4½x9-foot bed, perfect for firewood supply. I added a snatch block with a heavy sling that had loops on both ends. I could wrap the sling around a stout tree with one loop through the other, and hook the snatch block on to the open loop. I also added a modified tray from an old wheelbarrow so I could haul logs up inclines by slipping a cable loop over the end of a log, and pulling the cable through a hole I cut in the front of the tray. I cut away the back of the tray to create a slipper for the front end of the log. That allowed the log to slide up a hillside without tearing up the loam on the forest floor. I tied the end of a towrope to the cable, ran the rope through the snatch block, and looped it on the towing hitch on the rear of my truck. It was a whole lot easier to pull logs up a hill with a truck to a flat spot for bucking and splitting than it was to carry rounds uphill, although I did a lot of that as well when I could not easily get the truck through the trees. I was glad for all of the strength training I did back in New York.

I sold true cords, 4x4x8 feet packed solid, not a pile of wood thrown in the back of a truck. I didn't just dump it on delivery. I stacked the wood, and supplied a tied bundle of split pine sticks with a lot of sap that we called fatwood. You could light it with a match and it went right up. During the years that I supplied wood during autumn and winter I had a lot of calls and several dozen repeat customers, and that kept the rent paid and food on the table. I harvested all year round to prepare for autumn and winter, and during spring and summer I stockpiled about twenty cords in my work yard that bordered the forest behind our house. That was worth about $5,000 cash money. When you bake your own bread and cookies, barter for home-grown veggies and homemade jams, and help the local butcher keep his house warm in winter, you can live a good life. During the autumn and winter months I harvested, split, and delivered five cords a week, and sometimes more.

I received a call from a woman farther up the hill from me, on Upper Zayante Road, deep in the mountain forest, who heard about my firewood, and was out of wood and needed a delivery to keep herself and her kids warm. We were in the middle of a bad Northern California storm inspired by *El Niño*, heavy rain and cold, and the forecast said it would go on for days. It could be a dangerous trip, but the woman sounded a little desperate. There was no way I could say no to keeping a family warm in bad weather. I was not in this business just for the money. A firewood supplier has a sacred obligation up on the hill, although you'll never hear one admit to this side of the work, only to the challenges to body and equipment. The ground gets slippery with mud, and the wood gets slippery when it's wet.

You can slip and fall hard down a mountainside, you can get your hand crushed by sliding logs, you can get struck by lengths of wood kicked up by the chainsaw or get cut by your chain and get a good gash in your leg, and all of that is avoided by being very deliberate in your movements in wet conditions with heavy loads. I loaded up "a lady's cord" and headed out. I called it "a lady's cord" because I used to cut the logs only twelve to fifteen inches long for women with young children, instead of the usual sixteen to twenty inches, for safety reasons.

A woodstove or a fireplace insert does not have that big a firebox. So when you load it with the wood parallel to the door, you run the risk of the wood rolling back out on you when you open the door, or the hot logs or coals can fall out of the opening, roll off the stone surround and onto the floor of your house, and then you need a way of picking up that hot, burning wood real quick. Now imagine you are a woman with a crying baby on your hip, and you want to put wood in the woodstove or fireplace insert. I cut the wood short so a woman, with one hand, could open the door and put the firewood in with the end perpendicular to the door. If the wood was going to roll, it would roll to the sides of the firebox, and the coals would do the same thing. She could close the door and not let go of the baby for a minute. I got a lot of calls and callbacks from families on the hill for this reason. Although a lady's cord takes a lot more cutting work, more gas and oil for the chainsaw, and more time sharpening the chain, the repeat business makes up for it.

On this particular run I had to negotiate Upper Zayante Road, which is a pretty dangerous one-lane road with a lot of hairpin turns. Another driver and I avoided a head on collision by about two feet on one of its blind turns. It was kind of funny because I saw him take a deep breath at the same time I took a deep breath, and we both laughed because we saw each other have the same reaction through our truck windshields. We both backed up, and he made space for me to pass with plenty of room away from the downhill edge.

When I arrived at the house the woman was managing three kids and the house was very smoky. She had a window open, but I asked her if it would be all right to open all the windows, and I did. She had run out of firewood and in desperation tried to burn a chunk of telephone pole, which is saturated with creosote so it won't get attacked by ants or termites, and won't burn in a fire. Pole wood smolders with a lot of toxic smoke but never really burns, and it can release a lot of creosote into the chimney and clog it up and create the conditions for a chimney fire. I asked her for a metal bucket and some tongs, and took the smoldering chunk out of the house and put it in a deep puddle with a lot of pebbles away from her house and nowhere near the forest. The pouring rain would solve that problem. Then I unloaded and stacked the cord as close to the house as I could so she did not have to go far to get fuel for her woodstove. I asked her for a tarp and covered the wood so it would keep dry, and weighted it down with large rocks.

By that time the house had aired out, but it was really cold, and she and her kids were wearing jackets. She had a steel ash bucket, and I shoveled out the ash from her stove, because there were still bits of the pole wood that had dropped off the chunk, and there was a lot of ash besides, and I put that bucket out on the earth where it could cool and burn out. Then I showed her how to build a fresh fire with a fatwood lattice on the bottom and smaller pieces of branch on top, and brought in a couple dozen or so larger oak and madrone splits for when the fire was far enough along to take them, and showed her how she could load them in with one hand. I went around the house and closed all the windows, and while doing that I noticed that the wind had picked up. I went to the woodpile and checked to see that the tarp was in place and secure, and found that it was. Then I went to get my payment.

I knocked and she answered the door, and looked me in the eyes for a moment, and I remember the look was so intense that I took off my hat out of respect even though it was raining. She put the money in my hand, and closed my hand around it, and said, "You're a good man." I just nodded. I remember standing in the rain after she closed the door, and I was glad it was raining so she could not see my tears.

I realized in that moment that I knew who I was. All the nagging questions that a man can ask himself in his most private moments about his identity and his value had evaporated. I had taken my stand. I knew who I was.

We moved off the hill after about ten years. We had bought a house up there, put a lot of sweat equity into it, fixed it up neat and clean, sold it for a good profit, and moved into the town of Los Gatos. The economy had improved, and I was able to find writing work, and a good powerlifting gym, but I missed the hill and its challenges, and the brotherhood in the forest.

I still do.

If ever you find yourself in a moment when you can take on a part of life that you never thought could be yours, do it. Changing roles within the context of society, in a small a town, opens you up to all of the people and experiences that will expand you as a man. If you take this on, not as a con man, but with a willingness to create an alternate identity with integrity, it provides an experience in which you can see yourself as others see you, something that is difficult to observe within our habitual existence. It can take the form of a part-time job, a tradesman, or volunteering for community service. Self-observation allows you to understand parts of yourself that you can honor and appreciate, and to let go of parts that can bring you dishonor and rejection.

Holding the Ground (Mark)

Gary introduced me to The Hill gradually, as there were several natural landings along the trail. He showed me the kindness of a father who introduces his son to a challenge in a manner that minimizes the experience of failure or not measuring up, and makes it a compassionate experience. The part of me that was the lost, confused, lonely boy who missed having a father was gradually fed the healing he needed, and all of the muscle memory that I gained when I was living and working in the mountains came back as strength and endurance in a few weeks.

It also became very clear to me that Gary was a damn mountain goat, and he could hold a pace with the intense concentration and endurance required to meet this kind of physical challenge. This was my way was well, from marathon running and long distance cycling in my thirties, and building up my strength with heavier and heavier lifts and then working up in the dense forests of the mountains in my forties. Gary's hunch that we would be well matched for this twice or thrice weekly challenge paid off for both of us.

At some time along the way, after about six months, we talked about how a group of men, a men's group, can spontaneously form around a spiritual center with a commonly held tacit intention. "This is about holding the ground," Gary said. "It's about being consistent in showing up at the same place, at the same time. That energy will attract other men with a similar spiritual center. They will show up as men who are seeking connection. They will have a built-in sense of being present. They will know what that means."

So meeting up with Gary, whose heart is devoted to creating brotherhood among men, was an elixir to my soul. We had our Friday meetings, and we walked The Hill two or three times a week, sometimes on Friday mornings before going for coffee. At some point after about a year we started to "hold the ground" at Los Gatos Roasting Company along with holding a powerful, spiritual intention to form a group.

Six months later we were joined by Stacy Smith, then Bob Land, and then two men from Gary's last group, Barry and Walt, joined us once we got going. We had grown from two men to six, with another three or four showing up when they could. They included the president of a behavioral science organization, a Swedenborgian minister, and Kirk Watson, the marketing rep for a recovery program whom we were supporting to go to graduate school and become a therapist because he had natural talent for the work. Stacy left the group to form his own breakfast group, and then Adam Dorsay was invited in by Bob, and his energy was just right because it felt as if Adam had been with us from the start. As of April 2014, our group, The Flying Yahoos, had been meeting for thirteen years. Group members came and left during that time, but an original core of five men consistently made the meeting.

The group's name, "The Flying Yahoos," was suggested by Stacy after the Yahoos in Jonathan Swift's *Gulliver's Travels*, the men who had lost their heads and ran around looking for them. He designed a t-shirt that had cartoon caricatures of our faces as a circle of balloons around the name. Gary and I wore them proudly at every Vision Quest Feast, the special dinner that men of the previous year's Quest would plan and deliver to the men who had just come off the mountain and a three-day fast. This was one of the traditions that organically developed out of Gary's work as a spiritual leader in Vision Quest, and I was fortunate to be a part of it for seven years.

When I was hired to work at Fremont Hospital Outpatient Services I negotiated attending the Flying Yahoos 10:00 to 11:30 a.m. Friday meetings as part of my employment agreement; on Fridays I started work at 12:30 p.m. and finished at 8:30 p.m. My supervisor felt it was very important for me to have the support of the group while working with acute mental health patients. I have to admit I took great pride in wearing my hospital badge to our men's group meetings, dressed professionally, a member of the mental health community. In truth, if I did not wear my badge, I would have forgotten it.

The power of consistently holding the ground in a place and time, and the effect this can have on men's spiritual commitment, is priceless.

The Hill: The Place Is the Teacher (Gary)

The importance of a physical challenge to complement emotional growth cannot be overestimated in its positive influence. The Hill provides this for Mark and me.

Sometimes I hate this walk. I am like a student resisting the teaching, then finally, joyously letting it in. Sigh, thank you, mountain.

Every step here is a page. "Down" feels like I've been cleansed, "up" the holding and preparing for the release. "What would it take to be here, fully present to this place and my heart?" is a question I have asked many times.

You can't see a natural scene through the glass, feeling isolated and separated from the world, the way a latchkey child feels looking at the world through a window. The hardest thing in the world for me sometimes is to just be where I am, as Gary.

Unfortunately, many men I know hike only to time themselves from one place to another and credit themselves with distance and speed. They miss the beauty and the nurture of nature by just sitting. Try just sitting in an isolated spot in nature for a day. Not on a day. For a full day, morning to dusk.

I remember the first Vision Quest I ever did and how it brought me into nature in a way I had never experienced and inspired me to lead Vision Quests. My fiancé told me I was driving her crazy with my divorce drama and to go backpacking or something to go figure it out for myself. I decided to go backpacking in the Sierra's even though it was early June and there was still snow on the ground. Although I had spent most of my outdoor life as a kid in the woods, this was different. I stayed in one place long enough to really acquaint myself to nature and my place in it (rather small). That was a life changer. It inspired change deep within me and inspired me to learn more about this ancient way of gaining wisdom. Thus my Vision Quests were born six years later after working with some Native American peoples but the fire had been ignited by that time alone in the wilderness. Thank you Cielo Black Crow and Tommy Little Bear.

Childhood Survival: The Window to the World (Gary)

My mother's Victorian style home was three stories counting the basement, and it had four large windows in the living room. I used to sit on the sofa and look out the largest one. I would watch other families go to the beach or family outings while I stayed home. Occasionally another family would ask me to go with them and that was nice.

My favorite voyeurism devices were the Sears and Roebuck and the Montgomery Ward catalogs. They were my pictures of life before TV. Longing began for all those things. Before that it was comic book superheroes. So heroes and desirable stuff became my fantasy world. Later it would be the men's magazines. I am no longer sure of the names but they had pictures or drawings of beautiful women and adult adventure stories. Then, finally, there was Playboy with all the toys and the best pictures of everything. Even fantasy homes. Just plug in the pictures, and go for a ride. What is better? What something looks like, or what it feels like? I was programmed to believe in what I saw. It didn't matter what it may feel like. About negative feelings, my mother always said, "Oh, don't feel that way." So I tried not to. I just looked to the pictures for instruction.

We didn't have TV until 1956 when I was twelve. What a visual fantasy machine that was. It's pretty amazing when you tell your story, and find someone with a strikingly similar story. Again, I'm not alone in that one. Of course, I observe that happening all the time in my men's groups.

I reduced the voyeurism after my divorce and remarriage, but I continued with the fantasy mind and lust for pleasure. Now, with the help of some couple's therapy, and my wife's awareness, I am looking at my house, my home, in a different light. Maybe I can have what I originally desired. Home, stability, community, spirituality, and that can be real, I can finally trust it. I can come home to something that I was convinced at some level I had lost forever. I am writing the words. Part of me is more content, willing to rest, to let go, and trust again. I am tired of chasing false gods. I do enjoy the peace, and what we have been talking about in therapy: making a home.

Fantasy or Addiction vs Vitality (Gary)
Now there might be some confusion about addictions that can deceive you into thinking and feeling that you are being vital, but there is a difference. Addictions don't vitalize: they mesmerize. In other words they put you to sleep for a while because what you are experiencing is always a substitute for the real thing.

That's right. Think about it. You don't have to think or feel. Addictions disorganize it for you, and numb you out. It actually takes you away from your vitality or spirit. The physical feeling in your body is a distortion of reality in some way. It leaves you wanting and lusting. It steals the essence of who you are in order to have a sense of self. You have to give something up. Some part of you is stolen. It is a substitute for what, and is—real and could vitalize you. So what does vitality mean? There was still something missing. I have looked in many places, and occasionally thought I had it, but it wasn't there. I have touched it many times without grasping it. I think you know what I mean. There is something out there, but what is it? So much of therapy is finding a word that captures what is mutually felt; I mean feel it in your body, and all in the room connect with it. For me, most recently, in fact, in only the last couple days, I have found the word that expresses what I have been looking for: *vitality*.

The Merriam-Webster Dictionaries available in print and on line gave me several definitions of vitality: the state of being strong and active; being energetic; high-spirited physical or mental vigor; the capacity for survival; the pursuit of a meaningful or purposeful existence; the power giving continuance of life that is present in all living things – the vitality of seeds.

So much for dictionary definitions: What is it about the seedling pushing its way through the concrete? It is persistent and shows no lack of effort. It is not only consistent and committed. I see it as containing its own energy to move without any outside nurturance because it "feels" a strong sense of purpose within itself. There is also an edge of joy in going beyond its little self to become something much larger. Vitality contains within it "vibrancy." To me, it's a vibe or vibration that hits my body and chimes within my whole being like a tuning fork and energizes me to respond in a way that fulfills a need to magnify its pitch to the next level. If I listen closely, it is so intense that I want to feel it again and again, each time with a greater passion than the first. It becomes a hunger to go beyond the mundane. Once I get the right vibe I become hungry to hear it again and again. The vitality is so strong that it is self-generating, like a song that keeps playing in my head that moves me physically and spiritually.

So what blocks vitality in relationship for me? Sue says that I am split between the dark side and the light, that I fantasize on the left, the dark, music, dancing, trips, that I am never present, that I never connect because I am out there connecting with fantasy.

Vietnam (Gary)

Perhaps that is true. Before I went to Vietnam I believed in and wanted it to be an all-light world of my making: God, country, and family. When it all crashed, I knew I had made a decision that an all-light world didn't work. I lost faith in all of it, and decided rejection might be a better idea. Now, as she says, I am split.

Maybe I need an exorcism or something. At least I am now aware of it. In order to have connection I have to let go of my dark side romance with fantasy. I am afraid of the light because I feel it abandoned me. Again, what or who abandoned me? Susan; my elders on the dark side; my countrymen who were on the dark side; my priest; my lieutenant who had abandoned someone in the field; the dark side of war; living in a war zone.

The light was a man who befriended me. Chuck was the same rank but much older. He was the one who got me a job at the Enlisted Men's Club on base, who got me out driving around in his security police vehicle on an alert, out on the town in Nha Trang and into the bars to see what was really going on behind the scenes of war, and who got me out in the country when we were on R&R in Kuala Lumpur, Malaysia. There we hired a tour guide and saw all the Buddhist temples and shrines, went to the best restaurants where I always ordered something flambeau, drove to the coast and went water skiing mostly under water as the guide didn't speak English, met the ladies of the night, bought tailor-made clothes, and drank good beer. And we had our time as Kings and brothers bonded by war, fear, and a need to escape. Otherwise I would have grumbled, on base, on my top bunk fretting about life and love. Chuck, miss you. He retired from the Air Force as a security policeman and opened a head shop. Sadly, when I looked him up to say thanks he had passed at the age of seventy-one. I had posted a wish to find him on the Vietnam Security Police Bulletin Board and had a great conversation with another man who had served with him and also felt he had been kind of a big brother to him. At least it was somewhat gratifying to have another man validate his rich experience with Chuck.

Chuck dabbled in the dark side, along with my sergeant friend. God bless both of them. Maybe the light didn't abandon me. Maybe the dark side corrupted me. My faith was tested more than I could endure, and I sold out. It was hard, so hard, to keep my faith when I felt so desperately alone. I have witnessed the dark side of fantasy, and I know it is a desperately lonely place. So I have my fantasies but I am alone in them. I have been taught well, so well that I am split. Have I abandoned myself, or my soul, to the dark side? Is it so hard to choose light over dark? Those attached to the dark side shall live here? In fear? Connection or detachment? Dark or light? Relationship with or without any?

It comes down to a fear of relationship. With God or without? Light or dark? I am afraid of God. Sometimes I don't want to leave the house. Maybe that is actually a good thing. Leave me alone, Oh Darkness. Let me be. Quit tantalizing me. Let me live here in my heart rather than a war-torn land. Would I then be back to being a child looking out the window at what others have, jealous of what I project I do not have, or would I finally be at home with a house filled with presence instead of the empty house I grew up in? As they say, a house does not make a home. Maybe I can finally be at home in my own home, present with a Sue who loves me, with my daughter, a dog, a cat, and friends. I don't know.

Ever watch the James Bond movie *Skyfall* (Eon Productions, 2012)? In case you haven't, or you don't remember, James Bond is having a conversation with M and she asks him why he thinks he was chosen as a special agent. He doesn't know. She said he was picked because he was an orphan. Think about that. The point here is that many of us become heroes because we were abandoned in some way as children. Thus we become heroic in some contrived fashion in order to be valued and not at risk of abandonment. You can't be home if you are always on the Hero's Journey. The underside of the man who serves the archetype of the hero is an empty home because he who fears abandonment abandons others. The hero abandons because that is all he has ever known.

James Bond woke up in his confrontation with death and so have I. The ending of the movie is significant. He makes a choice. He comes home and so have I. He no longer needs to be the hero, nor do I.

Being Pulled into the Darkness (Mark)

On The Hill today by myself, thinking about "the dark side romance" with fantasy that Gary was talking about. It is so easy to surrender to the pull of the dark side. Gary experienced it in Vietnam, and for years afterward. I had an attraction to the Darkness. It's different from what Gary was talking about. I would see evil in a person and become so fascinated that I had to see where it led, and that became the source of some painful moments in my life. I was fascinated with criminal Darkness for a while. I studied serial murder for fifteen years in preparation for writing a novel about an army of hand-picked serial murderers. I did not realize until long after I finished the book that it was an echo of my family's past, the family I lost to the Nazis in the Holocaust. Dark side fantasy pulled me into a truth it was time for me to see.

Every once in a while I've run into a situation that perfectly represents what Darth Vader called "the power of the dark side." Vader is the *Star Wars* (Lucasfilm, 1977) character who fully realizes he has become a monster, and relishes the experience as a tool to satisfy his constant hunger for control and power.

The Darkness also has another side, one that Vader reveals to Luke Skywalker. It is so easy to be romanced into the Darkness by anger, or the need for revenge, or the need to fight powers against which we cannot win. Knowing we cannot win is, for some men, an aphrodisiac for self-immolation. It is as if the wound will be cured by cutting away more of oneself.

I learned from a number of patient cases, and from past experience in business, that the Darkness is seductive in the way it can move through a man's consciousness, as it is an archetypal agency unto itself that seeks life in the manner that any living thing pursues survival. Decisions made under the influence of the Darkness seem so right, as if they have a source of their own power, and feel like revenge and vindication all at once. That power of rightness is delicious to the ego, and that is where the Darkness feeds. Once a man is taken by it, he loses his moral identity and becomes an agent of the Darkness. This experience is paradoxical because in the presence of the Darkness men fantasize that they are in absolute possession of themselves and their internal power when in fact they have fully surrendered themselves to an external agency.

The key to noticing the approaching presence and power of the Darkness in a man is when he manifests or reports the simultaneous experience of (1) being isolated and (2) feeling absolutely right and (3) an undercurrent of anger—the combination of all three is the tell. Anger is a response to fear, so the immediate question to ask oneself with compassion is, "What do I fear in this moment that is driving me into anger?" Once a man compassionately knows his fears, and what is both rational and irrational about them, and can forgive himself for his fears, then the Darkness has no entry point.

Compassion is the active desire to eliminate suffering, and is a key tool in overcoming anger. The Darkness requires the environment of an angry struggle with suffering, coupled with a long-held grudge, if it is to flourish. Consider Adolf Hitler's book *Mein Kampf*, which means "My Struggle." A limiting factor is the power a man does or does not have to engage others in his struggle. If he is charismatic and his cause attracts followers he can lead others toward doing good or evil in the world, or both at once, where the murder of brown people would be good in one group, and evil would be a lack of loyalty to that violent group. Within this paradox the Darkness thrives as a cultural complex with its own morality claiming the right to have racist and violent groups target any democratic institutions that limit its power (Yoslow, 2007, p. 247).

A perfect example of a man who practices the extreme opposite of compassion toward his anger, who sees compassion and forgiveness for humanity, and any morality derived therefrom, as weaknesses to be shunned, who encourages the fears of his followers, and claims people who are different are the embodiment of dark forces that would destroy their homeland, is Donald Trump, and in this way he manifests a similarity to Adolf Hitler, Benito Mussolini, and Joseph McCarthy. The archetypal power of the Darkness is real. Given the opportunity, it can draw anyone into its own lines of force, even the forty-fifth President of the United States, and all those who follow him into his moral abyss.

This Walk, This Journey, This Process (Gary)

I know now that I had to do this walk, this journey, this process. (I always say therapy is a process, not a product). Before I could go on to the next chapter of my life I had to come home. I had to grow my values. I had to learn them the hard way. I am thankful for the people around me who gave me a new meaning. These include the quality people I worked with in law enforcement, the Sterling Men's Weekend, my men's teams, my professors, and my new wife who would not settle for a lack of value. I also give credit to Native American wisdom, my children, and the men's and women's spirits I worked with in therapy. They all helped me create new values. They gave me a foundation of hope and a sense of belonging and self. They brought me closer to home.

But I hadn't come home yet.

The Hero and the Victim on The Hill (Mark)

There was a twin fantasy that pursued me throughout my life, and I could not see it clearly until I was walking The Hill. In every aspect of my existence I was casting myself as either the hero or the victim. I began to realize that this was my way of making up for a lack of male identity. It filled the spaces left vacant by not having a model to emulate, a role usually fulfilled by a father, and the approving encouragement of a father regarding one's life choices.

Men need models to mold themselves. If they are fortunate the models will be of strong moral character, hardworking, humble, compassionate, and loving toward a partner. If they are not fortunate the models will create their own morality as needed, will be determined in the pursuit of goals defined by self-interest, will be guided by anger and revenge, and will see relationship as a source of whatever is needed in the moment. Both models can be seen as the hero, one light and one dark.

Is it possible for a man to flow between the two if he does not have a firm grounding in identity and integrity? As I trudged up The Hill I began to wonder if this was the way I saw myself, as the hero of the moment, resourceful at all times, loving at times, cruel at times, and without a sense of being anchored in either model, one light and one dark.

It was in pursuit of the hero within that I found the victim, the child who ducks, who puts up his arms to shield his face, who hides his bruises. That was my childhood experience. Given my out-of-control behavior, and being labeled regularly as a "pain in the ass," I would say internally, "I deserved it." I could not judge whether it was morally correct or incorrect to beat an unruly child. All I knew was it hurt. I normalized it by owning the blame. And to be clear, I *was* unruly, difficult, destructive, and had an after-the-fact sense of right and wrong. I was almost a delinquent, but not quite. To be a delinquent requires being able to take a punch, not fearing physical pain, and taking pleasure in hurting others. I was in a gray area. I was destructive toward objects.

I learned from working with patients who had been the victims of violent crime about a confusion that develops around the roles of the attacker and the target of the attack. The person grievously wounded by the unexpected event would look for a reason for its occurrence to normalize the experience when there wasn't any rational reason available. Irrational reasons for the event were created internally and believed, as these provided an anchor to an event for which a reasonable explanation could not be found. Fault needed to be assigned somewhere, with the intention of relieving the hurt. For lack of knowing the criminal who had victimized the person, or any reality-based foundation for the attack, the fault was often mistakenly assigned by the victim to himself or herself. This led to behavior that self-identified the victim as the source of blame: activities of daily living such as eating or bathing or cleaning house became unimportant, opportunities for friendship or meaningful work were avoided, startle responses to loud noises or sudden movement increased, isolation, anger, and panic grew in intensity, but there was no rational premise for any of these behaviors other than the lack of a reason for becoming a victim. "I deserved it," was the type of phrase, often held internally as a secret, which identified the victim's nightmare, and irrationally became the only reason available. This was at the core of the "It's not your fault" catharsis scene in the film *Good Will Hunting* (Miramax Films, 1997). When Will Hunting's therapist helps him realize that he was not the motivation behind his abuse, that he, in fact, had no control over his abusive stepfather, he releases the tears behind his rage.

I felt this wounding, had felt it for years, for decades, and had permitted this sense of impending repetitive wounding to color my existence. The role of the hero, in contrast to that of the victim, was actually the role of a rescuer. I began to wonder if this was the way I defined my identity as a professional working with patients. Was I working with the survivors of horrific events that resulted in post-traumatic stress disorder (PTSD) because I wanted to rescue them, and was my countertransference that I in turn wanted to be rescued?

I was very clear about the process of healing PTSD. The only person who could rescue someone afflicted with PTSD was himself or herself and no one else could take over any aspect of that work if it was to be successful. The role of the therapist was to be present with support, with information, education, encouragement, compassion, empathy, and deep understanding of the seventeen symptoms of the disorder, the process of defining the thoughts, emotions, and actions within the patient's experience, and the challenges involved along this journey.

There was clearly an element of the rescuer in it for me, but it was indirect. I placed myself as a group therapist between the person and the disorder with the intention of creating a conscious view by the patient of her symptoms or his behaviors within the context of a group, something normally done in individual sessions, but it seemed to me that the patients needed more support. The group experience permitted patients that moment of mutual perception of something that they could see in each other, something they could not easily explain to anyone not afflicted with this disorder that resonated among them as a truth they could share, and that experience was real and grounding.

Although Gary and I had completely different experiences, we shared this understanding of what it meant to feel separated from our lives by a *complex*, which, correctly defined, is *a combination of perception, powerful memory, and repetitive fantasy*. We needed to step away from it, stand apart from it. To accomplish that we had to become one with an experience so intense that there wasn't any room left for the complex's power over us. That experience was walking The Hill, in the middle of a winter rainstorm on a surface as slick as ice, or 107° and no easy way up or down, one dusty foot in front of the other, and nothing else in the moment other than freezing cold, burning sweat, and constant pain, again, and again, and again.

How often did I see my own shadow in the dust and embody it with the thought, "Don't worry, little brother. I'm here, and you and I are going to make it, no matter what." It was the fantasy that kept me going through marathons, through hundred-mile rides on the bike, and day after day on The Hill when I marched on my own.

In the moment, in the NOW of our walk, simply knowing that I was with my friend, Gary, who was in the midst of his own challenges, provided the sense that we were rescuing each other from something that escaped simple description. Great Nature, my rescuer, was there as we entered the Gate of Unknowing, as real as the mountain that gave us permission to call it The Hill.

Being Alone and Belonging (Gary)
Alone.
Learning a way of being.
Just being.
I ask what is natural?
What is real?
Questions that have been a part of my life for so long.
The hardest thing in the world for me sometimes is to just be where I am.

When alone as a child I always kept my set of toy army men in a special corner of the living room and I would spend hours playing with them around the room. My mother was okay with that as long as I always put them back in that special spot. It turns out another man in our men's group has pretty much the same story, and he tells me how he had collected over a thousand pieces of an army set similar to mine. It makes me sad writing this, but so it was. The army we wish we had so we wouldn't feel alone. The sense of belonging to something larger than our selves is sometimes comforting even if the belonging is an illusion of love and connection.

What have you joined that you project the fantasy of belonging onto? What sports team or corporate identity have you taken on belonging to out of a need to belong?

I have seen a number of men who drink together in a work or after-work situation as a way to self-medicate and feel connected. One of my favorite stories is of a high level corporate guy and ex-special ops academy graduate. He was in sales where drinking was part of the protocol. He got a DUI and it woke him up. I coached him and he began his recovery process for himself and for the sake of his family. He was a drinking buddy to a lot of other men. One of his first concerns was how he was going to tell them. How was he going to not drink in front of them or not join them in drinking? I supported him to man up and lead those men. I suggested that he and he alone had the courage and balls to do that—and he did. Last I heard he was doing very well in sobriety and had gotten a number of his colleagues to either stop drinking or at a minimum brought them into a greater awareness of the damage it was creating. "How do I quit? Everyone I know drinks like I do." I have probably heard that one a thousand times. It was extremely gratifying to have him call me over a year later, as traffic to his work diverted him by my office, and he thought to call. I had been thinking about him and he called just to let me know things were great for him and he was continuing his life of sobriety. What a gift!

Our culture is so very fucked up due to shame and guilt and too many medications to deal with it.

The Echo of the Hill (Gary)

Here I am at an ocean bluff vacation home and continuing to think about The Hill and what it means to me. It's amazing what it continues to stir up. I just finished reading the touching story of Skip Conrad in the October 2007 issue of *Backpacker Magazine* ("Vanishing Act," p. 68), and how Nature touched a lost man's soul. I know that feeling. I can understand how, when his life was at an end, he hiked to the place he loved, where he was totally accepted, and died without a trace. He was a victim of alcoholism and the resulting pain. Generational wounding can leave you lonely no matter what you do to try and fill the space. When you aren't given love and acceptance you can be lonely no matter what. I know for me (yes, there was alcoholism in my family history as well), the mountain—The Hill—feels like a friendly spirit that is always there.

Maybe it's the dirt we all come from and return to. It always feels like home. It feels safe. That is why I go back again and again. I feel I belong there. It is safe because there is no judgment. It is totally accepting. I don't feel alone.

If you feel lonely give this a try. Find a place in nature you love, truly love, not too far from home, and go there as often as you can. The place can become a friend.

My Body and The Hill (Gary)

I continue to battle a glitch in my side. I have been trying to unravel the cause for about five years. I am sitting here hoping (a word I don't like because most people hope rather than do) that the chiropractor I saw this morning has the answer. I am taking a pill once a day to activate some facet or part of my liver that has not been working properly. At least that is the conclusion I have come to. Some years ago I suspected that when I do therapy I restrict my breathing with my intention to listen. Later I realized it was probably more the result of living in a combat zone and staying clenched. When we are in fear one of the primary reactions to stress is to clench our muscles and organs. My restricted diaphragm has locked the

muscles next to it and caused digestive and muscular problems. My sit-ups have further tightened those muscles by putting even more pressure on the diaphragm. Now, today that is all resolved, but for seven years I have been somewhat disabled due to my PTSD and restriction. If the pill continues to work, it will definitely change my life. I can be hopeful.

I now understand what my mother used to say: "If you have your health, you have everything." HO to that. It has taken a great deal of my energy. So many times I have felt depleted because of it. I value my body having learned to use it doing construction at age sixteen and digging ditches for the utility company when I was eighteen. Now I have to exercise in some strenuous manner at least three to four times a week.

My foreman gave me this gift by example. He, in his late forties, led his crew by working ahead of them. We would try to keep up. Thank you, George Wettach. I would have to say I am continuing to follow your lead and my health is far better than most men my age because of it. I can easily do 9-mile walks, bench 135, press 60lb. dumbbells for 12 reps, and do 40 pushups, all with relative ease. (Note: Gary loves to brag when he's being humble. — M.Y.)

Hope (Gary)

The Hill is really hot today, until we get to higher elevations. Ah, that soft cool breeze feels good. It's pleasant and reassuring.

Hope is similar to that soft cool breeze. It's also pleasant and reassuring. Hope, when it's attached to action, can change my life. This is especially true of my health if I am taking action to maintain it. That comes from the experience of digging ditches that I just mentioned. Mark and I know about this. We learned it well for many years. It put us in touch with how to use our bodies. It made us value ourselves in a different way that had little to do with how we thought. We saw what it took to sustain ourselves very early on, and a strenuous workout today brings us back to that meaning. Now, in our sixties, hope is maintained with something more than ideas. I know I look pretty darn good for sixty-three years old. Sixty-three: that is actually a little hard to look at on the page but here I am. Those ditches not only helped me build a strong body, they motivated me to get a good education.

Half Moon Bay (Gary)

I keep attempting to walk but the Sierras are burning, and so is Henry Coe State Park, creating day after day of smoke-filled air in the Los Gatos hills. I can't even see the hills let alone go walk in them. I am super sensitive to everything, so not only is breathing more difficult, my skin breaks out. Today Mark and I have cancelled our hike again due to air quality.

Sue and I head for the coast. Half Moon Bay is clearing from an earlier fog. It is warm and the town is cheerful with tourists and locals. We eat in a quaint Mexican/Moroccan cafe with excellent food. Local musicians are playing in the square, and their smiling lead singer is pretty good. Of course I like that she is singing, smiling, and occasionally pointing at me. But I should be walking The Hill. I am getting out of shape here. Wow, look at that artichoke bread. It makes me want to rip off a piece of it right now even though I just had lunch. More carbohydrates, yes! No, I resist. The beach looks gray; hey, it's Half Moon (or is it Mood?) Bay. What do you expect? This part of the coast can be, usually is, dismal. But like I said, the town has a quaint appeal.

Vietnam in Half Moon Bay (Gary)

Well, we have to stop at the nurseries. So here I sit. Actually I am enjoying the spot in which I sit. Cars are zooming by, but the air is clean. Across the road is a thick forest of bushes. I imagine trying to push my way into them and go anywhere. It would be like hiding in the jungles of Vietnam. Yes, I can still go there. How would I hide from the enemy? Thank God I enlisted in the Air Force instead of being drafted by the Army. Good decision, Plep. But what are you going to do when you have lost your driver's license? I couldn't chase girls and I was tired of digging ditches. Three years, eleven months, seventeen days, and a wake up (until discharge, but who was counting?). I can't walk The Hill today but at least I am still here to walk it. I am grateful for fate's subtle shifts in direction.

The Long Journey Home (Gary)

No doubt my most direct contact with the ghosts of war happened to me while leading a Vision Quest wilderness experience. We had a base camp at the top of a ridge in the Ventana Wilderness of Big Sur, California. I picked this particular location to be removed from civilization.

I was milling around camp with my co-leader on a damp and quiet morning. I remember it as being slightly foggy and misty. I looked down the mountain simply to take in the always-gorgeous view. I was stunned and taken aback as I saw five Vietnamese carrying rifles on their shoulders and wearing the same garb as the Viet Cong, the traditional black pajamas and cone hats. My immediate thoughts were dark, and I was suddenly caught between two worlds. One I knew from being in a war in Vietnam, and the one in the present moment. I had to keep asking myself the question, "Are they here to kill me, or are they just civilians hunting for food?" Back and forth, back and forth, past to present, present to past. I wanted my gun and I didn't have it.

I watched them walk through the back of our campsite, and felt myself between two worlds of anticipation, trying to sort out reality. That was a scene I will never forget. I kept thinking, "How many of them can I get before they get me?"

Big breath.

The darkness stayed for a long time.

Belief and Distrust (Gary)

Today I was confronted by my wife's awakening to the realization that my fantasy life and need for excitement are a substitute for not having a family full of rituals and traditions, that my fantasies are a substitute set of rituals that fill up the space for me. Today when I walked I brought that up The Hill for me to process and shared it with Mark. It struck me when she said it, and I know that it is true.

Beliefs are a big part of the story. When I was a child my beliefs seemed to float. My ground was so unstable I wasn't sure what to believe in. Before I left for the military I had decided to believe in monogamy, the Holy Catholic Church, the sacredness of our bodies, family, the support of friends, John F. Kennedy, my country, family, and friends. That was my game board at the age of nineteen. Before I left for Vietnam I saw hope in being part of a large Irish Catholic family that my future wife offered, a religion that I could belong to, and a woman who could offer me the love I so desperately needed as I was an orphan of sorts. I thought I had found my place, my ground, my missing family home.

I so wanted to believe in something. I believed I was doing the right thing by serving my country and going to Vietnam. I was committed to my duties in the Air Force as an Airman First Class and felt valued. I went to church to be part of this new family, studied my catechism and was learning what it meant to be in relationship with a woman and part of a family. By the time I came back from Vietnam a year later all of it had lost its meaning.

I was thinking today life was like a game board and back then I thought I had accumulated all the right pieces. By the time I returned home it was like someone had swept their hand across the board, wiping it clean. I was bereft of any meaning in life. I felt I had lost all moral stability. I turned myself over to desire and fantasy like my elder colleagues in Vietnam had done. Whatever I desired I would attempt to do. I was in the abyss. If that meant alcohol or women I would go for it. If I thought marrying her would give me something I would go for it. I became a selfish (or more selfish), self-indulgent, dishonest prick: A true prick. At least I was most certainly a man without a ground and a compass.

Choose carefully whom you follow and don't let numbers choose you.

You see, I needed something to come back to or it wouldn't work. Everything I knew and wanted to believe in was destroyed. Even my culture, my country was not the same. No regard for loyalty to country, despised instead of respected, no one to listen, no one to care. Can you even imagine coming back from risking your life for a year, for your country, for American idealism and past heroic wars, to see kids your age running up a major street, blocks from your home, with the black North Vietnamese Army flag—the flag of an enemy that was killing your brothers, young Americans just like yourself? Strip clubs, drugs, and acid rock had become normal for my generation. That wasn't what I remembered. Where could I go? I was lost big time.

I have to admit that I had a fantasy of being welcomed home by people happy to see me, and pleased that I had returned. In my fantasy people would acknowledge that I had fulfilled some kind of patriotic duty, and they would all want to hear my stories, see my pictures, greet me with hugs and invites to celebrate my return. Virtually everything, save a couple friends in Vietnam, had dissolved. I felt left with nothing. My fiancée, my country, my friends and family had abandoned me. Even the culture I had known was no longer here. Everything had evaporated and I wanted desperately to come home.

I came back but I didn't come back to a home. There was no longer a home here. Everything I thought I could value was gone. My president was assassinated, my fiancé was no longer mine, my enemy's flag was being carried down my street, my "friends" were clearly more concerned with their little dramas than my experience of war, my music had been replaced, drugs and naked bodies on stage was the style. Miniskirts, hot-pants, and see-through tops were certainly seductive and exciting to see. No matter, I was lost but I was alive and looking with a jaded mind and a fogged lens. I couldn't go back and I didn't see a way forward so I took, and I mean *took*, what I could. I said okay to the new culture, I said okay to marrying, I said okay to the people who said they wanted to hear my story but then ignored me. I made the best of what I had. I was a lost child again, and I knew how to do that. I would get fed wherever I could. There is a greedy, angry tone to that. I searched for a place to belong. I was raised on chaos and disruption. So, I am back, but am I really?

God bless my fellow soldiers who never came home, who never had the chance.

Leading (Gary)

You know, as I truly relax the external world goes away. Stuff is unimportant, as in possessions. I am just here sitting on my bed in the comfort of my bedroom; I am warm, comfortable, and relaxed after having worked hard in my yard today. Was it the strenuous exercise? Is that what it takes to make everything okay and material desires go away?

What if I could just relax without the strenuous exercise, without walking The Hill for two hours? Less stress = less desire. Ah, to be in a state wherein stress and desire are dispelled. I've been here before. I know how good it feels. How do I hold on to it? Maybe this goes back to less is more? Part of me thinks of toys: Porsches, iPods, swimming pools. These thoughts are in the back corner of my mind, so now I let them seep in a little just to see what I do with them.

The first thing I detect is an energy, an excitement. It's tantalizing and seductive. It's not the fun, it's more the high, adrenalin, excitement. What if I didn't need excitement? But I have to have some, don't I? Doesn't everyone? "Everyone I know . . ."

Sounds a lot like an alcoholic. "Everyone I know drinks like I do. All my friends . . ." How much excitement do I really need? What does it take the place of now? Or what did it take the place of then? My first reaction as I write this is longing. That's quite a contrast. Desire less vs. excitement now. When I was a kid it was longing vs. excitement. It was an emptiness created by a lack of love and connection. I was hungry. That's a good word for it. I remember a beautiful Colombian hooker in Costa Rica approaching me and saying, "You are hungry for me, aren't you?"

That's in some ways the same. Desire that can take you to places you really shouldn't go. I said no to that desire back then, but my mind can take me other places. I know excitement can make me a little crazy, like out of control, anticipating the big "WHOOOPEEE!" Is this the Love vs. Fear equation? Physiologically it's a short shift from excitement to fear. I had a lot of fear and anxiety as a child in an unstable world: My parents' separation, divorce, and my father's death when I was three or four is a good start. If I could turn that dial just a little I would have excitement instead of emptiness. Do I still want to do that? It's a quiet slip into loneliness, loneliness slips into fear, anxiety, and longing, thus the desire for excitement comes up so I don't have to feel lonely. So the less I feel lonely, the less I will need excitement. I start desiring when I feel empty.

I realize that my little kid is resentful because he hasn't been getting what he needs. He is waiting for and expecting what my supervisor in clinical practice used to call "the giant tit in the sky." Thanks, Maria.

If you are resentful (it's very common by the way) in relationship, change course. Reverse what you are doing. Lead by loving her and she will open to you. Take the risk. Quit being a brat. I have witnessed this working for my clients far more times than not.

Could I fill up in relationship? I did before, but I was too needy and almost lost the relationship. Thus, I sealed off my deepest needs. I am scared to be that needy again. Am I just practicing not needing, not feeling, and it catches up to me? Am I scared to reveal how needy I am? How needy am I anyway? Shit! What is it I need? Well, based on my story, I need love and stability. I have that, so what's the problem? My wife spends a lot of time trying to make me happy, but it only helps, it is not a healing. The open wound is still there. Maybe if I loved more, rather than waiting; if I took an active role in getting it. I always say, "Lead!" Maybe that's the answer—lead. Better yet, Lead in the Relationship. Lead in loving and "being." That has worked.

If you grow up being deprived of love this will be hard. Take the risk of giving more rather than expecting more. Join me in having learned a valuable and contrary lesson that is well worth the risk.

It's also about taking action. Peter Levine (*Waking the Tiger*, 1997) would say that healing from trauma is running from the tiger rather than staying frozen in fear (fight, flight, or freeze). The way to heal any trauma is to get the energy of it out of the body. Mark and I are healing our trauma by taking charge of it, talking and walking, moving the energy out of the body instead of being stuck or frozen. It's our long way of healing from complex trauma but it has served us.

Lead in a loving way rather than suffering hurt and being resentful. Create what you need by giving it. Yes, by giving what you want to receive.

Examining What's in the Balance (Gary)

It's easy to convince ourselves that spending time in excitement is the answer. If we can feel really alive then we must be alive. It's how we define this feeling of being alive that starts things off. We can get excited about possessions, expensive toys, and that is not where our relaxation lives. We appreciate the way the world goes away when we truly relax. Somehow we need to pay for this relaxation. It often comes to us after a day of strenuous labor, or a challenging day on The Hill, a good sweat, a hot shower, a moment to regard the outcome of the effort. We ask if that's what it takes to make material desires leave our minds. Monks of every persuasion doing the work of a sacred place come to mind. It makes us wonder if there is a "stressless" desire, and if that is what it means to be without desires. Apparently not, as we can easily find the word *stressful* and yet *stressless* is not in our dictionary. How can we hold on to this "desirelessness" (also not in the dictionary), this basic concept of Buddhism?

The Meaning of Adventure (Mark)

As a therapist in supervision I learned that loneliness leads to anxiety in men. In myself I could see that the desire for excitement is meant to eclipse the loneliness, tamp it down so that it will be ignored. Gary and I know it never passes without an effort. Loneliness lives in the background, underneath the hunger for adventure. But I had to get the definition of adventure, the real one, to understand the connection, and to get beyond it. With that knowledge, could adventure become a spiritual practice, and more than a solution to anxiety and loneliness?

Adventure isn't an experience going as planned, with some exciting stuff to see, hear, feel, taste, and actions that one takes and performs skillfully, with everything going along pretty well. It's not that at all. The simplest meaning of adventure is "toward the unknown." When everything goes to shit and a lot of creativity and problem-solving and a strong dose of adrenalin are required to get out of a situation where death is a real possibility, that's when adventure shows up.

Adventure demands a conscious effort to maintain attention and concentration in the moment at hand. To me it feels like being wired. That state is normal for a child like me who was raised with fear and anxiety in an emotionally unstable home, who wasn't sure about what was going to happen next. I used adventure in late adolescent and adult life to purify that experience, which for me was colored by a consistent undercurrent of angry disappointment and resentment between my parents and toward me. For Gary it was an unstable home torn by separation, divorce, and the death of a parent. Both of us were out there on the edge early in life.

The hunger for adventure doesn't come out of nowhere, that's for damn sure. Adventure, real adventure, when an undercurrent of healthy anxiety and rational fear populates my thoughts, feels a little beyond normal life, that's for sure. My survival is an expression of dominance over all of this negative energy, when I overcome the anxiety, get behind it, find out what kind of crap I'm feeding myself to rationalize my world in the moment. Often it is the kind of anxiety and fear that a little kid feeds himself and feels it in his stomach when he is anticipating a beating. Getting beyond that fear is a relief. As I pull myself up and over a granite edge to see daylight, when I see that fifteen-degree diagonal line that will take me up and over the wave that could swamp my boat if I went head-on into it, as anxious as I might be, I know I have broken free of fear, put the energy to use, and I've been blessed with living in the moment. Acknowledging that the world is out of my control and that I must adapt to work with it becomes a prayer.

That experience of adventure is not available while reading a book, or going to the movies, or watching TV, or following a marked trail blazed by someone else. The aftermath of real adventure is a deep sense of accomplishment that isn't measured in money or awards or praise. It's about saving one's own life by learning how to work *with* Nature rather than *against* Her, to go with Her flow of energy and ride it, and become one with Her. For me it's a lesson in relinquishing ego, because there is no time to think about how cool I was in the experience, as the experience itself occupies my consciousness, and focusing on anything else creates danger.

If you've ever wondered why John Muir could spend so much time alone in Yosemite and never feel lonely, it's because he was the Olympic Champion of "Flowing with Nature." He climbed the big walls by himself, with the most primitive gear imaginable, and he was never alone. Nature was right there with him, and She owned his heart. To Gary and me, all of the "man against nature" themed media hype about adventure is bullshit made up by someone without love for Nature, for Her peace, serenity, and power.

If you're looking for a model in life of what I'm talking about, regarding adventure, a man who understands flowing with Nature is Bear Grylls, a survivalist who truly loves preparing for adventure and pursuing it. He is also a philanthropist who, bare-ass naked, rowed a bathtub up the Thames River in

London to raise money for a friend who lost his legs in a climbing accident. And in case you're thinking that a guy who named himself Bear must think a lot of himself, he got the name from his older sister who nick-named him Bear when he was a week old as she thought him to be a very spunky baby. So it's just the opposite of what a lot of men might think: his name is not about being the tough adventurer he truly is, it's a name that has soft, sweet love from his family built into it. He grew into the name. Does that give you an idea of where the seat of his courage and the depth of his heart come from?

Where does your courage come from?

Seeking Excitement and Searching for the Missing Father (Mark)

When I can focus enough to look back into my early childhood, all the seemingly complex emotional pain boils down to one process: I was missing my father, and I learned how to quietly slip into loneliness as the father I had was not present.

Gradually, the wearing character of loneliness taught me how to slip into anxiety, fear, and longing for a different life with a more positive tonality, in which my positive value would be reflected in my father's eyes. That is the gift from my father that I yearned for, to be viewed in a positive way, and my mother could not fulfill this need to be valued by the male parent, and no woman can do that.

I learned early on that excitement made any feelings of loneliness for my father go away, and that was one of the reasons for my being such a wild thing getting into trouble all the time. It ran deeper than a hunger for attention. It was a hunger for being valued. As I matured I desired more excitement so I wouldn't have to feel lonely. The need for excitement became an addiction that paralleled the expectation of being alone and without value. Excitement then became the status quo, as was feeding the feelings that excitement generated with greater risks and more demanding accomplishments. I ran long distances pushing myself way too hard. I took on jobs in which I could crash and burn, and worked my ass off to survive. I took on risks, like jumping off sheer cliffs in Jamaica into the ocean below, and had to learn in that instant how to wait for the right moment of a wave coming in before it broke on the rocks so I would jump out far enough and have enough depth to slow my momentum and just touch the bottom with my feet and not end up with my knees up my ass.

I found that the hunger for excitement or accomplishment waned when I found a partner and felt less lonely. The less I felt lonely the less I needed excitement and accomplishment. Then, feeling strangely fulfilled, I started to hunger for excitement and work out of habit, and began sabotaging the relationship out of a sense of feeling trapped by my own fulfillment.

That was my pattern. I would be loved, I would get close, and then I would feel trapped, pull back, become less available, less communicative, less caring, until my partner's feelings eroded into resentment and angry disappointment, or until she gave up and left the relationship, or until I told her the relationship was over.

I did not see the pattern when I was in it, and now it glows in the dark of my memory like radium. My key out of this pattern was finding a partner who needed as much independence as I did. I had to invest energy in the relationship to maintain it, and that needed to take a different form.

I learned from Gary that the key to having a sense of fulfillment from no longer feeling alone and an experience of excitement is to be the leader of the relationship. The goal was to invest the spontaneity or the planning that accompanies excitement or accomplishment into the relationship, thereby making space for both the relationship and adventures in life without having to sacrifice either experience. It does take some negotiation skills, I can tell you that, because today's woman does not seem to be so willing to be led, and would rather lead. I have a sense that the generation following me has a better shot at sharing leadership.

The Hunger for Adventure (Mark)

Upon reflection, I keep the hunger for adventure at bay with The Hill. It can seem innocuous, walking the same damn dirt trail up a mountain hundreds of times. Nothing could be farther from the truth. Take The Hill for granted, and Nature will provide a lesson in respect right quick.

In a sense The Hill is similar to a very prized and rare bottle of Armagnac, a contained adventure from which I pour a dram and consider myself fortunate to have it, and make the contents last as long as I can. The risk is always there, waiting around the bend. Playing along the boundary between respect and stupidity reminds me of honing a razor's edge: "The sharp edge of a razor is difficult to pass over; thus the wise say the path to Salvation is hard" (from the opening of *The Razor's Edge* by Somerset Maugham, 2003).

Gary and I were hiking a trail in Big Sur, and the regularity and control we had developed from hundreds of hours on The Hill felt like a limit I needed to break through. So he reluctantly agreed to do some bushwhacking into the forest, and we found ourselves looking at a shallow ravine that we were already about ten yards into. But we weren't in the ravine. We were above it.

We were standing on dense web of branches that were made of the tops of trees covered with a matting of dead leaves that during a bad storm (we thought) had locked into each other. The ground was more than twenty feet down. We decided that this was not a good idea. We headed for the nearest slope, stepping from branch to branch and testing each step for spring or snap before applying our weight.

I cherish moments like that because they help define the boundary of adventure. As I age I realize the time for risks grows precious, and Gary is clear on this as well. A few minutes of fun can easily result in six months of healing, stretching, taping, and gentle recovery. If that is the price of staying in touch with true adventure then there needs to be a willingness to pay it, even as the cruelty of time slows my step, grays my hair, and steals my vision of myself.

When Heroes Get Old (Mark)
>It was morning
>And I allowed myself to wake
>Out of the dream
>That was too sweet to be mine.
>
>The day spins and then whirls;
>Light burns into cool night.
>
>It was near midnight
>When I allowed myself to sleep
>Into the dream
>That was harsh enough to be mine.
>
>Near the heart-light
>That keeps enough darkness away
>That keeps daemons at bay
>I keep a memory
>
>I ask, is the image real?
>This place, this sense?
>
>And then the Hero appears,
>As he actually is,
>The one with burning eyes,
>A tattered cloak,

A limp that will never heal,
And a life lived always onward.

I asked myself
What happens when heroes get old?

And the Hero pulls
The cloak tighter against the cold rain,
And limps onward;
Ever onward.

I close my heart.

The Hungry Kid Within (Gary)

As we walk I am aware that I am processing out loud. I talk about my deprived inner child, and how he watched and listened to other children describe their trips to the beach, Hawaii, New York, skiing with their families or trips to Europe. I always felt deprived, and perhaps never knowing what it meant to have "fun." Now that I have the fortune to allow me to do almost anything I want, I find my little kid often dragging me around the world.

When I was a teenager I also spent a great deal of time looking at magazines and fantasizing. My world of fantasy was helped along by movies, Sears and Montgomery Ward catalogs, eventually TV, men's magazines describing wonderful places, and most certainly *Playboy*. (I was interested to learn that part of Hugh Hefner's journey was stimulated by being left by a woman during his time in the military.)

It didn't help that my first friend in high school was enthralled with Hillsborough, California, and what money could buy. He was also into stocks and educated me on the "possibilities" in the market. My little kid's fantasies went wild. The fantasy train was not only running but reinforced.

Now I find that the kid frequently takes me away from reality. I have to stop him and I think that is already in process, as sometimes I don't want to do anything or look at anything. I rarely watch TV or movies anymore because I find them so loaded with bullshit fantasy.

So what is real? I am escaping my child's fantasies more easily every day. Now, in the moment, I am desireless. I wonder if it is okay to be desireless. Of course I have to watch out for that little kid who is always waiting to go for a ride (yeah, maybe like the Sunday car rides my aunt and uncle would take with me when I was three years old). It doesn't take much stimulation from outside or inside to activate his unfulfilled desires or "hunger."

What if life was as simple as helping people, working on the house, playing with my dog, reading, and spending time with family and friends along with an occasional fun activity, or an adventure? What would it take to be still, to be present? I believe it will just take practice.

Tomorrow is another day of not walking The Hill and yet The Hill is with me wherever I go. It maintains me.

Hoka Hay (Gary)

I have been recruited by my wife to remove a vine from its trellis. My cousin Miguel and I work hard to remove it in the hot sun. At least I remove it from underneath rather than above, where I might fall through an eight foot lattice, and it is much hotter up there. We drive it to the dump, and we are done. Miguel has never been to the dump so it is fun to show him. We drive to the recycle area, and watch four deer hanging back about two hundred feet away. It is a good day. *Hoka hay* (today is a good day to die). I surrender to just being here. It's not so bad. Pretty funny how a garbage dump can be a source of joy.

In the evening I tour a friend of Sue's newly remodeled home. They have put a million and a half dollars into their remodel. Their house is beautiful, with many fine touches. I would have been envious to some degree in the past but today I let go. The house is beautiful but there is no land. It makes me appreciate what I do have: The Hill.

Just to Be Where I Am (Gary)

I find a lot of my writing happens before I get to the page. So this morning I find myself writing. In absence of myself I go somewhere else in my imagination. Where is that? Can I not just be here? I don't accept or like where I am, so I travel outside myself. It's an example of my old childhood habit. I struggle to be here. It's actually very sweet when I allow myself to just be where I am. I relax and meld into this place. I am present. I find it so difficult to just be still yet my creative mind is at its best when it is free of distraction.

Home (Gary)

I have decided today to stay at "home" and spend most of my time in the back yard. I have watched the ants, played with my dog, had my wife take a couple pictures of me for an application, helped her bathe her dog, cooked a fresh organic vegetable dish for myself, read, worked for ten minutes in the yard, and I am now laying in the sun with my shirt off writing this.

I observe that I am not waiting for anything nor am I anxious to do something. I am not missing anything nor forgetting something I "should" be doing. I am at home. My mind is blank and that is okay. Am I home yet? I don't know. Let me just "sit a spell," as they said in the old west.

Sadly this isn't Essie and Alan's. My mother used to board me with them during the week because of her work. They had a wonderful place with more of a country feel. It was about four acres with apple trees and a swing between two giant redwoods, a dog, and great cooking. I fondly remember the after-school date nut bread and the tapioca pudding, the essence of which I cannot put on the page. Yes, I feel the sadness.

The part I didn't want to write was that they initially scared me with their fights over Alan's drinking. I had nightmares and developed a stutter. I remember Essie finding a bottle of Four Roses bourbon under my mattress. Then one day all the fighting and drinking stopped. I am grateful. God knows what I would have been like if that had continued.

Now I am really sad. I remember digging a hole in the ground there just to see what I could find. It was my hole and my sacred adventure no one else knew. I also found interesting old stuff in their old burn pile. Why do I cry about that? I have to guess it's because I felt I had something that was mine and in my aloneness I found cool things to do and adventures I could create. I no longer have that. Was it a sense of home? Can I create it here? Maybe what I most miss is allowing that kid the freedom to adventure.

I have to recognize that The Hill is a large part for my child. My fantasy of bushwhacking through the brush and sitting under a tree no one else can reach, or has even considered getting to from the trail, really appeals to me. I often look off the trail and toy with my desire to cross the high brush to get to an old tree at the top of a hill, to a place where, maybe, no one has ever ventured. Maybe there will be a relic from the past there: a mountain lion's lair; a drug dealer's pot farm; the skeleton of an ancient mountain man.

Chapter 3

The Leafy Path of Gentleness and Compassion

Beginning with Beauty and Grace (Mark)

Today the beauty of this part of the trail is intoxicating. The sunlight glinting through glass green leaves creates a dappled dance on the dusty surface of the trail before us. And we are only at the beginning. It is easy to relax in this moment, and accept a state of gradual unknowing, a release from the day, from work, from relationships. This moment is colored with laughter and a little grace. I believe the grace appears in preparation for the challenges to come, as the mountain makes its demands.

As drivers toward a goal men rarely allow themselves gentleness or compassion. It is all about the price we pay for the effort, about paying our dues. The sacrifices we take on are not made out of the desire for gentleness and compassion but out of the purposeful pursuit of any kind of pain, mental, emotional, and physical. We admire combat if we are in the place of all knowing, and honor it as if it is the most sacred of realities, as it romanticizes the pain of our sacrifice. Here on The Hill, beyond the Gate of Unknowing, we change the intellectual and emotional pattern and honor gentleness and compassion as men in the world. Once we liberate ourselves from the need to sacrifice our lives to goals without humanity our task shifts to discovering where it is that we will invest these two gifts, gentleness and compassion, in ourselves, our families, and our communities.

The Bond with Adventure and Pain (Gary)

Time to round up my equipment; Mark is on his way. Got my heat socks on, my water with Emergen-C, stop watch, camera, StingKill, sun screen, sunglasses, knife, note pad and waterproof pen, cross training shoes that I have to replace every three months, and lastly my special pack for minimal gear. This is part of the fun, having the right equipment is *de*

rigueur. I grab it and head for the door. It's uncool to be late so I am in Mark's old BMW convertible within a minute of his arrival. It gives me a sense of relief to know that I am ready. It's a warrior and leader mentality and it also serves the magician part of me that makes things happen (see *King, Warrior, Magician, Lover* by Robert Moore, 2013).

This day we talk about why we process so much and come to realize both of us were restricted as children. Mark's mother was always afraid he would get hurt so kept him from many normal childhood adventures. He, like me, spent many hours watching others go and do things from the window of his home. We each recognize a large part of the source of our bond: a bond with isolation, frustration, and pain.

Why Can't People Love One Another? (Gary)

My liver (I guess it's my liver) is hurting (or at least my right side is) so I slept in today and have hung around the house doing simple chores. I noticed a thought that I simply wanted to know why people couldn't love one another and I felt very sad. I think that was a twelve-year-old's voice. I think that has been my quest for most of my life. Why can't people simply love each other? Why not?

Again, in the quiet I find much revealed. I know I must fully love my wife and risk trusting her without fear, resentment, judgment, or reservation in order to do it. I am also aware that the ego is the enemy of relationship.

Do you allow yourself to love? I mean really love someone. What would be the cost? Are you afraid that would mean you would be responsible for them? What stops you from loving fully? Fear? Judgment? What are your stops?

Connection (Gary)

When I walk The Hill I am often taken back to distant memories, fond memories of walking the logging roads in Oregon as a kid or walking the sand dunes in North Bay, Oregon, with my brother. When we cross a sandy part of the trail I always think of the time my brother and I walked a great distance until the sand dunes seemed to run out and we turned around. It was warm, it was an adventure, and my brother was leading the way. When I was walking the lumber roads it was with my buddies. We borrowed single-shot .22 rifles, bought a box of fifty rounds for fifty cents, and were off to explore and see what we could hit. My friend David Zimmerman (where are you David?) was a great shot. I watched him shoot the cigarette out of our friend Thorold Simpson's mouth. Those two were tight buddies and now I can't find them. Anyway, this is just one reminiscence out of many when I walk this trail.

Sometimes I want to smell those logging-camp aromas of fresh cut wood and chain saw oil again. Sometimes I want to recapture the moment with my brother and my friends. This is about connection. I feel most alive when I am connected.

Find the energy that makes you feel most connected and that is the best medicine. What from your history fuels you? Uncover what it is. Pay attention to what has meaning to you. No judgment; just the truth of what is.

For me it's like the moment at this morning's coffee meeting (tea, for me, actually) when my friend taps me on the shoulder and says evenly, "Shut your mouth." I used to be a mouth breather and he knows I am trying to break the habit. His simple act of caring means a lot to me.

Silence (Gary)

So often I forget that my creative juices moisten in the quiet rather than the business of life. Somehow I have been brought to believe that I am more creative if I am busy. In that state of being busy, thoughts and ideas come up and they only occasionally stick. But in the quiet, when I am still, I create an idea and act on it. It becomes substantial in the stillness. It's like most of these words. They have made it to the paper because I have been quiet enough to hear them. So the truth is that I am more liable to implement a change or creative idea if I spend time in silence. I certainly like the idea of more silent time. The author Carlos Castaneda called it the "do nothing" time. Most importantly, it is a time to feel. The one time I saw him, his departing words to everyone were, "Remember the most important thing you can do is to be quiet for one second a day."

Being In Silence (Mark)

Silence for me was the way through my shattered ability to attend to anything. If I could have complete quiet and a task that I wanted to do with complete absorption, I had the opportunity to be brilliant for that moment. So much energy crammed into one experience. I needed to seek out silence, actually demand it of my environment to be of any use to myself in what is usually referred to as "the normal world." I need to minimize contact with anyone because presence seems to be a license for communication among people who have no idea of how valuable the ability to pay attention actually is, and can turn it on and off like a light.

Gary and I need the quiet to be in the presence of an understanding that feels greater than us. We work together in this moment, writing in silence, side by side in the same position relative to each other that we maintain on our hikes on The Hill. I am on his right; he is on my left. We are in different parts of this landscape of our experience, and yet we are in the same place. In the current moment, silence is the gift we share.

Being Out of Silence (Mark)

Silence may be our requirement when we write, but our ability to split our attention puts us at a higher level of performance than non-ADD (Attention Deficit Disorder) people in other circumstances.

The ability to shift and split attention constantly is a gift in the midst of adventure. Also, the ability to focus one's attention on one event to the exclusion of any other event in a charged moment is a treasure in the midst of danger. These are truths that are usually ignored with kids and adults who have ADD or ADHD (Attention Deficit with Hyperactivity Disorder). The ability to place attention in a dozen directions and then focus completely on one point in exclusion of multiple sources of danger and its distraction is critical to life on a mountain wall, or in a kayak running rapids, or cycling over difficult technical terrain, or sailing in thirty-five knot winds through heavy chop. The people who want kids with ADD and ADHD to behave like the "normies" are not usually the ones who can handle these kinds of challenges because they involve high risk outside the norm. The "normies" focus on the risks rather than the gifts of adventure, and romanticize the risks to make an adventurous person seem special. This is where kids and adults with ADD excel. In other words, their ability to split their attention in a dozen pieces and then suddenly focus can be honed into a *skill*, and it gives them superiority when everything goes to shit. Hyperfocus that saves lives in the midst of disaster is a skill. The day I hear a kid praised by a teacher for his rapid capability to adapt to multiple, dangerous, sudden events because the teacher sees it as a skill is the day praise for the kids like Gary and I used to be will replace accusations such as "refusal to avoid risks and stay within a normal range of behavior."

A Different Hill Today (Gary)

This one I climb by myself, and winding through the dry blond grass to the top of a small mountain a short distance away from a major mountain artery. There is some traffic noise but I enjoy this piece of isolation. I am sitting amongst old oaks in a barren space. The ocean breeze whips around me. I can look toward the ocean, but smoke from a forest fire keeps me from seeing beyond a distant ridge. It's warm, about 72°, and few bugs to bother me, although they usually don't anyway. I find the more you relax in places like this the more they leave you alone.

I am here early, waiting for the men in our Men of Fire group. What a gift to be able to do my work here. It's a dream fulfilled to be able to meet on a mountain. Usually we meet in my garage (although I call it my barn for another desire). We have been meeting here once a week for about a month. Life is good.

Today I wear my new wedding ring (I have lost two). I am determined to keep this one. My wife gave it to me for our thirtieth wedding anniversary. I guess I am a keeper. I asked for this design—an elk in front of a mountain. The name given to me in a Native American Naming Ceremony is Quiet Elk, which I changed after my New Warrior Weekend to Wild Elk. Maybe it should be Crazy Elk. You can decide that.

"Don't let those people have died for nothing" (Gary)

Mark and I were supposed to walk The Hill today. He called and said he couldn't make it. That was a big disappointment for both of us. However, he just moved, and was down because he had to downsize into a marginal neighborhood. His wife is suffering from anxiety, and he is clearly stressed.

He is packing for Germany to speak at a conference on forgiveness. His presentation is based on his dissertation about the unique posttraumatic stress of the grandchildren of survivors of the Holocaust. Heavy shit.

I grab the picture of The Respite off my office wall to give to Mark. I am very attached to the picture but I know its better service at this time. It is also a token of my affection for him, and a sign of support for his mission. I drive to his house to send him off. He pulls up to my truck and I take out the picture. We both admire the detail offered in the watercolor paper I used to reprint the picture. He seemed detached, but I understood and allowed it to be.

We hug, I wish him well, and am motivated to say as I choke back emotions, "Don't let those people have died for nothing." I didn't expect that to come up. I will think of him and his journey for his twelve days. It will be a strenuous trip to do alone with a wife who is in the middle of setting up a new house after a tough move. I tell him I will check in with her.

Speaking for the Dead (Mark)

When Gary said to me, "Don't let those people have died for nothing," I realized he wasn't talking to me as an ordinary person. He was talking to me as a soldier. He said it in a voice and a tone that cut through forty years from Vietnam to this moment. I had a job to do and I was expected to do it. In that moment I knew he understood what I was doing for all of the people in my family who died for simply being who they were. I was going to ground zero, to Germany and Poland, to let any remnant of the Nazis know they had not succeeded.

I Have a Responsibility to Make a Difference (Gary)

Mark took off a couple days ago for Germany. He said he was spending a few days in New York with his niece and nephew before going to Europe. According to his plan he must be in Germany by now.

I drove home after work and changed clothes to do the hike up The Hill by myself. I was overdue and had to go. I don't like to have more than four days between hikes. I was a little concerned about the air quality as I hiked

but I seemed to be okay. I checked Spare the Air and it said the air quality was good. I was still suspicious. I found myself making pretty good time and I passed the Hill of Cruelty quite easily.

Here I was again with feelings coming up. I thought again of all those people who died in the concentration camps, for what? Somehow I feel I have a responsibility to make a difference. I just know I felt bad for a brief moment and felt a responsibility. The rest of the hike was a joy and I exchanged appreciation of the day with a group of bikers on their way up The Hill.

I look at myself and think of the sacrifices my ancestors made that have made my world just a little bit better than theirs. What sacrifices will I make and have I made that will make life just a little better for those I love and the generation to follow?

I advise you to look beyond yourself. How or what sacrifices did your ancestors make that helped make your world just a little bit better? What sacrifices will you make for the sake of the generation after you?

Being in "Ground Zero" of the Holocaust (Mark)

I have not written a word about my trip to Europe beyond the notes I wrote during the journey. I have fully forgotten about them until this moment. I even wonder where they are—maybe in the envelope with all of the receipts and materials from the trip—that is how overjoyed I am that the experience is over.

I did my best to live among the dead for about three and a half years. I called them The Six Million, knowing full well that all of the dead totaled more than eleven million and included Catholic priests, the mentally ill, the disabled, homosexuals, the Romani people (insulted as Gypsies by the Nazis and most of Europe), and political enemies of the state, among many others, and that I was focused on the Jews alone.

I did not write about the second generation, the children of Holocaust Survivors, except as background to help define them as parents of the third generation, the Survivors' grandchildren. Writing about the children of Survivors was part of the work, an important part, as they were the people who had the most influence on locating participants for me. They wanted to have their children help me in my study of the passage of a terrible trauma across generations, an echo of the experience that haunted their lives, and at the same time gave the third generation, the grandchildren of Survivors, a strength that the second generation did not have: a greater ability to forgive others in the present. This surprising discovery was the outcome of my research.

I looked through the large, white envelope containing the evidence of my trip to Europe: ticket stubs and guides, maps and tour information, my speaking and hotel itineraries, and found my notes from the journey. I checked the dates of each entry and did not, could not, read beyond those parts of the account. I had folded a sheaf of white paper in half to form a signature, and had written on them as if it were a book of sorts. The only thing that gave me joy in the moment was that I found the notes. I simply needed to know where they were, that they existed, that I could go back to them, as they verified that my experience was real.

The fact that I cannot read more than a word here and there tells me I am not ready to go back through my journey to London, to Berne, to Auschwitz, to Oswiecim and the poverty of Poland, to Freiberg and the wealth of Germany, and to the fear in my gut as I walked through the streets of these last two cities. These countries were known to hate the Jews with so much energy that they slaughtered Jews in the millions for a dark purpose. This purpose extended far beyond the mass murder. The hidden purpose was to satisfy two deranged, spiritually motivated goals. (For more information on the spiritually motivated goals of the Third Reich see *The Pride and Price of Remembrance* by Yoslow, 2007.)

The first goal was to capture life energy in enormous quantity and direct it into the power of the Aryan Reich. The second was to ensure that the messiah of the Jews could never appear. Thus Hitler, who believed he was the reincarnation of the god Odin, could dominate the world. These were the closely guarded reasons for murdering millions of Jews, and ridding the world of the Romani people, the developmentally disabled, the mentally ill, religious leaders, and enemies of the state.

Millions were murdered. The number is so huge and is normally associated with the population of major cities, with economics, with money, real estate, and investments. It is difficult to concretely imagine millions of dead people because most of us do not have an experiential reference for mass slaughter. The closest example may be an aerial view of several miles of beautiful but crowded beachfront anywhere in the US on Memorial Day, except everyone would be dead.

Imagine how many cows and pigs and lambs and chickens are slaughtered every day for human consumption. Don't get me wrong; I'm not a rabid vegetarian proselytizing that lifestyle change. It just helps to see the bloody product of slaughter that is usually provided in its neat plastic wrap as something more than a piece of a living thing now dead, but instead as the whole bloody corpse to get a clear image of the murder of millions of people in bloody horror. Imagine the meat aisle of a supermarket expanded to fill the whole supermarket, and then imagine one thousand supermarkets, and that represents a fraction of the mass atrocity. If you find yourself in grim silence while considering this comparison, remember that leaders of European nations and the United States who knew the Holocaust was happening not only turned their back, but also saw this as a solution to a number of social conundrums including "the Jewish problem." Breckinridge Long, Assistant Secretary of State under Franklin Delano Roosevelt, had every plea by a European Jew for emigration to the United States sent to his office where they were all held with no action taken (Long, 1940) and summarily destroyed. This is not conspiracy theory. It is documented US government history not taught in school.

I remember being at Auschwitz II Birkenau, and seeing a forest of chimneys rising out of the outlines, the stone footprints, of buildings beyond the still-standing wooden barracks and chimneys of the death camp. The Nazi SS had burned most of the wooden barracks to hide the evidence of what had been done at the death camp. But each barracks had a heating system consisting of two chimneys near the ends of each building, and a long, low, brick, heating duct that ran the length of the barracks between the chimneys. The idea was that the heat from the two chimneys would be passed along this containment to radiantly heat the entire building. Nazis claimed that this was the way barracks for horses were built, to keep them warm through Poland's icy cold winter nights. It was part of Nazi disinformation to make it appear from the air that this was a huge storage facility for horses, cows, and pigs to support the army. In actuality, the fireplaces were rarely used, as it did not matter how cold it became for the Jews. These brick structures survived the fires set by the SS to destroy the evidence of the camp near the end of World War II in Europe.

I remember walking through these barracks. There were about twenty of them, and I promised myself in the moment of my arrival at Auschwitz II Birkenau that I would walk through every one of them. I entered the front door of the first building, walked passed the first chimney and along the heating duct to the space beyond the second chimney, and up the other side to return to the front door. It was a slow march, up one side and down the other, examining every square foot of the interior, noting the width of the stalls, remembering the levels of bunks in the stalls where people slept four or five on a level to maintain a maximum, efficient use of each barracks.

In one of the buildings there was a very old piece of dry and tattered striped clothing draped across the concrete shoulder of the chimney where it met the run of the concrete heating duct. I imagined from their appearance that these rags had never been moved since January 27, 1945, when the Ukrainian Army liberated this death camp. I could not help but wonder who wore them.

The SS fled the camp knowing how Russians would treat them until the Russian interrogators learned anything they could. The leaders of the Soviet Army were informed of the camp's existence by local Polish townspeople. The prisoners of the camp who were just barely alive would never have been discovered otherwise.

I looked up at the peaked ceiling in each of these buildings, and noticed that the top plate of the walls did not meet the roof, and sunlight did its best to slip in between this space and enter the building. There was a light drizzle falling outside, and a cold, harsh, gray light at Auschwitz II that day. It was a dampness that, upon exposure for hours, seeped into my bones and kept me cold without any hope for warmth. I had no doubt that these were the conditions that existed for people in the camps. I trudged through building after building in the same way, with the same slow pace. I managed to make it through five barracks.

I exited the fifth barracks in a state of emotional exhaustion I had not known before, characterized by an experience of accumulating emptiness. I approached the sixth building and started to feel ill, a cold nausea filling my gut. I opened the door of the sixth barracks, took one step in, and found myself struck by a wave. It is hard to adequately describe it beyond saying it was pure Evil, yet now it seemed to have substance. I could not press through it.

I had encountered this Evil for the three and a half years as an idea, studying the death of millions, and writing about, and reading the responses of the grandchildren of Survivors to my research questions about the Holocaust. I experienced it very powerfully near the end of the work, when one of the professors on my dissertation committee demanded that I write into the introduction a descriptive, experiential section that would cause a person to feel as if he or she were a Jew in a death camp.

Now, with one foot in the door of the sixth barracks at Auschwitz II on this cold, cold day, I encountered a taint of Evil within, knowing in fact that something beyond any commonplace idea of human cruelty had occurred there in deed rather than thought. Try as I might, several times, I could not press through the energetic barrier to this space. I felt the accumulation of a deep sense of failure at not fulfilling my promise to myself to walk through every barracks, and at the same time could feel a sense of deep warning that I was standing at the boundary of an experience that could cause me harm if pursued.

Standing in the doorway, I looked up at the interior, at the place where the wall nearly met the ceiling, at the cold light forcing its way into this cold, shadowy interior. I did not realize at the time the significance of this cold light, and how much it resonated in my conscious reality and my unconscious memory. I stepped back; closed the ten-foot tall barn door of the building, and took another step back to stand on the lumpy earth dotted with wild grasses, regularly mowed, that color the grounds of the entire complex.

I realized I needed to leave this place, but I could not until I had walked up the stone stairwell and into the watchtower at the main gate of Auschwitz II Birkenau, and took in the view of the camp. The forest of brick chimneys beyond the standing barracks told of how massive the effort had been to murder so many millions of people, and this was only one site of the slaughter that took place throughout Germany and Eastern Europe. There were over 15,000 concentration camps where hundreds of thousands died of starvation, exhaustion, exposure, and execution, and 6 killing centers where more than 6,000 people were killed every day, from 1941 to 1944: close to 4,000,000 people per year.

Reluctantly, I walked to the site of the showers that preceded the crematoria, and saw where trucks had been parked in rows on both sides with their engines running creating a din of noise that covered the screams of the dying in the showers after tablets of poison were dropped into wire baskets below the roofline, tablets that were activated by the water vapor rising from dozens upon dozens of bodies crammed into the space. The roar of revving the engines was just another form of disinformation for the thousands held captive in the camps through the cold, cold winter, and the steaming summer.

When I returned home I was ill for a couple of weeks, ill and exhausted. Gary invited me to walk The Hill, but I could not go, and he walked with another man from our group, Stacy, and I was glad he did not have to go alone. When I was finally able to walk The Hill again I went alone.

That day I drove home from working with the men at Goodwill Industries Silicon Valley, the homeless veterans whom Dennis Hayesly, a drug and alcohol counselor, and I had invited to become a men's group, and get the support they needed to pull themselves up and out of homelessness. Dennis himself had lived in a tent under a bridge for eighteen years. This was his way of reclaiming himself as well as every man he could rescue from that life. This was some of the most rewarding group work I have ever done. Dennis named it "The Lifeboat Group," because it was the mission of the group to pull men who were drowning in the sea of homelessness into the boat. A number of graduates of the group moved on to stable jobs within the Goodwill family, or moved on to positions in companies that had programs in place to hire veterans, representing a sincere effort to make a difference in these men's lives. As I left the building that day I felt that Dennis and I had done good work, but slowly the emptiness returned, and the perception of Evil, the echo of Auschwitz.

It took me a while to put myself together for the hike. I gathered my clothing and my gear in a slow, one thing at a time, linear experience, moving in slow motion, almost deciding to not go several times. I was surprised when I arrived at the place where we park for the walk, as I had covered the experience on automatic pilot from my equipment locker to the parking spot. I made the internal decision that I would maintain a moderate pace, stay focused, and avoid injury.

Starting up the blacktop was an exercise in resistance beyond its physical steepness. I focused on each step, on taking one step after another, on my breathing. I paid minimal attention to the difficulty, the pain, the sweat, the unrelenting up and up and up with each step. I welcomed the effort.

It took nearly the entire climb before I was consciously on the path I knew so well, before I could see the birds, smell the wild sage, feel the cool October wind on my face scented with wet leaves and damp earth, and see the rows of mountains in the distance, and the glint of sun on water of the Lexington Reservoir down below. The accumulation of positive energy on the hike up was replaced by a gathering emptiness on the way down. I slipped a couple of times because I was not present, but was not injured. Something was feeding on me, eating at me, and I did not know what it was. I focused and made it down safely.

I went home that afternoon to the property that my wife and I had toured and purchased before I left for my journey through Europe. I parked the car in the driveway and walked back to the garage. The house had been built in 1928, but the garage was built in the 1940s. I opened the garage door, stepped in, and looked up at the top plate, at the wall and the peaked ceiling. I recognized the light struggling to find its way into the building. I closed the garage door behind me. In the semi-darkness of the windowless structure I looked up to see the light struggling through the space where the wall did not meet the roof, the cold, cold light, and felt the echo of millions of souls rattling through me.

I lifted up the garage door and left the building, went into the house, and made a phone call. Three days later the garage was reduced to rubble by a demolition crew with heavy equipment and the last of it was hauled away leaving nothing but bare earth. I stood in the middle of the demolition site and prayed for the eleven million lost to the death camps.

I called the chair of my dissertation committee, Dr. Robert Morgan, a few days later, and told him about the experience inside the garage. He responded in a very serious tone. He told me I could not close the door of the garage behind me, that it invited the same energy into my consciousness, and that the archetypal exposure could be very dangerous for me. We agreed that it was the Archetype of the Apocalypse, an element of the collective unconscious. I knew its Darkness was powerful enough to draw anyone into its own lines of force.

It was this archetype that had overcome the decency of the people of Germany. It had overcome their powerful sense of what is right and good, and allowed the apocalypse to become a reality led by a self-proclaimed superman, a man driven mad by a power over which he had no control. His personal weakness toward Evil had become the servant of the Archetype of the Apocalypse within the collective unconscious of Nazi Germany.

When I told Dr. Morgan I had ordered the demolition of the garage, and that it no longer existed, he paused, and I waited. He asked me, "Do you think and feel that your journey in this is complete?" I allowed the question to resonate within me.

In that moment I was certain that what I wrote in the introduction to my dissertation was true, that there is no returning home from this journey, and that is why companions on the journey are so important (Yoslow, 2007). I saw the significance of The Hill in my life, and its ability to reveal the truth in my mind and heart. I said to Dr. Morgan, "I'm done."

I spoke to Gary about this experience during our next hike up The Hill, and he also was taken aback by my account of stepping into the old garage, and closing the door behind me. Of all the men I knew, he had the clearest understanding that there was no way home from this journey.

We were companions in grief as we tearfully trudged through the dust, remembering all the lost. We mourned all the good men and women lost in Vietnam and all the slaughtered in Auschwitz, all those we loved in our lives, now gone.

Neighbors on the Walk (Gary)

I recently met Corrine and Bob, who have a home at the trailhead, and made immediate friends with them because I took a liking to their old dog. I think it was because the dog took a liking to me as well. They showed me the house that was for sale across from theirs and even invited me to come up The Hill with them while they changed the community water filter. What a treat. I didn't go with them but instead took their suggestion of a shortcut down The Hill along with information regarding a closer and legal place to park. Wow, it certainly pays to extend oneself. I always say to my clients that everything happens out of relationship, so here it is. What a pleasurable return on investment. Sometimes we can get a little selfish in how much we interact with people because we become consumed with our full minds. Yes, that includes me.

Speaking of others on The Hill, there is Hanna the Akita whom we pass on most hikes. She is there to bark at us, as that is her job, and occasionally when she is lazy, she just ignores us like we are old news. We were blessed to have her on the trail with her master, a delightful lady and her new baby, one day last year. I took their picture and emailed it to her. That was sweet. Most times I would just say hi and keep moving, but this day Mark and I took a minute and I made the offer of a picture. Now she has a pleasant keepsake of herself and her baby in Nature with her dog. Simple gifting can delight the soul. It was Bianca, Hanna, and Jessie, and now, a year later, it's Bianca, Hanna, Jessie, and Paula. Another picture, another email. We now seem to have a ritual of doing this twice a year by running into each other by chance.

Another time I made a good attempt to get what seemed to be a lost dog back home. Initially he startled me a bit—okay, a lot—as he came around the corner. I am always hoping to see a mountain lion so when I saw him come around the blind bend it was a relief to see he was a dog. You know how that is: Watch out for what you ask for. I read his name and the phone number off his tag, and called the owner to rendezvous at the trailhead, but the dog took off again. I had to let him go. I called the owner and that was it. Then I ran into a biker and asked him to assist. We ran into each other on another hike and he said the dog had followed him to the top and he seemed to have found his way home. We now share that little saga every time we meet. That's another sweet story from The Hill.

I got it. This is all about proving myself. The climb, the hardship, the heat, the cold, the pain; I get to keep proving myself on a regular basis. There is no moment lost. And maybe I will make a connection along the way. Maybe that is why I notice whether Diane, or whatever her name is, and her daughter notice me at the end of the trail because they have seen me before. Sandy, who lives on The Hill, talks to me. Then there's Corrine and Bob who say hello. I am seeking validation of existence. I have always known that but not known that. Ah, the value of connection and not feeling alone.

I have found that life is much fuller and richer when seen as a series of shared experiences and a validation of the value of each other. Sometimes it's a simple smile or nod. I get just a little high from the smile or nod back that tells me I am not alone.

I encourage everyone to reach out to the small spark of life that passes from one soul to another as it energizes and lifts the spirit. It's also a reminder of your humanity.

Looking For My Tribe (Gary)

Most certainly one of my heroes in this regard is one of my clients who after much personal pain, abuse, and abandonment by his father, and twenty-three years of recovery became an incredibly loving man. He didn't graduate from high school yet has a very successful contracting business. I don't know about you but I have worked in construction and most contractors have a hard edge. John can have that edge; however, he greets his men with a hug. Sometimes they don't know what to do with that. Those who have known him for a while will stand there and wait until he is available. He also spontaneously engages strangers, one of my favorite things to do. I call it "not being a victim of circumstance."

The lesson this man has taught me is to lead yourself into the life you choose. Wait for no one or for any thing, validation, acceptance, encouragement, or sign.

I know now that when I accepted Michael Gurian's invitation to visit his 105-acre country estate north of Spokane I wept there because I felt accepted. At first I thought it was my response to his total acceptance, but that wasn't all of it. It was the embrace of the alder trees that surrounded me, the warmth of the sun, the gentle cooling breeze, the butterfly that landed on my shoe. There, as well as here, I am not alone, and I am blessed with total acceptance. So where does this hunger for benign acceptance come from?

I remember the first indicator. It was first grade. We were supposed to draw something for some kind of art project. It seemed we were all trying really hard to get it right. Somehow it was challenging. I remember giving it my best, but Johnny next to me wasn't taking it seriously. I remember now he was drawing a duck. Wow, that just flashed into my mind (the value of writing from a "let go" position). He was fucking the duck, so to speak. I loved ducklings as my aunt and uncle had frequently taken me to the park to feed the ducks and I had a string of toy ducks to pull around on the floor. I loved ducks. How could he do that with no respect? It was so wrong, and so awful, I took his drawing and ripped it up. I got in trouble for it, but I knew what he was doing was bad and wrong, and now I reflect that I must have had a fear of destruction of beauty, which for me may have been the equivalent of abandonment.

I think it had something to do with security because I had found something beautiful and sweet, and I treasured it. I was so emotionally bereft, so insecure and fearful of abandonment, that little things meant a tremendous amount to me. As a child I guarded my little treasures with a passion. That fuzzy yellow duck must have been an anchor of sorts.

There was another time when my uncle's brother came to the house, and I thought he was wearing my uncle's cap. I got really upset and adamant that he couldn't be wearing my uncle's cap. It was actually part of their shop clothing, but I didn't know that. Everyone evidently thought this was cute, but actually it was another example of me trying to maintain a sense of security, a knowing that sacred items would stay as they were; if they did it meant everything was going to be okay and I would be safe.

I know as an adult that what anchors me or makes me feel grounded is <u>being or doing</u> what my mother initiated in me: my father was dead when I was three years old, and I was to take care of her. Thus the hero was born.

What anchors you?

Fathering the Warrior Servant (Mark)

I ask myself what this journey up The Hill is about for me. If it is all about following Gary, or if it is something I need for myself. Having been without a loving father as a child I look to Gary for that fathering within his role as mentor in my work with men.

Since I am childless I have no experiential idea of what it means to be a father, and so I cannot reach the good father within myself for more than moments at a time. I can do so with my niece and nephew, and it breaks my heart whenever I am with them. I have missed most of their childhood out of not being able to connect with my family, as they are in New York, and wished-for emails and phone calls are no replacement for in-person contact.

Facing my work of being in relationship with family is part of being a warrior-servant. It is part of my struggle to become the man I hope to be, the man I strive to develop within me. I am clear that this work never ends.

As much as I would like to believe that I can reach a state of completion, I am as certain that there is no real ending beyond death. Even that may not be the end. At least that is my human hope for another shot at cleaning up our mess.

Chapter 4

The Respite

A Source of Will (Mark)

Every time we reach this gentle path, lined on both sides by birch and maple trees, our breathing changes as the grade decreases. The natural beauty that surrounds us is punctuated by the view of a rough-hewn corral style fence at the far end of the path that turns right and slightly inclines out of sight. This path allows us to relax before our next challenge, which is suggested by the upward angle of the fencing ahead of us.

Usually this type of restful path comes at the end of an arduous journey, but for us it shows up just before the climb starts to kick our asses. We often remark that The Respite is that marker between turning back and going forward. Its beauty is so satisfying that going home makes sense. But actually, The Respite shows up the way a deep breath is taken before a great effort is required. It is a moment to reflect on the Will that is required to continue up The Hill, an opportunity to make an internal check on our commitment.

I sometimes wonder, if this path were not as beautiful as it is, would we have the same impetus to go on? It is almost as if The Respite ignites a hunger for more experience. Its beauty feeds us an energy that goes beyond this physical moment.

A Sacred Object (Gary)

My mother before she died would often say, "What does it matter?" In her depression, nearing the end of her life in convalescent care, she gave up. I now understand what she said at a different level. I see the value not of giving up but of surrendering to what is. I like the Alcoholics Anonymous saying, "Let go; let God." She could have been at peace by letting go, but instead she was angry and bitter that she wasn't getting what she wanted and

that her life was over. The point is it doesn't matter. Nothing really matters unless you make it matter. In a sense she was right. Even then there are often times when you do so much better by surrendering and letting go. Just like it is on The Hill. Some days I just have to surrender to the heat, the rain, or the fog, and I love it.

Since the fire trail has been graded recently there is little if any glass or garbage to pick up. I consider it my duty to keep this trail pristine. It's a sacred trail, and needs to be respected. Yet there are years of broken pieces of glass that litter the way. I will say much of it is gone, thanks to me. To me it breaks the spell to find a shard of green glass sticking up from the ground where there has been peace. Peace: that is a good word to describe this for me.

I now connect the dots. The Hill has become another sacred object, like the ducklings I loved and cared for with my aunt, and like my uncle's hat. They all have given my life a sense of stability and meaning: a true grounding.

What grounds you to or in right action? Without something to ground you, you will spin, moving as fast as you can. Thus is born the Addiction to Hurry (Jones, 2003).

Acceptance and Transformation (Mark)

It is 110° on The Hill and we are training with full packs in preparation for leading the next Vision Quest. Gary speaks about surrender and challenge in the moment, and although it makes sense to me, I do not see it that way. To me it is an opportunity to focus on the work of not paying attention to the heat or the weight or the stress. It is about being in the moment with complete acceptance. I see surrender as something else, or at least different from what it is to let go. To me this experience is a conscious allowance of everything that seeks to stop me from accomplishing my goal, working *with* Great Nature rather than *against* Her, and respecting Her power in all of its forms. Maybe that is surrender, yet it seems a far more active process, as surrender seems so passive and, for me, has to do with giving up or giving in. I prefer total acceptance with a sense of appreciation for the powers of heat and gravity.

This is a transformation for me. I used to feel burdened and oppressed by whatever was offering the gift of conscious acceptance, and felt I had to fight whatever it was and dominate it in my reality. It is the difference between "being against" and "being with and within." To know transformation requires the liberation from battling life, and instead, welcoming the gift of the moment, right now. The transformation from struggle to acceptance is mirrored by our experience of The Hill, as we meet its unrelenting ascent with appreciation for our bodies and what they can do.

There is a sacred moment, a Respite, when I have disappeared from my egoic self. That takes the form of looking over my shoulder, and, in the view of the trail I have just climbed, seeing myself as I was, and in the view of the azure sky above the mountain crest I am approaching, seeing how far I have come.

Grace is alive in all of it.

In a moment of stress do you join with the nature of things or do you fight? A wise man knows the ego is the enemy of relationship with all, including himself.

The Hawk Comes Home to Die (Gary)

There are little saplings everywhere here on Gurian's land, and I am listening to the creek. Again why do I cry here? Now I look at the meadow and I cry some more. It is tall green grass and a forest of trees just beyond. But why do I cry? It feels so sweet; I have missed it. My heart hungers for this so much my head cannot know. A white butterfly wings past. My heart seems to sing behind it until it disappears. The wind opens the trees to more sun, and it feels for a moment as if I am in heaven. The sweat lodge is fifty feet away. Perhaps I am home again.

Michael tells me this is where the hawk came to die a couple weeks ago. Mike was coming to his meditation spot on the creek, and this old beat up hawk didn't move from his spot only a few feet away. The next day Mike saw him sitting in front of the mountain house, and in the morning he was dead. He had come here to die. It is a good spot to die, or die into, as we all will or could.

Butterflies continue to visit and the sound of the creek is soothing. This is similar to the place I grew up, years before I started my walks on The Hill in the clouds. It was there on logging roads that I hiked and became lost in marshy creeks with skunk cabbage abounding. And water skippers who hopped around in the water. This was where I learned to explore and hike. My friend and I would go to the war surplus store to get our gear. Our packs were WWII vintage. My brother did the same but his were WWI vintage. Ah, the aroma of the fresh cut trees from the lumber camp, and the scent of the chain saw oil. You could smell it from a distance. I realize more than ever why my hikes in the hills of Los Gatos mean so much to me. Even fighting off the flies in the hot sun brings me back—back home. This is a respite.

Completion (Gary)

I notice a slight pant as I edge up The Hill, and in just about the center of The Respite I let out three big sighs as if on automatic. It has been a heavy day in my private practice, and I recognize the sound of my own grief, like carrying a heavy emotional load. One man has threatened suicide, one told us last night he may have cancer, and another didn't show up for his appointment and may have relapsed, again, into his alcohol addiction. No sooner do I realize my grief than I see a hummingbird slip its tiny beak into a pretty red cylinder of a flower. Everything is okay now. I leave The Respite and begin the steeper climb. Ah, life is good, and I take in the air. I notice this week that I am feeling good without my usual fantasy wonderings. There has been little thought given to cars and real estate. I am enjoying each moment there is to enjoy. I occasionally ask myself how I am feeling, and when I stop to answer it has been to just notice that I am very comfortable.

How often do you allow yourself to "just notice" where you are? It's a way, with practice, that you can know yourself, or you can become a "human-doing," as they say, rather than a "human-being."

Men of Fire (Gary)

At this moment I am sitting on a hilltop waiting for my Men of Fire group to arrive, a heart centered group of men that I have led for eighteen years. I have a slight ache in my side (still trying to cleanse my liver) but I am comfortable in my inflated camp chair, sitting atop a slight mound of gravel and moss between two large oaks, with a view down into dry grasses and a forest of mostly pine.

Ah, smell the clean air. Life is good. I don't need no stinkin' fantasies. I am HERE, and my wife says I am important. How about *that*! I have actually prided myself on being unimportant. I have to laugh a little. Somehow that is a funny part of my journey, another piece of the past that no longer serves me. I choose to let it go and accept (perhaps) that someone really loves me and thinks I am important. Okay, so I am still absorbing that possibility. Big inhale. It's good to be important to someone. I just don't want it to go to my head. I've had practice at this so I think I am good. I wish I could smoke a cigar here and maybe have a glass of champagne, a little celebration of self. Why not? No fires or smoking, high fire danger. Darn, I had to bring that up. Maybe in another place like this soon. That would be good, HO! I don't know why it was so fun writing this today, but it was.

I've been reflecting, and I've come to see the trail as no longer dirt and stone, but ironically as a mirror, flattening my illusions and countering my false beliefs.

Find ways to practice experiencing and, even better, seeing and feeling. It has been a big part of finding my way home.

Respite: The Experience Inside the Name (Mark)

Before I left for Germany to present my research on what I call "essential PTSD" and its outcomes (which for some can be a deeper sense of forgiveness or for others a deepening anger and desire for revenge), Gary provided me with a photograph of the part of the trail I named "The Respite." I named each part of the trail that is our walk on The Hill because of this place, I think. Or perhaps it was "The Hill of Cruelty" (but that comes later in this chronicle). I can say that all the names grew out of a spiritual center.

I named this place The Respite not because it is a resting place (yet in a way it is) because it does not come at the end of the journey but at a place just before the trail begins to get really difficult for those who are not at all ready for the challenge. The Respite is the place that offers a little bit of kindness before the continuation of unrelenting ascent. It provides

The Respite

the opportunity to reflect on the will to move forward, and to hold that as having greater value than any doubts about having the commitment to face the difficulties to come.

Gary's photograph of The Respite that he gifted me before I left for New York and then Germany, hangs in the office I share with my supervisor in San Francisco. The men who meet with me in that space look at his photograph and say, "I know that place," or, "I've been to that place." The photograph has captured an archetype of the central and northern California landscape, which could be almost anywhere from Santa Cruz to Eureka, and more importantly it captures the essence of what it means to be at peace in Nature, a brief moment of reflection that makes the journey worthwhile.

The scene is of a bend in the trail with a short run of rough-hewn wood rail fencing in the distance that follows the curve as it bends out of sight. It is clear that the trail continues but the journey beyond is not visible. That is the mystery of this place. The tone and color of the afternoon are inviting. I look at it and I immediately want to know what is around the bend, even though I already know what is there, and have been there more than seven hundred times. It still holds a sense of the unknown for me, and asks the question that only The Hill can answer: "Who are you here?" The Hill will tell me.

Take a moment to remember when you found a respite in your day, or your life, a resting place that arrived so perfectly before a major challenge. Be in that moment when you permitted yourself to see where you were in the time, space, and experience of your life, and what a gift that was. Create a respite for yourself before major events so you can be all the more present to them, conscious of who you are in them, and the gift you will bring to that moment.

You are the gift.

Chapter 5

The Quick Rise of Gentle Persuasion

The Challenge of the Climb Reveals Itself (Mark)

At the end of The Respite, after that curve with its rough-hewn fencing, there is a sudden rise. It is not a significant distance uphill, just long enough to cause us to feel a little winded, just enough to inspire the thought, "Do I really want to do this?" as the challenge of the climb has begun to reveal itself. "Maybe I'll turn back now. I've come a good distance. What time is it? There is so much to do . . ."

The key in this moment is a gentle persuasion that allows the path to convince us that we can go forward just as easily as we can turn back. We can return to the ways we know or move forward into what is unknown. Persuasion has curiosity built into it. Gentle persuasion is the inner smile that permits us to go ahead, go forward, go on.

As we climb we see something in the distance and know a little of what it might be, as we have been here hundreds of times. We may or may not recognize what it is as the seasons change. The value of this experience is a willingness to be drawn forward into the unknown, to be pulled along with the gentle persuasion of The Hill.

The Quality of My Death (Gary)

I walk the hill alone today. There is gusting rain and fog on The Hill. I must go. I am pulled by The Hill and I must respond. I ignore the blacktop leg of the hike to the trailhead, and look forward to entering the sanctuary of the open space.

I brought my iPod, which quite normally I would judge as an intrusion into Nature, but to me it's a new toy that I must play with. I am listening to David Deida (*The Way of the Superior Man*, 2017) lecture on love, passion, and heart. It is an intrusion on the soul of Nature, yet it blends by subject.

I am wearing Levis and a rain jacket. My pants are buffeted by wind and rain, but that's okay; I am warm enough on the inside with a long sleeve pullover and a Polartec top. There is no one on the trail, and I am loving it: the closer to the summit, the more severe the weather and the denser the fog.

I feel a sense that I would be an unconscious easy prey for a mountain lion as I am cocooned inside my rainwear. I hear only gusts of wind and rain outside of my iPod lecture hall. I reach into the outer pocket of my fanny pack and pull out the scabbard containing my razor-sharp knife with its ten-inch blade and molded grip that I carry for safety, and place it in my right rain pocket and keep my hand on the handle. I am totally contained now. I am safe and "snug as a bug in a rug," as my mother used to say.

I have another realization in the writing of this that I pulled my knife less for safety and more for not wanting to risk embarrassment. I feared being killed only if I didn't protect myself. This was akin to the situation I was so chagrined to realize in Vietnam.

I was put in a possible attack situation where I was alone and couldn't really protect myself against what I understood to be overwhelming odds. I didn't want to die a fool or in shame. Believe me or not, I wasn't afraid to die in a fight but I had some pride in how I died. Dying was a given; dying alone in shame and embarrassment was not acceptable: a BAD feeling believe me especially having experienced abandonment as a child. This was my worst moment. At least on The Hill I had some control over the quality of my death, here and now.

Playing Hooky as a Spiritual Quest (Mark)

I appreciate Gary's reliance on his razor-sharp hunting knife which he always carries for a feeling of safety that goes far beyond any fear of mountain lions in daylight hours. Gary prepares to face death when he grabs that knife since he has actually been within that risk in Vietnam. That has nobility in it. But I also appreciate that neither of us has any field training in the use of a survival knife against a wild animal. I used to enjoy being invested in a fantasy like facing a lion with a knife when I was a kid, because it almost always felt so good to read about it in Edgar Rice

Burroughs novels and act it out. It's a fantasy for me but Gary is ready for the reality. The real encounter is a very different level of existence with its own set of questions.

But in this moment I am living with questions that draw no benefit from fantasy and have no immediate answers, life questions:

"Where am I going?"

"Am I truly capable of loving anyone?"

"Do I celebrate connection, or do I silently fear it?"

"Where can I find a really good corned beef sandwich?"

There are no easy answers to these questions, except for the last: Gunther's at Hamilton and Bascom in Campbell, California, has a great sandwich, but it's a drive from Los Gatos, and the best in the world, Katz's Delicatessen, is at the corner of Houston and Ludlow on Manhattan Island in New York (big sigh).

Regarding the other questions, all there seems to be is a gentle persuasion that where we are in life is real, and that we may be fortunate enough to keep on making decisions that will not cause us any harm. I am amazed by the power of this gentle persuasion when it takes me out of my normal and sometimes grinding existence into something that opens my heart, that draws feeling out of me, normally restricted, in the manner of tears shed at the ballet, when Misty Copeland dances as if gravity does not exist, and I feel my heart break when she leaps, and all of her practice and her brilliance and her devastating smile float on her power and determination. But that does not happen every day. Every day is not a Pavarotti aria. That's why we have elevator music.

It is on The Hill that much of this shifts. To be clear, I never have time for this experience of hiking The Hill. Unlike Gary, my life is not as well organized or appointed as that of a therapist who has been in practice for the last thirty years or so. I am just starting out on a career that I began too late in life. I have spent the best years of my life in crushing depression and have shifted into determined redefinition to build a doctor out of a mediocre man. Strangely enough, I may have at least partly succeeded in the transformation, and it has given me an appreciation for gentle persuasion. How else could I have gone through all the years of grad school and internship, and my second adolescence, unless some persuasion was involved, even if it arrived just before senescence and incontinence?

Anything that is of an essential value in this life seems to contain an element, an experience, an internal note of gentle persuasion that offers a tone of its own. I see this as my encounter with anything that challenges me and draws me forward at the same time. It also needs to have an element of "playing hooky."

Maybe Gary roped me into this experience of climbing The Hill so he could justify playing hooky as a spiritual quest. If he had a witness then it could be made more than okay for both of us. Ego aside—as ego often has this need for excuses, justifications, lists of proofs, and never-ending wants, and has a tendency to demean the deeply meaningful to avoid deep feeling—without The Hill my life would be more ordinary than it already appears to be on grey days such as the one currently outside the window.

My last encounter with The Hill has been very painful. An old knee surgery has reached the limit of its lifetime for the repair to be of use.

That's the fine print of arthroscopy and arthrotomy that my orthopedic surgeon never seemed to make clear. The fine print in 1-point font says that the repair lasts about ten years, then it begins to break down, and this is somewhat dependent on the mileage accumulated on the joint, and any hunger for adventure. On top of that, recent discoveries have suggested that the practice of cutting away cartilage rather than repairing it causes a more rapid onset of osteoarthritis.

There's another piece to this, also often unknown to the arthroscopy patient. The puncture wounds required for the surgery create scars that can join the layers of skin, fascia, and the joint capsule where these tissues normally slide over each other during movement. Before the last hike I felt the stitching pain that comes from this scar tissue separating so that the layers can move again. As this surgery happened in 1984, a twenty-five-year-old set of scars was pulled apart. I asked myself when this tissue separation happened, and I think it was when I jammed my knee into a deck cleat as I was taking down the jib sail on the heaving bow of the boat in heavy chop. Once the sail is coming down in a fresh breeze it is not a good idea to stop gathering it on the deck as it can end up over the side. So instead it is better to just yell in pain while pulling down and furiously flaking the jib so it can be rolled up and tied securely into the forward pulpit with highwayman's hitches in the jib sheets until the sail can be properly flaked and bagged at the dock. This deck cleat saved me a lot of money. The amount of physical therapy and massage that would be needed to break up this scar tissue would total thousands of dollars, and I got the job done in one quick movement at the end of a day of adventure on the water in high winds. I suspect the pain will decrease over the next few days or weeks. Or, at least, that is my way of letting go of an injury acquired while training for the 1983 New York Marathon, and letting go that I ran it anyway, and letting go of the surgery that followed a year later.

Does this pain mean I will stop hiking The Hill?

That's what gentle persuasion is all about.

Chapter 6

The Field of Sage

Profound Impact (Mark)

The reward of completing the Quick Rise is the passage through a doorway from one environment to another, forest to open field. The deep breathing that follows the minor challenge of the rise is blessed with a gift. On The Hill this is a large open field of golden grass encountered upon leaving the forest behind and the powerful scent of wild sage on the wind. The opening is profound in its impact: the spaciousness of the field is an invitation to spaciousness within ourselves. Taking a deep breath is far more than just breathing. Sage is a healing influence.

We have wondered if sage has a chemical effect on the brain that supports the flow of confidence. The reason I say this is because at the other end of the field we can clearly see the trail suddenly rise up at an angle that does not make any sense at all. Somehow the scent of sage assures us we can continue on even though we know by sight that the path will soon rise upward with unrelenting verticality.

Sacred Moments (Gary)

As I walk The Hill several times each week I try to lock each experience into my memory as though I may never be able to do it again. Just like the way I am playing ball with my dog right now. Yes, as I write this I am playing with my dog, Cedar. He loses the ball under the cabinet, and I have to get down on my knees to retrieve it. I will always remember these moments because it is a part of "our" game, a sacred game wherein life is precious because I know that his life is short. Not because he is ill but because he is a dog and he maybe has four years left. That kills me to know but at the same time keeps me conscious and holds "our" time as sacred. Not so different is my relationship with Mark.

We share much that I treasure, and I hold each walk sacred because that too may end. Either because he moves to establish his career, or moves away, or one of us becomes ill or dies. It all happens. Staying conscious is part of the walk, the walk of life. I could choose to ignore my feelings, but I choose not to because I also enjoy more of what I have. I am alive to walk and feel life fully, living each moment to its crest, rather than the way I used to do things, which was to feel like someone had to pinch me in order for me to believe the experience. Disassociation is another way to avoid pain.

I felt outside of my experience much of the time. I know I am not the only one who does this, so that makes it okay for me to disclose, right? I can feel my ego again. I certainly don't want you to hear that I have any flaws. Ha, that's funny, because I always tell my clients that I prefer humility, but now, with you, even though I probably don't know you, I have to be humble. It's a good thing. I know I have been a successful practitioner partly because I am real and willing to share my wounds, my teachings, what I have learned, and laugh at my flaws. It's also a way of screening my clients for motivation. I only want those who are willing to join me, in a sense, and do their work, otherwise it is a waste of time and energy for all. I know with all certainty that is what makes my men's groups so rousing.

Choose the Light (Gary)

I'll get back to the point. I notice that any time I go somewhere, I do people's inventories. Part of me is always contrasting and comparing, evaluating and judging. Hell, I do it just driving down the street comparing houses, cars, people, almost everything in my field of vision. Recently, I have made a real effort to stop this dark practice of projecting shadow on everything, realizing it's the ego that is always on alert to protect, defend, or fight for itself. I notice when I stop this mind chatter I automatically shift my focus to more productive aspects of life. It's a positive shift. In other words, I bring in light rather than dark energy. When I do this I am automatically more productive. So sometimes I walk in the shade and shadow, and sometimes I choose the light. Today I choose more light. I am separating from my mother's shadow. I end my allegiance to her cause. I fight the negative imprinting we all have from our parents rather than surrender and be just like them. I had to choose: Will I be awake, or be asleep and unconscious of choice? That is part of the work of therapy.

Earth School (Gary)

I believe we are all here to learn something, otherwise what the fuck. Life is a school for the soul and if you don't get the lesson it will be repeated. I hate those repeats.

I wasn't hungry for the learning. I was starved, literally starving.

I feel that past generations were forced to choose more of a shadow way of thinking in order to survive. We have the greater luxury of conscious thought to choose which one will predominate.

Walking The Hill

Some go numb, some awaken,
some are just shaken—by Nature.
It is the God-given caldron that blends
the best and worst of a man to go deep if he allows.
To stretch, wither, and die if he chooses.
I prefer awaken.
It chooses me and I choose it.
I am open to every smell,
every breeze, tree, flower that varies with each season,
the colors and shades, feathers, scat,
a rush in the brush.
It is all vital to me.
Clean air, blown in from the coast,
blue skies, cloud formations always changing,
shadow and light, blackberries,
early morning feeding birds,
my track upon the ground.
It is here in the dust I am most alive.
I live here; I exist in the city; but I live here.
This is where love comes from.
Its origin is here and I can feel it.
We are born here and this is returning home for me.
Thank you.
Thank you for Love.
It originated here and I feel in my heart that we all did.
Home is in it.
In the earth.
Maybe that's the body.
The soul seeks a higher place, and as yet unknown to me.
What might it be?
Maybe it's flitting in and out of all of it,
the whole spectrum of the universe.
As I look out over the expanse of ocean,
breathe in the air,

> I am enlivened:
> to pull it all into my body and—soul.
> Drink in the river. Swallow it whole.
> I am it, and it is me.
> Ah, so close to God.
> It is an energy that moves in all things.
> Spirit, Holy Spirit, no, Wholly Spirit.
> I soar with thee.
> There is a God for me and She is in everything
> but clearly seen up close.
> Most clearly seen up close!
> Thank you.

This reminds me of *Mothers, Sons, and Lovers* where Michael Gurian talks about drinking in the sea of the feminine. I now think of the Universe as the Divine Feminine or Divine Mother. That is where I walk. I walk with the Divine Mother. She nurtures my soul. She feeds me light and dark energy and makes me feel at home. This is where I come from and this is where I go back to. I am a part of it and it is a part of me.

> I have had my nap and now
> I drive south with my wife
> (who has also been sick)
> and I am parked in a shady spot
> behind the shopping center.
> It's a good spot,
> very quiet behind a cinder block wall.
> On the other side of the street is
> a field with acres of bags of potatoes.
> I have never seen potatoes freshly bagged
> and waiting to be picked up for delivery
> like so many orphans waiting to go home.
> Squatting on the ground
> wearing their gunnysack clothes,

and sitting silently waiting in the warm sun.
Maybe sitting so close to one another
they are comfortable to wait
and not wanting, just
waiting.

The Gingerbread Pan (Mark)

The Hill does not provide very much time for reverie because its challenges keep us in the present most of the time. When memories enter that space it is because they have accumulated so much emotional momentum that they can no longer be contained. For me they burst forth as complete images, a film rolling in my head that demands viewing.

A scent rising from The Field of Sage baking in the sun brought back the day I was introduced to homemade gingerbread. The house was full of this delicious smell, and I saw my mother pull this big, deep, white enamel pan out of the oven and set it on the stove. By standing on my toes I could just see the underside of the pan, which my mother took off the stove and held in front of me so I could see a sea of golden brown goodness. I remember I was given a square as big as my hand when it was still warm. Eating it was an experience. That's when I was first trusted with my own cup of milk, the cup with the special handle that fit my whole hand.

More than forty years later, when my mother became very ill and was near death, I traveled to New York to stay with her for her last two months. Then she was hospitalized for a couple of weeks. During my visit I stayed at the old house I grew up in. On the evening after my mother passed I went back to the house and felt like a voyeur uncovering someone else's secrets. I looked for the big, deep, white enamel pan, the one that held the gingerbread, and found it in the back of one of the cabinets under the kitchen counter. It was worse for wear, stained and chipped at the corners. I went out to the back steps and sat where I'd spent many an hour as a child, and held the 12-inch by 12-inch pan in my man's hands, remembering the enormity of the gingerbread it held so many times when I was very small. That was a happy time of imagination and discovery, just my mom and me out on the steps in springtime. And a few hours ago I'd heard her last words, a kind of childlike mumble as she passed, and had seen her last paroxysm of pain as her heart gave out, and the last great pulse in her neck as she died. I had whispered in her ear, "*Schlaf wohl*, Momma," sleep well. I replaced the pan in the cabinet. A day later she was in the ground.

The Song Within (Mark)

When I lived in the Santa Cruz Mountains I developed a relationship with Nature that I had not known as a city boy back in Brooklyn, New York. There is a big difference between seeing a perfectly pruned elm tree on a front lawn in Brooklyn and owning a hillside covered with live oaks that are three times as tall and whose branches have grown around and through the surrounding bay trees to create gnarled living sculptures. Cut down all the bay trees, that grow like weeds, and the result is a monumental sculpture garden. I created that view and enjoyed it every day.

We had a seasonal storm spring on our property that collected the winter rainwater and ground water coming down from three surrounding hills. It ran through a culvert under the one-lane road leading to our house, and gushed out of its twenty-four-inch mouth like a fire hose during and after midwinter storms. Water is really precious in California, and, where there is an abundance of water, wildflowers, ivy, and poison oak grow as if possessed, and that was the case in and around the storm spring on our property. A previous owner had wisely dumped a few yards of loose rock along the ditch in front of the culvert to control any erosion by the gush of water downhill. It was at night after a week of storms that we would be lulled to sleep by the sound of that rush of water.

One winter I noticed a lot of pooling in the ditch, and that can saturate the surrounding soil, so that the downhill flow can create a flood plain and cause significant erosion. I had to get down into the ditch and remove whatever had accumulated that was causing the blockage. As I walked down the steep hill along the ditch I began to sense an aroma that I knew, but in the moment I could not name. I realized there was a whole field of it, and as I walked through it the scent was hypnotic. It was wild sage.

There are at least a dozen varieties of sage in central California. It likes the sun, and shows up in and among wild grasses like the Field of Sage on

The Hill. Whenever we come to this wondrous place in our walk, especially on really hot summer days, the sage bakes in the sun. As soon as we leave the tunnel of the trail that is covered by trees and the scent of the forest floor we step out into full sunlight, and we are instantly enveloped by air fully perfumed with sun-warmed sage. It is one of those perfect moments that repeats itself in various intensities throughout the year, this sharp boundary of scent between the forest and sage-invested waving grasses, green in springtime, gold in summer through winter.

Sage is also about healing, and about blending with Nature. The ritual of smudging with sage is used by Native Americans to cleanse themselves or a space of negative energy, and for centering and healing. When we reach this field we have left enough of our lives and our world behind us to meet The Hill at a different level of being. The perfume of sage on the wind introduces healing into the journey.

This boundary reminded me of the scent on my property up in the mountains as I walked along the spring that directed the water from three hills down into a canyon below us. I was carrying a pick mattock and a shovel, searching for the cause of the pooling in the ditch. The downward flow had pressed a large amount of earth, rock, and branches into a dam, as if the heel of a giant hand had pushed a couple of yards of it all together. I set to work to clear it, and allow the downhill flow.

>   Pick and shovel break stone and earth
>   Blisters bubble up and weep
>   Sweat and blood mix and mingle
>   Within the rhythm of the work
>
>   Great Nature
>   Whispers a secret
>   As one clod of earth splits to reveal
>
>   A treasure . . .
>
>   The skeletal
>   memory of
>   a leaf
>   Pressed into
>   the earth,
>   Whole and nearly
>   transparent,
>   A memory and a
>   memoriam all
>   at once.
>
>   For one sweet moment
>   We are in and of the leaf
>   Hidden within the earth
>   Waiting to be found:
>   The seed of a song

Reverberating with the
holiness of this
silent prayer
from a long-gone tree,
I drop to my knees
down in the ditch
And the world whirls within

And tears fall
And tears dry

Pick and shovel
Resume their rhythm
Blisters bubble up and weep
Sweat and blood mix and mingle

But now there is the song within.

The Field of Sage on The Hill changes with the seasons, with great gouts of color, blues and reds, pinks and pure white, as flowers in late winter, spring, summer, and autumn take their turn in painting this field with wonder. It is fitting that this field shows up just after the steep rise from The Respite, and just before the challenge to come.

The Field of Sage says to me, "You've come this far, boy-o. Now it's time to learn who you are, and what you're made of."

Chapter 7

The Hill of Commitment

The Quest for Meaning (Mark)

Gary has been doing group work for more than thirty years, and I have been in groups for as long, and have begun leading groups in the last couple of years. Perhaps the most rewarding characteristic of group work, whether I am in it or leading it, is the sense of commitment. I believe that commitment is the foundation of the new beginning that men often hope for when they pray for rebuilding their lives, especially for men who have been through trauma and loss.

When men attempt to work through very challenging experiences on their own they search for answers within and consistently find themselves looking back to where they came from. Group work ends that loop. It is the presence of other men facing the same challenges, each in his own way, that allows a group to begin moving forward with the spoken intention and commitment to each other to not go back. They see parallel energy in each other, and it pulls all of them forward. The commitment is not only to the journey. It is to take strength in choosing to not be isolated and instead to be open and truthful with other men. In a strong group, being truthful and bonded, the shared journey becomes a quest for meaning.

Support (Gary)

What I loved about Mark Ruskell was that he was a straight shooter and if you needed a hand with something he was there. We had many honest conversations about our feelings, and we had a boatload of adolescent fun together. We went on a couple team trips to Mexico and a canoe trip in which he was the only one to come back and save my ass from spinning in a circle.

Remember that old science experiment where you put a pin on top of a cork in a bucket of water and watched it spin as a compass needle? That was me, and that was our first adventure since our Sterling Men's Weekend. I had decided to be macho after the Sterling Men's weekend, and took one of the canoes by myself after a water fight. Well, I got in the middle of a lake, and the wind just kept spinning me in a circle like the pin-on-the-cork experiment. I spun from east to west and back again time after time. I was exhausting myself trying to move forward only to be blown in a circle. Mark came back for me, and we somehow got me to the dam where the trip ended. His weight and strength saved the day. I never forgot that.

To have a friend who will come back for you is a treasure and a measure of someone you want to walk with throughout life. Do you have friends who will do that for you? If not, seek them out. Those are the kind of friends I have chosen, and it most certainly made life's struggles much easier.

The Hill became more than a hill, or exercise, or being in Nature—it became a relationship: a relationship with Mark(s), and a mirror to reflect back an image of myself and my relationship with me. Each chapter reflects part of my, and our, struggles for wholeness. Sometimes those are the most beautiful times.

It's amazing that we always fall into a pace that is mutual. Maybe it's just that, but I add the word respect. It is a pace of mutual respect. This walk is many things, but I think our pace represents a mutual respect for each other. We have melded. Why so? Is it the walk? I think it is because this walk is a catharsis for two, sometimes weary, older men. Notice I didn't say "old." Fuck that. I am tired of people referring to themselves as old. Especially when I know we are in better shape than most forty-year-olds.

We are trekking through our past and into the present through our babble. I really shouldn't call it babble because that might give you the wrong impression, but sometimes it is just that. That is what catharsis often is: just a lot of babble. The mind seems to need to occasionally relieve itself of too much gas (yeah, that is often part of the walk as well) or something. Yes, brain fart now has a new meaning. This is either because we have pressed the mind too hard, or because it's in an infinite loop. It's stuck without any way to free itself other than by babbling. Simply put, the mind needs to detox from all the input it gets from the world. Eckhart Tolle, author of *The Power of Now* (1999), refers to this as "the pain body."

Shadow (Gary)

I notice that sometimes we are in shadow and sometimes in light. What a great metaphor. This walk is a perfect exposure to all the elements, most particularly those within our self. I also came across a black feather today, and wonder what bird has left a part of himself, and was it from grooming or from trauma? Is he alive? That, too, is symbolic to me.

Can we rid ourselves of the dark parts? It seems to me we can, but it is usually only through grooming ourselves to a different level of understanding, and letting those parts go, or through some trauma that forces us to change. Most of the time it seems to me that we are forced to shift through some form of trauma. Maybe this is a message for me to let go of something dark. I don't take everything I see as a symbol or sign, but I feel quite often it happens the other way, in that there was a sign and I didn't pay attention to it, and should have. So I look at today's sign and ignore it only to look at it again now as I write. I have slowed enough to observe from a deeper place and ponder the question.

Is there a deeper sign here? I play with it and have to say there is some truth in this possible message. The more I let go of what fantasies lay in dark shadows, the more productive I am in writing this book or getting any task accomplished.

I pick up the black feather and reflect on what magic it may carry. As a matter of fact, it was resting in the shadow of the trail. I carried it with me into the light. It doesn't seem to hold much for me now, so I let it go. How perfect, I think now, as so often I embraced something in a dark way, and when I thought about it—and by doing so brought light to it—it didn't have any value. Of course, you deserve an example.

Surrender (Gary)

"God damn would you stop whining! You are becoming histrionic." Mark is testing my patience around surrender. I say, "Ye of so little faith." Yet ONLY he has ever been in this place. That's my job just like it is his sometimes. Not to fix but to listen, although I would claim he has more fixes than I. Sometimes he doesn't want to listen long enough for me. I surrender and listen.

You see, I believe that it is useless to fight, or try to control certain events. It feels to me that things always seem to provide a lesson or a better way that you won't realize until later. Enough people have told me stories that were tragic yet in some way the outcome made sense. Obviously, some things are just tragic, period. My side hurts, yet I am setting too fast a pace for Mark. He invites me to go on alone. I slow up and tell him I will follow his lead. I will walk with him. We are not as fast today but we still make it to the tree in a great time. We turn at the tree for the downhill, and our physical energy is spent as well as his angst. We float down. It has been a good hike. We have seen only one bike rider and at least one of us has left a large piece of our load here. We are quiet now. Thank you, spirits of the mountain.

My Birthday Wish for Mark

MY GOOD AND TRUE FRIEND,

WE HAVE HAD MANY ADVENTURES TOGETHER. WE HAVE CLIMBED TALL MOUNTAINS. CROSSED VALLEYS AS HOT AS HELL. AND WEEKLY, WE CLIMB AND DESCEND 7 MILES OF RUGGED ROCK AND 1,450 FEET OF UPHILL. WE ARE PLANNING MANY ADVENTURES, EASILY AS CHALLENGING. YOU KNOW WHAT THIS MEANS.

HAPPY BIRTHDAY

Ego vs Acceptance (Gary)

Mark and I walked on Friday. That finishes my exercise for the week. I talked about my frustration and pain in dealing with recent clients' addictions. I don't usually get worked up over such conundrums, but the ego involvement was so pronounced.

One man is a survivor from Vietnam. He is a boat person whose ego helped him survive, and now he is a multimillionaire who looks very successful, with multiple symbols of success, and multiple addictions that are leading to the end of his marriage. My other client relapsed, and had to go through a hospital detox because his ego didn't know what to do without the sustenance of alcohol.

Often, people without their addictive substance end up anxious and relapsing because they don't know how to survive without it. They have to be taught acceptance. I know this fires me up because I am still learning self-acceptance, and I can say that because I have become quiet enough to get the ego out of the way. When the ego is quiet life can be pretty sweet. That is why I walk The Hill with my brother, continuing to collect more evidence for further change in my own psyche.

Hoka Hay (Gary)

    I am sitting in the sun
    in my beautiful back yard
    with my dog,
    looking at my thriving plants' colors.
    It is Spring.

    Hoka Hay:
    Today's a Good Day to Die.

Ego (Gary)

I wrestle with ego and beauty. I will start with ego: my fear of it. I don't like too much acknowledgment. This comes up as I have recently received significant acknowledgment. I find that I don't like it. Yet I have been touched by the differences in men's lives because of something I contributed.

Is it because I don't value myself enough to let it in? I always say I despise ego because I have seen what it has done to people. Am I afraid of my own? That is what the mirror could be telling me.

Let's explore this. Maybe it's a cover. Maybe I don't want the responsibility of having made a difference. Then I would have to show up more. I would have to stand out, and there is a risk to that. Is it the risk of making a fool out of myself, or being shamed, or looking stupid? I have to be with this, but I talk it out loud to Mark as we walk together. Mark attempts to help me see that I don't abuse ego. I get that I have been hurt many times by others' egos. Disappointed and hurt. At the same time I can get in an ego state that creates arrogance, and then I awaken and stop myself. I don't want to separate myself. I prefer to join. My goal is to not feel alone but rather to feel connected and loved.

Ego Always Wants More (Gary)

Sometimes I am just pissed off. I don't feel compensated. My little kid feels cheated. Yeah, I am a good man doing good things, but so what? Where is the gorgeous estate home with a pool and land, great parties, tons of people around who love me and invite me all over the world, a Porsche, a home in Tahoe, friends in Europe, on and on. So, "Who cares?" Is this all I get? If it is, then I can stay pissed off or surrender to what is. What are my options? Talk about ego! Here we go. I can only see writing a book, at least more public exposure. Seems like a lot of work. Much of what I have done creates aloneness. It's done for love but being a leader is lonely and if I can't have more love then give me the toys for all my efforts. Yet I know with all that you can feel alone.

The Fear of Ego vs The Gift of Legacy (Mark)

The way Gary hides out frustrates me, as I can see he is very uncomfortable with the demands of public success that can come with being a known source of knowledge in a field of endeavor. Ours is *menswork*. For me it is spelled just like that. One word.

If you believe the stereotypes handed you by your mother or your first girlfriends as to what men are, and use these as a means of defining yourself, you are totally fucked for years to come. Menswork is not done with women or by women, who know very little about being a man, and a lot about observing, evaluating, and judging men.

I imagine myself leading a women's group on menopause, and all of the expert opinion I could have on the matter, all gleaned from observation. How much of what I say would ring true to women who are going through the experience? Would I come off as an idiot? You betcha!

Gary has learned what it means to be a man working with men by simply modeling what that is in groups of men and supporting men in a struggle with the model he presents. That is why the notion of ego is so toxic for him. If he allows the voice of ego to inform him, he automatically questions his integrity and his motives. So in this work he struggles with maintaining a voice free of ego that feels more like a battle between ego and superego, or, "being completely conscious of integrity."

Here's how I picture that battle between Gary's ego and superego: it's a sly-looking skinny guy in a zoot suit (the ego) being beaten up by a gorilla wearing a tuxedo (the superego) for whom the formality of integrity can never be violated.

The battle that characterizes getting a man such as Gary to accept that he must share his knowledge or it will die with him consistently borders on the absurd image of Einstein refusing to believe he has a gift for mathematics applied to physics. Gary would rather just be left alone to do the work of modeling what it means to be a man, and tell me, and every other voice claiming he has a responsibility to pass on this work, to shut the fuck up and go home.

Rather than allow myself to be convinced that he needs to keep his voice private I have encouraged him to write for several years and coached him along until he started to do it. The music of his soul now revealed on paper suddenly and fully makes clear the value of sharing the subtlety of his work with men. Most importantly he enjoys the work of writing, and is often surprised at the product of this process that allows the unconscious to speak with fewer boundaries than it does in conversation. He is describing the model for menswork, only one among many possible models, and the only one he trusts enough because it is his own.

Gary remains good and true, holds on to the depth of his heart, senses comfort with his condition of integrity in the moment, and keeps in check the ego that puffs us up and makes us want and compete, and those are some of the reasons why he is able to share himself and his work in a rewarding way. Gary has learned to enroll his gorilla-sized superego in a deep mission, and as long as that mission—to help men save their own lives—is served he will pursue it with much less self-criticism and chagrin, and will gain support from a concrete product of the endeavor that he can read and employ for reflection and teaching.

And that, friends, is the real reason for this book: so that a great man's work with men does not die with him. It is communicated in a form that is not about instruction, but about being a man in the moment, with courage, and a good heart, and an iron will. It is the way ancient men learned from tribal elders whose mission was the continuance of the clan.

Through it all, Gary appears to be a basically ordinary guy, when actually he is deeply critical of his thinking and feeling, as he is willing to practice a disciplined self-observation and self-remembering that draws him into himself, and continuously builds an internal resource for observing the men within his therapeutic circles. He remembers his history, as well as the histories of all the men who do the work in the groups he leads, and calls on the spirit within each man to be a good and true companion on the journey.

Disappointment (Gary)

I have to look back to where I got that sense of feeling cheated. I spent a great deal of time alone as a kid, either looking out the window to see what others were doing or simply looking outside of myself. Then I spent a lot of time watching TV, which we did not get until I was twelve. I spent an enormous amount of time dreaming, and picking my world out of pictures. Then at puberty I created pictures in my mind and hedonistic ideals. I created my world from these images. My move from a small town in Oregon to a large city high school in California and the "greed teaching" of an elder friend didn't help. I began to believe that everyone should have these ideals. Didn't everyone? I don't think they fantasized to the extent I did, as I had little other stimulus. Now I am plagued by all these images, which I must put in their proper perspective, or go to my grave with a visual lust and feast that can never be achieved. I must consider the source. I placed these images in my mind out of scarcity and probably anxiety for lack of something else. I altered my situation with fantasy. So now, IF I can fill myself with what is real (Sue, Sarah, Heather, Chris, Eric, Cedar, friends), grasp the abundance in what I have, and relax without fear of missing something, IF I can be here now, and enjoy what

I have, I will be okay. I have to wrestle with the fantasies. Maybe if I don't wrestle I will be okay.

The fear of missing something comes up. I like excitement. It, too, is a drug. Lament: I find anxiety when I consider letting go. Maybe if I could find joy instead of excitement? I find myself sad and fearful of being still. I never could. I was moved around so many times as a kid. Then there was my fiancé, and the hope that I could make a "still" life work. I could build a peaceful place. At the same time there was my deployment to Vietnam where my world became foreign and ripped apart by the men senior in rank to me and older than I who didn't adapt well to living in fear. Yet we all shared a certain amount of excitement of living and surviving in a war zone. Physiologically, fear and excitement are two sides of the same coin. Alcohol and sex were the drugs of choice. My squadron commander said laughingly that we had the highest rate of venereal disease on base, WOW. I was twenty-one years old and I was going to become a good Catholic boy while I watched even the priest, who was teaching me the Catholic religion, drop out an essential part of the mass. All the while the letters from my girl were changing and I was hearing about her "friend."

I came home to a whole new culture where my story was not wanted, my pain not recognized, my woman with someone else. I lost all hope. I recently asked my wife sincerely if the war was over, as in my heart I have never settled. I am not back. This is why I have to go back to Vietnam and to the Wall. You see, ever since my mother and father separated when I was three, I had been looking for some kind of order I could rely on. I thought I found it until Vietnam. Now I don't trust what I have. I gave up all hope. I recently visited a Vietnam veteran in the hospital and he said Vietnam left him not trusting anyone.

Wanting to include some history of the Vietnam War, I opened a book offered by another therapist who is a Vietnam vet and participates in one of my men's groups. I thought I might find something revealing and perhaps soothing. I just flipped to a page, and found a Vietnam veteran writing about going to a veterans' organization after the war and getting into fistfights because the prior generation wouldn't legitimize our war because we "lost." That was one more stab in the heart. I had to put the book down.

Alone (Gary)

I don't trust anything. I am scared to be here. I have seen so many people give it all up for false gods that I have come to believe it, too. Part of me doesn't want to, but part of me does. A practice, a discipline of just being here with Sue and my Cedar, but even that can change. My Cedar will go away some day and I will be alone again. Everything leaves either through will or age. Even me. Maybe the recent acknowledgments from men are telling me it's okay to be here. That it is enough. That I am enough. *That* was it.

When I came back from Vietnam I was hit hard with ALONE AGAIN in a strange world. ALONE, yet I preach not doing it alone. Here I sit, still alone, not home, as the home I was to come back to wasn't here anymore. Where is my home? I have searched my whole life for a home. I have been in this house for twenty-one years this month, but only now am I considering making this my home. Not "be here now," rather, "be at home now." Claim this home and be here.

Too bad life takes so long to achieve. I could achieve life here. Quiet, oh Fantasy Mind. Stop. Is it too late? So much of what I do is an attempt to make it be safe where I am. Maybe I don't have to keep at it. Maybe I am HOME.

I realize that I am sitting in our new and beautiful wicker chairs with my feet up and my dog lying nearby. It sure looks and feels like I am at home. I couldn't walk The Hill today due to a wild fire and its intense smoke polluting the air. The house smelled like smoke and outside was like being close to a fire and having the smoke blown toward you, except it didn't go away.

The State Military Reserve finally called, and I guess I may be "in" with the answer to a few questions regarding my medical history. It will require my attendance one weekend a month. Maybe that will force me to be home. Maybe the exploring I want to do is done, unnecessary, and less valuable than showing up for someone else. Maybe I am almost here and The Hill has brought me home. That feels right in my heart.

War/Vietnam (Gary)

I talk about Vietnam to someone in my circle at the Roasting Company and what it holds for me: "You know you can look at that place on Google Earth." I think I have heard of this before but chose not to look. Today I finally download Google Earth, and I am blown away at how the whole earth can be put on my computer.

I enter "Nha Trang Air Base" in the search field and I get its history. Then I go back to Google Earth and enter "Nha Trang Air Base or airport." I don't remember which but there it is. I feel my body shuddering as I look closer and closer.

It's not there. What I remember is no longer there. The only building I recognize is the large steel roof of the base church where the priest forgot part of the mass. I am dismayed, relieved, and in some sort of state of shock. How could something that affected me so profoundly no longer be there, and how could I be looking right at it? To me, it has been alive and active in my mind for forty-one years. To me it is like last year. It's gone! It is hard for part of me to believe, but at least part of me gets it now. My story no longer has a physical presence, and it's hard to comprehend. Maybe now can I be home and be free of Vietnam?

I think I am done. I am finally home, but there is one more episode that makes it all complete for me. It is hard to type this because the emotions are so strong. This happened last weekend.

I show up in uniform for my first California State Military Reserve Meeting. I get my first salute at the doorway to the armory. I shadow the lieutenant and take emergency readiness classes. Then it's time for lunch. A group of us decide to walk three blocks to the fast food place. It's hot, we are all in uniform and someone honks their horn. I think it is someone making fun of us. Then I notice someone is waving at us. On the way back from lunch someone is waving at us again. Then someone stops and wants to take our picture. The police officer waves as he drives by us. I finally realize these people are proud of us, and acknowledging us. I discreetly wipe my right eye and hold back the emotions as I connect with what I so missed when I came back from Vietnam, a "Welcome Home." I got it. Thanks America, I finally got it.

After the weekend drill at the armory I am driving home in my tight new uniform, and wearing my cap with the captain's bars. It is a warm summer day and a man ahead of me is driving his red Ferrari with the top down. I used to envy that or fantasize what that might be like. But today it means nothing. I feel only pride and a sense of satisfaction. I am home. I am happy driving my truck and I am home, at last I am at home.

This July 25th makes it 40 years and 341 days for me to come home, but who is counting? Ha, ha, ha. I am home. HOME AT LAST.

"A man afraid of himself has no place to hide." — Gary Plep, 1976.

Yet whenever I think I am done with something I am not.

It is Monday evening's group three weeks later. I have supported one of the men to journal. This evening he claims time as he has something he wants to share. I am thinking it is something about his childhood or relationship.

He says quite flatly, "I would like to share a story about Vietnam that I have never shared." I tear up just a little as I have an idea now of what is coming. He asks if it is all right with me and I tell him, "Yes, please do."

He describes flying a helicopter in Vietnam to pick up dead and wounded, and it is a hot landing zone, meaning there is a lot of incoming enemy fire. He lands, picks up dead and wounded, and before he can pull up a sniper with an AK-47 in a tree directly ahead shoots out the bubble of his helicopter sending shattered pieces of plexiglass everywhere. He is hit twice. He yells to his copilot to pull the chopper up and out of the landing zone, but as he turns to yell at him he sees he has been shot dead between the eyes. He is on his own now, and pulls up and out and flies to the hospital landing zone some fifteen minutes away. He makes it to the zone, falls out, and hits the ground unconscious. He wakes with Nurse Molly (actual name unknown) holding his hand, and telling him they didn't think he was going to survive. She visits with him daily until he recovers. One day a staff officer comes to see him, pins a bronze star on his chest, shakes his hand and leaves. He is back to the war zone and flying out dead and wounded again. He and his colleagues are angry with the copilot for doing something stupid to get himself killed. That is post-traumatic stress disorder syndrome for you. Not logical. He states, "I am still angry, not at him. Just angry."

Both of us wiped a tear or two from our eyes, but I was surprised to see I could just be there and he could tell the story so calmly. He said it was the first time he had told anyone this story. I tear up a little now as I write, and have great respect and appreciation for the women who saved our souls: another piece of the healing and coming home.

Too many movies. I guess I will never be done, but I am HOME. It has been hard to feel whole while part of me has been in another country. I needed to be welcomed home by strangers on a street, honking their horn as they drove by. I needed to welcome myself home.

Welcome home, brother. You have traveled a long distance to get here.

Not Being Enough (Mark)

I have been in a battle of my own for years. Not as dramatic as warfare by any means, and it is as real as war for me. I am at war with "not being enough." On hard, dry days it shows up on The Hill as doubt in the face of unrelenting ascent.

Gary has been struggling for decades with being a lonely kid and not having the sense of being home from the Vietnam War. I have created roles for myself conferred and supported by a combination of academic and professional degrees, hard won expertise and fantasy to cope with "not being enough." It has never really helped me feel comfortable or accepted.

The way my family treated me led to my need to be someone else, to split away into a fantasy life that portrayed what I believed was expected of me because I was "not being enough." I felt less than, and could not appreciate what I was. The wish to be someone else was so preoccupying that I could not get comfortable with, and did not develop the ability to witness, my own integrity. I knew I was not being myself, and was more comfortable internally pretending that I was someone else, a meta-self free of the loneliness and rejection that populated my childhood.

I was raised to believe that I was guaranteed to screw up anything that had meaning for me. I grew up being told thousands of times that I was a failure, a schmuck, a loser, a waste of time. When I received accolades from someone important, like a teacher when I was a kid, or a boss when I was a young adult, I had to stop myself from looking around to see who was getting the compliment. I wondered if a fat bully in the room was going to punch me in the head because someone said a good thing about me.

To this day I still have difficulty believing that I have any value at all, and perhaps that is my greatest source of what looks like humility in the face of success. My posture is not about being humble. Actually, I'm waiting for the slap in the face that will follow a smile aimed at me. Whenever someone smiles at me, I internally get ready to duck. It's a leftover from being abused by that smiling face as a kid.

Today, whenever I witness a kid pulling back a lot with a fearful look on his face when someone he knows smiles at him, I know I'm looking at an abused child. Shyness and fear are different expressions. Shyness is normal for little kids. Fear means there is trouble in the kid's house. I lived in that house.

My father was a very bright man, a surgeon, and he seemed to be able to do everything as if by magic, a set of capabilities that he carried in his pocket and could withdraw at a moment's notice. He never involved me in, taught me about, or explained the stepwise process of becoming a man when I was a boy, and derided me for not knowing. He was a narcissist with a sadistic streak who was disgusted upon seeing his son's inability in comparison to his own maturity. I could not learn fast enough, so it made sense that I was shit.

Being raised that way left me without a sense of timing relative to a challenge—the time it takes to get really good at anything, a sense of practice relative to the presence of expertise. I would try anything and fail for lack of experience with it and not invest the time to get good at it. Instead I had entitlement and failure. I had the fantasy of perfection and brutal realization. If there were ever a "not getting it" leading to a painful life experience, this was it.

My father's desire to get projects done around the house did not include teaching me how to do what he was doing. Rather than treat me as the son he wanted to teach, train, share with, he consistently told me to "Get out of the way." He did not have any patience and felt justified in holding that perspective, as it seemed I was a painful disappointment to him.

I knew for a fact that this was not the way he grew up. I am sure that he fully remembered, by my mother's report, that his father, my grandfather, consistently bragged about "my Wilfred" to others, unqualifiedly told him he could do anything he put his mind to, and was always there with a sense of pride in his son. This is an enormous gift. My father did not share this gift with me as he did not have the patience to work with a very inquisitive at times hyperactive child. Although my father grew up in grinding poverty, he had a father who was strong with a form of wealth: encouragement.

Encouragement is simultaneously the least expensive and most valuable gift any father can give his son. It costs nothing and it buys the world. For lack of this energy, which creates accomplishment and wealth, there is a trail of failure and loss that does not end. I struggle with this every day.

Years later, as I was moving toward pre-med in college, my father permitted me to attend one of his seminars for his residents. I envied them as they received his attention and close camaraderie. I envied their brightness and their response to being supported in the learning process. They were his sons. My father's attitude toward me in that moment identified me as the kid he was stuck with, and I would never be as good as those young doctors.

Near the end of her life my mother regretted the way my father treated me, and she was sorry she had not stepped in, in a number of circumstances, to prevent any further emotional or physical injury. At least she communicated that she was aware of his deficits in the raising of his son, yet I had to balance this with her total love of literature and her total lack of support for my own goals as a writer.

If you knew my mother you could understand why she read Shakespeare aloud with me when I was seven years old. I asked her to do this after I heard her and my older sister reading Julius Cesar aloud for her junior high school assignments. I loved the sound and power of the words. All of my wildness simply stopped for those hours of reading aloud. The experience built a deep love of poetry and the human saga in my very young mind. It was years later that she strenuously objected to my desire to work in the written arts. She was a well-meaning, crazy-making, desperate, Jewish woman who was so risk averse that she could not conceive of anyone becoming an artist and being successful at it. That only happened to other people, like Shakespeare or Homer, and they were dead. The fact that there were thousands of successful writers in an industry consisting of dozens of genres did not qualify as an acceptable reality to her. In his silent way my father reflected my mother's highly vocal concern about my becoming a professional writer, my early choice of profession. She would moan, "You'll never make any money and you'll have bad eyes and wear thick glasses," as she wrung her hands in terror. I figured that this was the support that all parents gave their kids, meaning that we were all fucked.

How much blame could I levy on both my parents for my own lack of backbone in the pursuit of an art form? Could I blame them for the fact that I gave up when the people closest to me made it their business to identify my goal to be an artist as "idiotic," "stupid," and "a waste of time?"

Gradually, I developed a life of increasing isolation. I did not trust men at all. I did not trust women at all. I took all of my writing talent and jammed it into advertising so I could make a living. I despised the environment and the work but it kept the rent paid and food on the table. In the background I pursued my writing for myself, never told anyone about it, never submitted it for publication, never allowed myself to share my identity as an artist with other writers or artists. I feared and loathed opinion and criticism.

I worked my way up the ladder in the ad business to executive positions, but I could never completely fulfill their demand because my heart was not in it. I looked at my roles as those of a character in a story, rather than living fully in them. I had moments of real professional and financial success, but knew I was on the road to failure. In my early fifties I burned out, got fired, and realized I had to do something meaningful.

There was a moment when I thought I would pursue my writing. I would put everything I had into getting known and published. I put six months into it, and once again lost faith. Once again I sought another road that was more in line with old parental judgments. I had spent so much time in therapy over the years that, after being fired from my Chief Creative Officer position, the top job in my business, I talked with my therapist about becoming a psychologist, as I had spent most of my life working with and managing crazy people in the advertising industry. She took a long pause, and then agreed with me, and encouraged me with the idea that I could make a difference. So I went for it. And that is how I found my way into the profession.

Training for the profession allowed me to see what happens when a boy finds himself without a father's love. I have had to become my own father. Ironically I have become a doctor, and that has been a slow transformation. The greater irony is that in that process I learned to love my writing more than any other endeavor. In this way I share a little bit of what it means to come home, in the way Gary finally came home from Vietnam more than forty years after his arrival in the US.

Transforming Failure into Compassion (Mark)

In taking care of people with acute mental illness in a group therapy environment, given my history, I could fully accept whatever processes or events had led to their condition. I came to them without judgment or superiority. I could see the people they were beyond the severe disorders that held them in their grip.

The lack of support I experienced in my family became the window through which I could see human beings desiring to transcend their illnesses and transform into people who could manage their weaknesses with the recognition of their strengths. Their fantasies of failure that they had of themselves were opened up and explored, and the people they could be, if they chose to work at it, shone as a candle's flame in the darkness.

In the process I was transformed. The more sincere my efforts became, the more I could support patients to make themselves well on their own terms. I became far less broken and far more determined to make a difference. Maltreatment by my father fell into the background as a condition to overcome by the daily application of spirit for the good. By becoming the encourager of wellness, I, in turn, received the encouragement that comes from the good father within. I had become the good father. My transformation was occurring in parallel with transformation in the patients.

Every time the outcomes of my work were described in very positive terms by my supervisor, my medical director, and by patients, I knew the truth about myself within my heart: I was fortunate to be just far enough away from the conditions my patients manifested; I was just close enough to truly know their struggle and remain conscious of their efforts toward transformation; I was removed enough to respect and understand their illnesses within the objective realm of clinical psychology.

With ego held aside, it became clear to me that people in the world were just a step away from madness, and I saw how fortunate they were to have the resources to maintain their grip on reality, having lost my grip in the past, and the decades-long battle that was required for me to regain my perspective. I was no longer broken. I was one of the lucky ones. I was good enough to do some good for others. I was good enough. The father within me was proud of me. I believed that my paternal grandfather, if he knew me today, would be proud of me.

After forty years, I, also, had come home.

The Hill of Commitment

Chapter 8

The Hill of Cruelty

Expectation and Entitlement (Mark)

This part of the trail is so similar to the challenge of change, especially when it's painful. This experience of unrelenting ascent becomes downright cruel. It's a metaphor for the steepest part of conscious resistance to full awareness. It's easy to hold the cruel fantasy that the ascent up this part of the trail will lead to a plateau, right? But, as we reach the top of the rise we see another rise that was hidden by the steepness of the first. At this point the challenge is far greater than we expected; surely there must be some relief on the way. As we reach the top of the second rise we see there is yet another beyond it, and with this discovery there is an understanding of

what makes this so painful, and the lesson is so powerful that we encounter it every time we reach this part of the trail.

It has to do with expectation and entitlement. It is expectation of what we want, of relief, of ease, of a break with a cup of coffee and a doughnut, right up here on The Hill, at a table with a table cloth, and an attractive server to deliver it, just for us. Letting go of the expectation, letting go of entitlement, and accepting the trail for what it is resolves the sense of cruelty we projected onto its challenge and its beauty. The fourth and final rise becomes an encounter with the Fourth Way, being awake, with self-observation, self-remembering, and self-awareness.

Truth Defeats Denial (Mark)

The path now has no cover. Open to the sun, dry as bleached bones, dust and polished pebbles combine to create a surface as slippery as ice on a twenty-five-degree slope. Every inner voice that ever stopped good growth and good new directions now speaks louder and with greater intensity than ever before. Gary and I are in this together and it might not make any step easier but we have the laughter that comes with pain. The path angles up and then slightly flattens, giving the illusion of a crest, and turns and twists up the face of the mountain and angles up again, gives a very brief and relaxing downhill dip, and then angles up very sharply yet again, and after a blind bend, angles up again, enough to drive us to our knees. Each time the path gives the slightest indication of easing up we are tempted to relax our commitment in the way we used to, when we were much younger men, at the first taste of accomplishment, when our commitment was tested in a way we did not expect, again and again.

The practice offered by The Hill solidifies commitment so that the relaxation that used to show up when things got easier has evaporated. The Hill of Cruelty makes our resolve as tough as a five buck steak fried hard, left in the sun for a week, and pissed on by an angry coyote.

We are certain now that there is no turning back, and certain as well that we have found within us a Will we did not have before, with full packs on our backs in 107° heat, two aging warriors who refuse to give up. The cruelty of The Hill that teases us with the feeling of accomplishment at reaching the top brings us back to the feeling of spaciousness, of allowing good growth, and The Hill becomes a part of the journey, a challenge of a different sort. We have tested our limits and learned there is no limit to inner growth, especially when it is witnessed by another man. That awareness is a whisper, at first. The significance of having a witness to this type of challenge, someone who can vouch for the fact that you never gave up even once, makes it impossible to deny the reality of the moment.

Denial can get loud as hell in my head. I might hear it, but I pay no attention to it. It drifts away as truth defeats denial with a mixture of sweat and dust. That is no small feat.

Suffering (Gary)

The heat helps. It can be brutal but Mark and I seem to love it. It claims us and we give it all up moment by moment as we think we might drop. It's kind of like our lives. Both of us have tried so hard to have life be different from what we have known: 107° and no shade and a 25 lb. pack go steadily up hill. It forces us to do our best at what we know and can do. It's really more of the same.

I know that has been my life, to always be struggling up some kind of hill. Somehow this is more gratifying and tangible as we have a finish line. We can see it, it's achievable, and almost immediate compared to other things in life.

The tree is our goal. Just to get to the tree. The last hill is a bitch and we seem to push each other faster. The pace has changed, and we are now competing against our last time. Awe for the mountain, the tree, and to pee. Maybe something will grow better here due to our efforts. We check our stopwatches and give ourselves an "Alright!" and a high five or "Oh well, still pretty good" and a fist bump for the day, then a gentle hike down.

Sometimes I am depleted for three days. Other times I want to go to the gym and continue the work out. It seems kind of crazy as I write this to walk 3.5 miles up The Hill and 3.5 miles back and then want to go work out. Maybe this is true masochism. Now that is something I haven't studied.

Maybe I am addicted to a certain amount of pain. Where did I possibly learn *that*? Well, the military teaches you to survive pain with your buddies. I most pointedly remember basic training, and a bunch of us sitting in a room full of tear gas after a 4:00 a.m. forced march. It was cool doing an ordeal together. I also remember the times I have sat in a sweat lodge with a group of people and "sucked dirt," got closer to the floor and cooler air, or continued sitting upright in a "warrior sweat." Is it good or stupid to be the last one sitting up when you notice even the Shaman is down once the steam clears? I don't know. I felt stupid, alone, and not liking it. Being the lone survivor sucks, again. And being the hero . . . eh.

Maybe it's the group experience, the shared suffering that is so addicting. I certainly know how it is to suffer pain alone. This doing it together is very satisfying. I always tell my clients that doing it alone sucks. I believe that.

I learn as I talk and as I write, yet in the past I couldn't write, and it is only recently that I seem motivated, maybe because, here again, I am not doing it alone. This could be another difficult journey, but because it is shared I relish the hardship. I know Mark, who is a writer, is going to push my ass hard to get it done. "Writing is a commitment to do something very

The Hill of Cruelty

difficult and productive that requires discipline and sacrifice." How often did he warn me about that? I am in. Wow, that actually feels exciting. Okay, I am addicted to pain and suffering, as long as it is for a good cause. Maybe our ramblings will influence others to take on a challenge or maybe just enjoy the story of two crazy bastards who love to push our edge physically and emotionally with vibrancy.

The Hill keeps it simple. It's grind rocks, pick up glass. Don't fall on your ass.

I can recall The Hill breaking me down several times. It's hard to be resistant to emotions here. I get vulnerable quickly, especially before something like the Hill of Cruelty.

Mark on grief: "Go deep into the darkness until you find the pinpoint of light."

Or, from Gary: "All in to the light through surrender."

Mark: "Honor the light. Use it to turn loss into honoring" (said just before The Hill of Cruelty). Another form of connection.

What does it for you? What opens you up to life and grief? I challenge you to be awake and connected. Connected to what? Yourself, the core of you, and what awakens you and keeps you awake.

Is it a race or my stream of consciousness carrying me up The Hill? I love breaking from the shade into the sun. I find myself in a sauna. It's the feeling of being baked by the earth and the sun. I am like the earth here. The mud and water God put together. I am cooking like a good bread. It feels right. Not at all punishing, as some might hold it, but rather a form of aliveness I feel to my core.

God, my gut hurts today. My stomach muscles that I worked out yesterday are talking to me today since my hill hike. Ah, time to take the shortcut down.

Be Prepared: Gear Up (Gary)

I've got my Cool Max socks and shirt, my water bottle with Emergen-C, camera, stop watch, knife, Sting Kill, sun screen, note pad, pen, clip-on sunglasses, and lastly my special pack that Mark bought me that just holds my water bottle and a few of the items. The rest go in my pockets. It's

The Hill of Cruelty

funny because I am always critical of sports that require all kinds of special (especially brand name) gear. Yet this is de-re-gore for me. Here I am with all of my special shit. I realize it is fun to carry all my equipment, and that each item has become almost sacred. They work, and they can make a difference. I despise the culture of wanting, yet I have perhaps played a part in what I most resent. I want so I walk. That does seem to be a part of it.

Is it okay to just "want" to be alive and live well?

My great mystery is unraveling. I am discovering things about myself in the walking and the writing. I walk because I want something. That rings true. I know I crave the contact with Nature, and the energy I get in my body, but yet I continue to talk about what I want. Maybe I am struggling with the conflict of wanting, and never having enough, like everyone else. Hmmmmmm. Could be true, doctor. (Is the word really "want?" How about "starved?" My mother couldn't even remember if I was breast fed or baptized. Obviously I had no one to feed me everything we are starved for beyond food.)

The weather dictates the changes in my gear, and I have a number of other items I add or subtract depending on climatic conditions. And before I go out the door I check Air Now on the web to make sure the air quality is considered safe. It's the shits to be on a good start to a hike and realize my lungs are heavy, burn, and I cough because I know I am getting something in my lungs that doesn't belong there. The wood smoke rising from homes on the surrounding hills on cooler days can be debilitating and a nuisance.

I grab my gear from upstairs and do a quick trot down to the door. Neither of us wants to be chastised for being late. Mark's old BMW convertible pulls up shortly or he is waiting with his bandana on his head. Oh, one of those things I forgot to mention.

When did a bandana become cool? Actually I think it looks pretty stupid (you will find our judgments throughout by the way). Like you're a fucking pirate or a Russian cleaning lady who is out to pick up a new broom or something. I am sure some athlete started this, and now everyone has to follow, much like the backward baseball cap. I know I only wear the bandana under my hat when it's hot. I soak it with cold water and slap it on my head. It helps. It has become another somewhat sacred tool, certainly on hot days. (You fool, don't you know you will be rejected and won't be loved if you wear that? Mom has a set of requirements for love. Pay attention.)

Looking Stupid Is a Good Idea (Mark)

Gary often replaces common sense with judgment when it comes to appearances, as he is very sensitive about his appearance, and will never admit it. That's why he's sensitive about the bandana on my head, and that's why he wears one only on hot days and only under his hat so no one can see it. Of course, he is unaware that the corners are hanging out so that he looks like a drunk who blew his nose and, seeking a place to store the snotty rag, shrugs his shoulders and sticks it under his hat. Nobody can possibly know that he looks just as stupid as I look. Then again, there is a possibility that he looks stupid every damn day, but that is another insult for discussion at another time.

I wear a bandana year round to keep the sweat out of my eyes, as the hatband of my old sombrero no longer absorbs anything but Gary's derision. I don't think I look cool with it on. In fact, the *shmata* on my head can look reasonably stupid at times, especially when it gets twisted around and the sun symbol on the fabric, which is supposed to be positioned in the middle of my forehead, is halfway between my forehead and my ear. Duh. However, if I have to make a choice between my really acid sweat getting in my eyes and looking like a cleaning lady, I'll be asking for a new broom any day.

One More Thing About the Bandana (Mark)

A few years ago I organized a family trip to Yosemite. I wanted to share the magnificence of Nature with my niece and nephew, and have them understand why I would often say that when I went to Yosemite I felt as if I was going home. That is the feeling that the big walls of Yosemite engender in my heart. I have been in that valley more than twenty times, and had the privilege of being taught how to climb the talus fall at the base of Half Dome by Peter Mayfield, a really talented big wall climber. His coaching on how to solve the technical problems of scaling an apparently smooth rock face gave me enormous respect for Yosemite, and helped me conquer my fear of heights. I cracked that fear in half, and out of it came a gentle confidence. And the *shmata* on my head helped to keep the sweat out of my eyes when I really needed to see where the next crease in the rock was waiting for my fingers or my toes.

When I took my niece and nephew out for a hike up a moderate ascent out of the valley, and they saw me don my bandana at the start, they each wanted one, and I had extras in my pack. I showed them how to tie it so it stayed in place, and up we went. I didn't see how much they loved me, and how much they saw me as a model, until I realized that they wanted to copy everything I did on that hike and scramble.

Taking my nephew on the challenging hike up Yosemite Falls during that trip was the closest thing to being a father with a son that I have ever experienced. He was terrified of heights, as I was before I learned to climb with Peter, and I was able to support him as he proved to himself that he could make it. We took a break on a short rock bridge about three feet wide where we looked out over the valley, with a granite wall rising three thousand feet behind us and a two hundred foot drop in front of us.

He wanted to turn back, and began convincing himself of his own fear. We talked about his fear, and I asked him if he thought that the rocks were going to jump up and grab him, and of course he said no, and I was able to show him through experience that he was in charge of his body and his movements, and that he could trust himself to make the right move at the right time. I explained that his body will move where he places his eyes. If he is focused on the path, he'll stay on the path. If he stares over the edge he'll walk over the edge. The idea is to focus on the path ahead, give it all of his love and appreciation, knowing where the edge is and avoiding it. I asked him if he wanted to learn how to scramble over rocks and he said he did, and we continued on up. I saw the confidence build in him the rest of the way up and all the way down. I could sense his courage. All he needed was encouragement, the thing that costs nothing and buys the world.

His pride in making that climb and descent could not be contained. He just glowed for the rest of the trip. A few weeks later he sent me a letter in which he shared an essay that he wrote for a class at school that described his experience, and it cracked my heart in two. He remembered every detail, every turn, every challenge, including seeing another hiker jump four feet in the air over an uphill rock when he heard a rattlesnake complaining about the traffic near his home. His description of making his summit was entirely focused on the beauty of the climb, of Yosemite Valley, of the perfect blue sky and the colors of the granite, and did not contain any ego. I was so proud of him.

A bandana was the catalyst for learning to be the father I never had with a child I dearly loved, so that *shmata* has a lot of meaning for me.

The Blessing of Good Gear (Mark)

Gary is correct about the ritual of gear for any sport. If I were to line up all of my gear for my three favorite sports, sailing, mountain hiking, and bicycling, I could sail to a distant shore or hike to a mountain base camp or ride 100 miles in any weather. Yes, it's really cool to have everything you need in terms of gear. That is a very special knowledge. It comes from the experience of being over-prepared and over-packed. Then, through the hands-on encounter with a mountain, a forest, a cliff face, an ocean, a questionable source of water, or a situation where you will need to hunt or fish for food, boil water, or cook over a small fire, experience helps eliminate or replace gear to create the lightest, most stripped down set of stuff that will permit survival, and do a good job of it. So, I also have "all my special shit" for the hike, and I don't have Gary's aversion to mentioning the trade names of my gear. The good stuff is the same as good tools. You want to know the maker.

Clothing that will not bind or chafe, and can be worn for days at a time if necessary and still stay comfortable, after sweating and drying out a few times, is a very big deal. Having insect repellent can also be a big deal in black fly, flea, tick, and mosquito seasons. If you can combine both, in clothing made by ExOfficio that has insect repellent built into the fabric, you eliminate something to carry, and you stay comfortable and bug free. I'm into high-tech gear, a conversion that came from people I emulated in marathon running, long distance biking, mountain hiking and scrambling, and sailing. My clothes have to support the event, keep me dry and comfortable in heat or cold or rain, and have a positive impact on conditions for endurance.

Everything, from my underwear out, is high tech material that never bunches or binds. If we are in 100°+, my clothing has a cooling, wicking feature. If it's 35, additional gear will be an ultra-light fleece vest from Patagonia under an impermeable windbreaker/rain slicker with a breathable liner from Mountain Hardware. My pants, depending on the temperature, are always lightweight or heavyweight nylon from REI with a weave that prevents snags on branches or rocks. I also have rain pants to wear as an outer layer in case of a downpour, as well as the waterproof, hooded windbreaker, and they have come in handy a number of times. Both fold down into the hood of the jacket and pack as an 8x8x10x2-inch pyramidal shape.

I wear a belt made of high-strength webbing over my clothes that supports the carrier for my one-liter, non-reactive, Nalgene water bottle. (It never has a plastic taste, and when I wash it I know it's clean. Those are the two reasons I do not use a Camelback.) The belt can be used as a tourniquet or a sling or a method of carrying firewood. I have a mini first aid kit that contains bandages, antibiotic cream, serious pain meds, antiseptic wipes, tick-removal tool, complete suture set, three pairs of plastic gloves, and a sling. (Anything with an expired date is tossed and replaced.) The whole thing measures 5x3x2 inches and fits on the back of my belt. I have a Victorinox Swisschamp Swiss Army Knife with thirty-three functions that provides blades, a scissor, can opener, tweezers, toothpick, and all the tools I need for field repairs. (Get a thorn or a splinter in your hand and you'll be happy to have a sharp pin, a pair of tweezers and a magnifying glass, all of which are in the knife.) I have my iPhone, which triples as a compass, camera, and emergency phone. I keep it turned off until I need it, because the battery can be drained by the constant search for a signal in mountainous terrain. For Vision Quests I added a 5.11 Tactical Headlamp powered by four double-A batteries. It's a little heavy, but it can cast a really powerful 338-Lumen broad beam combined with an LED array that provides a dual floodlight. It can run for an average of forty hours (check out the specs) with a ten-foot circle of bright light in case we need to find someone and provide assistance in the dark.

Boots are a very big deal. They have to provide good support, but need to be lightweight, and must be comfortable when you put them on and for many hours when your feet swell up with very challenging activity and heat. I prefer Lowa boots, a little expensive, but you get what you pay for. The company makes a shoe style and an ankle-high style. I have both, and the one I use depends upon the terrain and the weight of my pack. If I'm carrying less than twenty pounds on a reasonably maintained trail the shoe style is fine. If I'm carrying twenty-five pounds or more, or if I'm going to be in rough country, I use the ankle-high boots for added support. Lowa also makes incredible heavyweight leather mountaineering boots, and I used them for a couple of years. The lightweight boots do not require any break-in time, but the heavyweight boots need weeks of breaking in before they mold to your feet.

The last thing is a hat for protection from the sun. A regular baseball cap is a half-assed solution for sun protection, as it does not really protect your nose, cheekbones, ears, or the back of your neck. Gary loves to bust my chops about my Mexican straw sombrero. It provides all the shade I need, as the second half of the hike up The Hill, and most of our trail into Vision Quest terrain, is in full sun. The hat has begun to break down where the brim meets the crown, and Gary is waiting for the moment when I put the hat on and the brim gets pulled down around my neck. I've sewn it together several times using a canvass hatband for backing, but soon the straw will fail, and then I will need to go searching for a replacement.

I use another hat for deep woods. It's made by ExOfficio, and is a cap with a longer and wider brim than a baseball cap and has panels that drop down to cover my ears, the sides of my face, the back of my neck, and these panels loosely button under my chin. The hat is impregnated with bug repellant. It is amazing to see a cloud of black flies staying six inches away from my face. The flies would normally be attempting to clean my nose, eyes, and ears, a service they perform for many animals in the woods, especially deer. A true test of self-control is to let the flies crawl into your nose and ears and do their work.

I have my gear for our hike organized and ready in a bag in my gear locker, so I can be dressed and out the door in five minutes. I can't be late. It's a show of disrespect for Gary, and for The Hill, and Gary loves to bust my chops when I'm not right on time, which happens with regularity.

Loneliness and Perfection (Gary)

Reflecting on my neediness. I am afraid of it, as I know it pushes people away. Maybe I can reformulate it some way.

I believe most men are lonely because of their programming to be providers in excess and absentia. Then we become even more needy. Like my client who worked hard to make a fortune, and is now unhappy in relationship, so he travels the world, seeking and empty.

What would do it for me? Hot sex helps, but so do hot cars and . . . choose from the list of wants and toys, you can name it. Maybe it's working less and being quiet, as I wrote earlier. I thought I must be unlovable, so I try very hard to do all the right things, and be a good person. Fuck. Who now abandons whom?

I get it. I have abandoned myself, an abandoned child who learned how to abandon himself. Just like an abused child learns to abuse. The quiet has certainly opened Pandora's box. These walks are killing me open. So what would it look like to not abandon myself and to no longer follow mother's directives?

I just now lost my words to write about all of this. Guess I will have to ponder on another walk up The Hill. What if I was, what if I am . . . lovable? Would there be nothing to do?

How about you? If you were lovable would you no longer have any work to do on yourself?

Change for the Better (Gary)

Hey, it's Mark, and me, and Stacy, another man from our group whom I invited along today. All of us are struggling up The Hill at a snail's pace. I thought it was just me. With a better view at higher elevation we soon discover the smoke that clouds the valley; no doubt from the San Diego area fires. Regardless, it's another beautiful day, yet Mark continues to unload his darkness from the bowels of German persecution, the foundation of his doctoral dissertation on the Holocaust. He is very dark and intense. I attempt to remind him of the beauty of the day but he refutes it with an assertive, "I am always intense, what do you expect." I assert back with a loud, "Lighten up!" Interesting that we are close to the last stretch of the Hill of Cruelty.

We continue on to the tree and make a poor but better than expected time of one hour, nine minutes and some odd seconds. We turn around to take in the view. Smoke and haze cover the valleys. It is good to be up here looking down on it. I actually feel better up here than when we started. We rejoice in our time, pee on a bush or tree, and slowly descend.

I am not sure what today has brought. Stacy is quieter than usual. Mark is his usual intense being. I point to each one of us starting with Stacy and labeling him "relaxed," me "medium relaxed," and Mark "not relaxed," as we head down the hill.

So what do I take from today? I know that I always want people to change for the better. I know I need to let go and realize this is it. Little if anything is going to change in my friends. I don't like this. The truth is I don't want things to change, but I want people to change. They won't be able to love me if they don't change. I can't stand that. Let's extrapolate on this.

It goes back to ripping up my classmate's fucked up drawing of the duck in first grade because he didn't do it right. You can't have love unless it's perfect. Only the perfect get loved. Only the good child gets the candy from Santa. If you are deprived of love you must not be good enough or perfect enough to receive it. Okay, got it.

Fuck. Another lesson from The Hill. And from a commander who when I voiced my expectations of certain commanders said, "Remember, Gary, they are just people." Thank you, Col. Turos. That keeps vibrating in my head.

How accepting are you or have you been just as critical as I?
Thanks for the gift mom—NOT.

The Cathedral (Mark)

> Leadership with honor resonates
> Heart speaks without words
> And the shadows of the circling hawks hover
> And move on into remembrance:
> The Quest is life and death and life again

We often joke about this hill: the Hill of Cruelty. Gary and I share good humor about it. We also know it can kill us.

It is a very steep incline in full sun. The surface is broken stone and eroded soil that has turned to dust, which gives the surface the same feeling as ice when there is too much contact with rounded pebbles and dust and not enough with the parched earth below this erosion. At 100° or more with a full pack the Hill of Cruelty is a warning: if we can't do this we can't be present for the men who are too weakened by a three-day fast to hike out of the valley that we descend into from the Ventana Wilderness. We need to represent the resolve required to meet the challenges of the mountainside between the road to civilization, where the trail starts, and the marker that identifies the place where we arrive for the Quest: The Cathedral.

The Cathedral can be seen only if one is familiar with it. Two giant oaks at the crest of a golden hill that join together two lines of oaks, rising on the right and left. Their heavy, full-leafed branches reach to the ground.

The invisible entryway is at the base, under a hanging branch that dusts the pathway in, with the wind encouraging the branch to sweep away any footprints. It keeps the secret safe. It is the first sign of magic in this place.

I am saddened when I think of this gateway to our base camp, because it may have been burned away with the most recent major fire in the mountains behind the cliffs of Big Sur. I am hoping the power of Ventana, God's Window, has been able to resist the flames. I pray for this.

The Hill of Cruelty is good when it comes to grief. Unexpectedly, at an uphill moment in full shade or full sun it will wake us up to the thing we must let go to feel the expansion that this journey allows, a journey that Gary and I have shared more than seven hundred times. We are attuned to every stone, every nuance of color, every snippet of sound, every scuttle of movement, and the occasional disappearing tail of coyote or rabbit, deer or bobcat, snake or lizard. It's a place where deer and fox travel together if you have a chance to view their run.

When I first hiked the Hill of Cruelty I thought that it was done after the first rise. Then the second helped me see my vulnerability in this harsh environment. The third drained the last of my energy. The fourth reduced me to tears and brought me to my knees. Today I walk it as I would any other hill. That seems to be the gift of this brand of cruelty when visited with regularity.

Gary and I will often comment on how well we took this hill when it is done, almost always with a tone of surprise, because we know the mental toughness with which this hill has gifted us, seven hundred times. This hill is a gauge of our personal resolve, of how much we can take on when Will is all that is left.

The Hill of Cruelty taught me to see something I had not fully appreciated throughout my adult life: the power of personal resolve in the face of something that at first inspires fear and then deep respect. There have been a few times when I felt pain in my left shoulder, arm, and wrist as I climbed this hill. I had to ask what was more important, my daily life, or this moment of communion with something so timeless and so much larger than myself?

It was clear that I chose each time what I preferred to have as my last memory if my heart were to give out. That's what killed my mother, and my father, and my maternal grandfather, and my paternal grandmother. None of them ever attempted the physical challenges that I choose to face each week. If my genetic price is early death, it will not be at my desk or in my bed.

This is the lesson of the Hill of Cruelty for me: to press on and to not permit fear or self-loathing to prevent the exquisite vision of myself as a grain of dust on this trail.

Chapter 9

The Hill of Awareness

Finding Readiness (Mark)

The Hill is a great leveler when it comes to comparisons. It is practically impossible to adjudge myself better than anyone else when the realities of gravity, heat, and elevation reduce my efforts to that of an aging man's struggles on a mountain. Even if being outwardly humble is not one's way, sarcasm about one's athletic prowess is soon to follow in response to the environment of The Hill.

What is even more interesting to me is that this part of the trail is, in part, even more difficult than the Hill of Cruelty, and it is the accomplishment of climbing this series of elevations that makes climbing the Hill of Awareness that much easier. Most importantly, for the first few years of climbing this mountain, I thought this portion of the trail was easier. It wasn't until I became aware that the Hill of Cruelty prepared us for the next challenge so well that it only seemed easier. Lastly, I cannot help but enjoy the irony of the Hill of Awareness metaphor, that awareness is not immediate but the result of exposure to life's cruelty.

The brief and gentle downhill following the Hill of Cruelty announces that the obvious tests are behind us. Now it is the level and quality of awareness that will determine where Gary and I are in this journey. If the Hill of Awareness had been encountered any earlier it would be too difficult to attempt. In the perspective of the aftermath of the Hill of Cruelty, readiness for truth is a near certainty.

The Gift of the Wilderness (Gary)

Mark and I hit the trail and I think of our walks as a rock crusher. Not only are we grinding tiny rocks into the earth, we are talking through our own rocks. We process stuff out loud for the other to hear, but much of what we are saying is for ourselves to hear. The hard stuff goes into the machine whole and comes out a much finer compound, laying down a softer ground upon which to walk. Life is somehow easier having dumped our load of rocks into the machine and allowed the earth and sky to work it out. Nature has a way of doing that. She is the silent observer. There is something alive and working all around us as we talk and walk the earth.

We often put out our fantasies so we can gnash our teeth about what we wished we had. Those fantasies, too, seem to go through the rock crusher and become fine sand. What we used to talk about is rarely mentioned. The earth has claimed it.

I look over the valley and am aware that very few of the million people below ever get this perspective. They may see this expansive valley from a plane, but to see it looking down from the ridge is quite different. It is the shades of green in each mound of foliage of each hill. On rare occasions, it gives you the total expanse from San Francisco to the south end of the East Bay. Now is the height of summer and we see the green and the red coming in. The red is the poison oak in its glory.

The flies love me today. They try hard to bite me. I am not used to this as they usually leave me alone. But today they are particularly hungry. It is morning and they search in vain for their breakfast as I flail away at them with my hat. They are persistent even when I know I have hit them. No more shorts and short sleeves for the season. But it's just another struggle I somehow enjoy, as I keep moving up The Hill, now focused only on the ground and my shadow. I can see them circling back. Hah, it is all part of the struggle for life, and I endure it with that feeling of aliveness. Perhaps like Moses in the desert. I would bet he enjoyed eating *manna*, the sweet deposits on twigs produced by insects at night (Guttman, 2019), because he knew in his struggle that it gave him spiritual energy and a sense of purpose. In the same way John the Baptist ate locusts and honey (Matthew, 3:4). That is it. It is a spiritual energy, a greater sense of my own spirit when I struggle a bit. My body thrives on its aliveness. It keeps saying I am alive and I thrive here mentally, physically, and spiritually. Getting bitten by life once in a while awakens you or keeps you present.

Ho, brother. I say go into the wilderness and find your spirit. It does not dwell in the city. The city is to exist; the wilderness is to thrive. Spirit is nurtured here.

You see I was an original latch key kid. My mother had to work and she didn't have a car. That meant I had to spend a great deal of time alone. It was just the two of us after my brother left for the Air Force. I think I was nine or ten. I spent most of my time evaluating things. I remember walking upstairs and going down and doing it again just to defy logic and feel what that felt like. I studied the clock on the stove to the point of being very accurate about time without needing a watch. I became, very often, accurate to the minute in guessing the time. I had my chemistry set and microscope as well, but wasted little time doing homework. That was boring. I was most interested in introspection.

What was love? I was twelve. I figured I would learn that later on. I remembered the query. Ah the gifts that come from our wounds.

Honor (Gary)

Mark calls me late. It is his anniversary, and he calls later than we agreed. I wish them both a happy anniversary. Mark agrees to pick me up in forty-five minutes. I prepare not thinking too much about it until he arrives. I jump in the car and pick up on his energy, and his run-out-of-the-house (hair on fire) look. I get it immediately. Yeah, ladies, sometimes we are a little slow. We drive up to the parking area to start the hike up to the trailhead.

I say, "Hey, Mark, it's your anniversary. Want to make a hundred points? Go home and tell her you realize you need to be with her, and take her to breakfast. You love her dearly . . . blah, blah, blah." Mark asks me, "You don't mind?" I reply, "Hey, drop me off, and I'll walk back to my house or have Sue pick me up." Mark says, "I'll come back and get you in what, two hours and ten minutes?" (That's the length of the hike at a good pace.) I say, "Forget it." Mark says, "Awright!" I can sense his relief after having to choose between honoring his brother and honoring his wife and their relationship.

Hey, the walk is beautiful, and I am feeling spry. My side seems totally relieved. Hey, maybe I'm cured. I am free to ponder life's questions by myself. Today I ponder marriage and divorce, having been through both.

When is it okay to divorce? Suppose you are no longer attracted to your partner or whatever? I always tell people that it's important they give it their best to make the relationship work. Internally, what I do not say, is if they have given their best, and it still doesn't work, then it's time to consider letting it go, and that needs to be said by them, first.

Actually the question I am resistant to ask is, "When is it a 'sin' to divorce?" No, that's not it. Is divorce a sin? Most people aren't aware that the word "sin" in Latin simply means "if on the contrary." In Old English it's used in archery and means "missing the mark." But for Christians today it means you have violated your relationship with God. Let's look at that.

I "feel" (okay, now we are going deeper) it's a sin unless we have battled it out. Most will immediately take this as expressing anger with each other, and that is not what I mean. What I mean by "battle" is a strong inventory of the truth and the expression of it.

What is my foundation for considering all of this? Internally, where am I coming from?

Marriage and divorce are issues that depend on history. But that is not what I'm about; I'm not about being haunted by the past and old decisions. With my relationships, my clients, friends and acquaintances, I know where I stand about the past. My past is no longer important; now it's my present I hold dear. It's a simple philosophy. Strike from the heart of passion. The time for fantasy is over. That window is closing. And if I don't close it, time will.

Five steps later I find a tail feather of a red tailed hawk and retrieve it. Grief, aha. Tears release as a wounded warrior finds the luxury of feelings inside the battle of the ego.

My Wednesday night men's group is an example. I am sitting in the circle next to a man who relates the story of his father who was a charming, gambling, womanizing alcoholic, and a wife abuser. He had just described my father. Ironically (or is it?) the man next to him has an almost identical story. One of his issues is making a decision about his relationship with his wife from whom he has been separated for two years. He has told us she is overweight. In his story he tells us about his mother and father getting drunk and fighting, and both of them falling down. He had to pick them up, except he couldn't pick his mother up because she was too heavy. He suddenly had an Aha! moment. We then discuss how he was there to rescue his parents, but learned to abandon himself. I learned that one too well myself.

Another gentleman in the group, sitting next to the man who just shared, is over seventy and has told us how difficult it has been for him to share his feelings. He has just recently, after many years in the group, become razor sharp in his expressions. His wisdom has nailed some men in describing their situations to the appreciation of all of us. It's a bonding moment when all of us hear it and become silent in appreciation of his direct hit.

Most often divorce happens out of allowing a negative pattern from the past to live in the present. We unknowingly allow the past to be in charge of our thoughts, emotions, actions, so that what is happening right now takes a back seat to something that no longer even exists. The thing that holds a man (or a woman) in check is an old source of pain, and once that is clearly seen as something he is defending against, he has a choice; he can let that pain continue to be in charge, or he can break that pattern and become the leader of his life.

What will he do without the pain? It has run things so well up to now. It's comfortable because he knows how to do it. What will **LEADING** his life look and feel like NOW? We are all creatures of habit, and it is scary to change. Even if it's dysfunctional we prefer to *follow* something we know rather than *lead* something new. The habit of maintaining old patterns is an allegiance to the parent imprinted in the brain at an early age.

I preach "**LEADING**," rather than following an ancient script that is no doubt centuries old, a negative script that has been passed from generation to generation. No shame, no blame, just dysfunctional now. A Native American belief is that we are affected by seven generations before us. We need to be conscious of what we are doing in the present as we will have an effect on seven generations after us. It is never just about us. I used to think it was. My wife, Sue, corrected me and she is right (yet again).

What are the sins of your past? Make a list and see if you are leading or following. Are you a leader to the future or a follower of the past?

Perfectionism (Gary)

All beings don't have to be perfect to be loved. I guess that's why today I eat my beets from a can. My wife hates that. What can I say or do (smile, laugh)? I am still lovable aren't I? Aren't I? Maybe that's where my anger comes from.

In a perfect world everyone would love one another. So I try for another day to be perfect, and strive for a perfect world. But I am constantly frustrated. Let go, and accept what is shown. Love Mark's dark side as I love my own. Can I quit my assignment with "The Perfect Police?" Imperfection is everywhere. What would I do with all that extra time and energy? Ha. Sounds good. I Quit! Or at least I am off for now. I am off. I am off duty.

As I begin to sign off from perfectionist duty, I look to my left and notice a newsletter from Massachusetts General Hospital, and my eyes go right to: "Research published in the June issue of the journal *Neurology* suggest that reducing negative emotions may be one way to significantly reduce the risk of developing memory troubles" (Feldman, 2008). God is always watching and willing to teach if you pay attention to your surroundings.

"Notice, just notice," I say to my clients and I have to repeat the phrase to myself on occasion. It sometimes feels easier to just follow a familiar old script rather than open up to noticing the world where we live, and see it in a new way.

The Battle for Freedom (Mark)

I often ask myself, "What are you doing?" I spend most of my time feeling driven. I am seeking something that will shut down my preoccupation with the darker side of existence.

The men I treat, some of whom are homeless and hopeless and deeply wounded by war, violent crime, and substance abuse, some of whom are wealthy and seeking a perfection of self and life that is untenable: they act as signposts along this trail up The Hill. Amid the pebbles and dust there is an answer to all of the tragedy we create for ourselves.

It is to *be here now*.

I can put down the whip of the past, and the can of black paint that eliminates every guess about the future. I hate the phrase, "What if . . .?" Instead I focus on what is happening right now. Most of what I do seems to be in reaction to the past or in preparation for the future. (If anyone is interested in getting as close as possible to these extremes I suggest pursuing a doctorate in a clinical field between the ages of fifty and sixty.) Even as I climb The Hill with Gary I am so ready to criticize, to judge, to name, blame, categorize, worry, project, disrespect, and belittle so as to carry out the perfect confabulation of the neuroses previously owned by my mother and my father. Finding myself in all of this was impossible until I began to enjoy the moment, and could tell the streaming sometimes screaming side of my brain to "Shut the fuck up."

When I get wrapped up in multiple layers of minutiae everything suffers. I forget to pour the Oolong tea because I am so wrapped up in this writing, and the tea is over-brewed and bitter. I drink it anyway, and internally state the wish that I will remember to pour it on time next time. The only way that works in my kitchen is if I set a timer. I need to have an agency outside myself to hold on to the things I want, even something as simple as a cup of tea.

Could I stand by the pot and wait the two minutes for the tea to open up its initial flavors, the ones that are so dear in the moment, in the now? It means I will need to pay less attention to capturing the flow of ideas for this page, yet I know I can have another thousand ideas that are as good, possibly better, and possibly not as good, and that the edit will perfect all of it anyway.

This letting go of perfection is so easy to say, so easy to recommend. The truth of it is that, when I say this to a patient, I am asking him to turn off his past as if it were a light, and walk out of his darkness into a new, clean, well lit space that is fresh and free of concern for the future. *Perfectionism is that desire to harness the future by defeating the past. It is absurd—the idea of doing battle with something that no longer exists to change what does not yet exist.* And yes, it is important to plan, and yes, it is important to learn our lessons from the past so that we do not repeat it. It is just as important to not be owned by it, day after day, enslaved by what no longer exists to change what does not yet exist. I battle for my freedom from this preoccupation with perfection on difficult days, and then sometimes from moment to moment, second to second.

The battle for freedom becomes superfluous when torment over past failures and my imposed illusions of the man I am supposed to be become conscious and visible and no longer drive my beliefs, feelings, thoughts, and dreams about the man I am and can be. This is what lives on The Hill, in summer swelter, autumn color, winter downpour, and spring flowers in the grasses and trees. It is the end of illusion and being here now. Just two hours of this challenge to free myself from the *illusion* of being a man and to experience simply *being* a man three times a week is enough to maintain a view of what is possible.

Gary and I trudge side by side, me on his right, he on my left, in the exact same way as we have for seven years. We share all of this as part of the process, each of us invested in our freedom from whatever it is that limits us, both of us looking forward to the view of the valley below from the tree that is our marker. We are on a path that is ours alone because there are not many people who know about this fire road beyond that it is unrelenting in its ascent when seen from a distance, and when attempted by the uncommitted is given up at the start.

The tree that is our marker lives just before the summit of The Hill. It is a big live oak that, as a sapling, chose the most precipitous place to exist, on the very sharp shoulder of a steep ravine. Its position defies the laws of physics by dint of effort, its roots gripping with steadfast resistance to the scorching drought of summer, the howling winds of winter, and floods threatening mudslide. The enormity of its bulk, perched on the edge, is a reminder of what is possible in the face of the desire to call such wonder impossible.

The tree tells us what it means for a man to make his stand in the face of those who try to take away his power. It is a living, courageous, and undeniable symbolic response to opinions inspired by fear and denial.

Gary has said many times to the circle of men who are preparing for Vision Quest, "Do not share your reasons for the Quest outside of this circle. Don't talk about the rituals and practices we use in preparation for the Quest. People will challenge your intention to endure a personal test. They will try to take away your power. They will try to take away the meaning and purpose of the Quest. Hold the Quest silently in your heart. That is where your truth and your purpose in the Quest take root."

Chapter 10

The Tree of Truth

Being in the Moment (Mark)

Near the summit of the Hill of Awareness the live oak stands on the outer precipice of the road, growing where a tree of this size seems an impossibility, yet there it stands all the same. The Tree is who we are in the moment, in the now. To accept the truth of who they are in the moment, men have invented any number of contests, and very few have provided the hoped-for reward. To stand beneath the Tree of Truth, and know who we are in the moment, free of any measure save our own, is to understand the favor of inner growth. The Tree is merely a reminder to take stock, get our bearings, and allow ourselves to know where we are in the moment. This is the precursor to healing that lasts.

Important Companions (Gary)

Just back from a couples session for my wife and me. Yes, I believe in therapy enough to do it for myself. And today I got from my wife how important I am to her. I needed our therapist, Beth, to say that to me, translating what my wife was saying, in order for me to get it.

I never felt important as a child, so even when I felt I was doing something important Sue would put me in my place by saying, "It's not about you." I understand now that was about my ego, not about my "self." Tears run as I lay on the bed writing this. She wants to make me happy because I am important to her, very important. So at this stage of my life I have to decide what will do it. I think I have been waiting for that someday when I – "Big *I*" – deserve to do what I want.

On The Hill today the horizon to the west gives us a view of the sky above Santa Cruz and Monterey. It is clear, a sighting that is usually clouded

from here. The perspective is grand, to know the beaches are warm and sunny as well, which is not always the case.

A man from our group waits for us just above The Respite. We invited him to join us for the hike today. He is leaning against the fence that keeps people from short-cutting and eroding the trail. He started out early with the plan of meeting us up here. He looks spent and his shirt is soaked. It is not his day to do a timed climb to the tree. Here, his back to a fence post, he has processed his grief. Not that it is done, but he makes a sort of impassioned plea for support. I retell him what I know of his story as a way of letting him know I empathize. I also tell him that I support him doing grief work. He says, "The way you can support me is to call me to hike with you." Basically he doesn't want to do life alone. He had a lot of aloneness in his life, as Mark and I have known in our lives. That must be our bond, or certainly part of it.

I always say, "Doing it alone sucks." I ended up having that conversation with my good friend's husband this same day. He had relapsed into alcohol and lied about it to his wife. He was dealing with his wife's anger over his dishonesty, calling him a liar. He said, "I lied, but I am not a liar." This is another time when a man feels alone and needs the support of other men. That is why the fellowship of Alcoholics Anonymous can make such a difference. Many in recovery try to do it alone; most tread water for a while and then relapse, or become so intense about their sobriety that no one wants to be around them. I told him my theory and suggested a men's group. This time he is ready.

Death (Gary)

It seems I am ready to write this time. I could never focus in the past but now I am ready. Perhaps I feel I now have enough wisdom, enough proof from my learning that I am clear I have something to say. Or perhaps it is knowing I will die. It always felt like death was something other people did, especially older and unhealthy people. Another fantasy dispelled.

I recently saw myself dead on a table in a dream that quickly brought me awake. I don't know if it was an omen or an inspiration. I decided to take it as an inspiration. I like that idea better. I have had times when I have felt my heart might stop. It was probably part of what I have determined to be my digestive disorder, or was it? I just know I hit the wall, and had to have naps.

No matter the cause, I figure it's time I get it done. The book, that is. I would like to leave something behind besides pictures, memories, and a few thousand bucks. I want to feel I made a difference. That has been important to me since I was twelve.

Just Fix It (Gary)

Anyway, I felt the world was in chaos, and my mother's whining about work and relationships (be they friends, coworkers, or lovers) certainly reinforced my feeling that the world needed to change. I wasn't sure how I was going to do it, but I was going to search hard for the core problem so I could fix it. It must have been the beginning of the search for manhood because God knows men love to fix shit.

Even now, as I grind my way up The Hill, I am plotting on ways to fix it. The world, that is. What can I do to make a greater difference? I don't even think about what I have done being a therapist. That's just what I do. I want a sign that tells me in big red letters, or something. Good question. How will I know I've made a difference? I think I will see something somewhere that quotes me, repeats my lines and moves a whole lot of people to action. Yes, and, I really like the idea of something I say on a big billboard somewhere. Red letters would be good: "World Peace now effected by *Walking The Hill*, written by the clods, Mark and Gary."

No, I don't necessarily need my name on it. I just like knowing that I created a ritual that is in use by the local men's organization, Momentum, which formerly was called Nation of Men. That's pretty cool. I don't see my name, but I see my imprint, and see the energy that comes from it. That works for me.

Have you ever asked the question, "What will I leave behind?"

Money is fun to spend, and it can fill your bank account. But filling my spiritual account means more to me. That never goes away, and that matters, not when I'm standing at the gate of heaven: It matters here.

Relationship (Gary)

While hiking today a mountain bike rider suddenly appears and tells us there is a wild cat a short distance away. I pull out my camera hoping he is in the light and that he hasn't gone back into the dark brush, which is his protection.

Let me see the tiger! Let me witness this darkness! I go to fantasy about all he might be. But he is not. That which I wanted so much never appeared in real form. As my mother said, "What does it matter?" It matters not mother, for you are dead. I am alive and it matters not. Thanks, Mom. I learned how to witness darkness in relationship.

She said, "What does it matter?" in her depression many times before she died, but I think she realized a deeper truth, that there is little in this world that really matters. What matters to me in this moment is the light connected to another soul besides myself. You see, to me what matters is not doing life alone. She was very alone because, being in survival all her life, her ego and her fear pushed people away. She kept herself in a dark place. I understand why, and cast no judgment on her, and thank her for helping me choose light over darkness. It helped me to understand the darkness in relationship in my work with couples. Feelings expressed aggressively or passively have the contrary effect of pushing people away from each other. Alternatively, it is hard to resist hearing the truth spoken from a caring place if it is delivered eyeball to eyeball, with ownership of one's feelings and using "I feel" NOT "You feel" messages, accompanied by a touch of the hand: I, eye, truth, and touch. That's communicating with love. The partner has the other half of the job, which is equal, and that is to listen without anger or repulsion driven by ego, the ego being the enemy of relationship. The listener has no obligation to give an immediate response, but, rather, has the opportunity to take it in, and consider what is true for them, and respond in kind after consideration. It is not a battle to see who wins, as is almost always the case with couples.

We live in a culture that worships logical, rational, linear thought processes, and disdains and ignores feelings. Feelings are seen as uncontrollable, unnecessary, and dangerous. Yet, it is our feelings that make us human. That's what I learned from the book, *Women Who Do Too Much*, by Patricia Sprinkle (2002).

I ponder the "sin" part, and my first marriage, and here's my thinking. If you communicate from a place of love, which I've just described, and you still think you should leave (as most leave too soon) remember that you made a commitment. Ah yes, a commitment before your community. You gave your word to witnesses—including God—that you would hold this as sacred, yet most take it as just something to get through. Then, when up against it, the vows fold because they were never taken seriously and owned, truly owed. And there is no accountability other than to the court and financial institutions. No one in the community stands up and says, "You made this commitment. Now you go the distance." We quit too easily in my opinion because we don't know how to work through the hard times, and no one holds us accountable in more than a financial sense.

Where do you quit? When do you sell out on yourself and the relationship? What are your stops?

Our society needs to return to the basis of all life: relationship. It starts with a spiritual relationship, with a higher power, elder, parent, and community. Ideally, all of the above stress the meaning of relationship. It is interesting to me that this reinforces my belief in a need for God. That is, a higher power invested with wisdom tells us the way. Unfortunately, religion has failed, or the people who organized the religions have failed. What we need are wise elders who show us the way with conviction (that's an example of commitment) to communicate and hold us accountable to what we commit to. I sure wish I'd had that.

I think it is only due to family dysfunction that my first marriage failed. At the age of sixty-three, I now see the need for a higher authority, and I see what is created by its absence. Now, because of the obvious corruption in church, state, and family, we have turned to other higher powers for direction, or one could say, false gods.

Video games and starlets are modeling directions and consequences for actions, and kids are eating it up. Starlets don't necessarily give us the consequences directly, but they sure do show us the result of their actions in the bright lights of their own lives. Video games, just in case you haven't played one at all, require a strict set of guidelines that you have to actually study and integrate or you don't get very far, and the whole idea is to be able to stay alive by figuring out the rules.

So where did I leave off? My humble opinion is that it is never okay to get a divorce unless you have exhausted elder direction (okay, therapy). Unfortunately for us, our elder direction either came too late or, in my opinion, was not forceful enough to get us to look at what we, each of us, were doing that was wrong. It wasn't just a failing of the marriage. It was our individual failings that were never addressed. That would only bring us back to another failure in relationship between others and ourselves. How sad. Fortunately, it brought me to about eighteen years of off-and-on therapy to overcome most of our generational inability to promote healthy relationships.

I don't blame anyone. I only accept responsibility for what I can do now. Now is what matters. I prefer conservation of energy. Life is too short. I am committed to learn and grow until I die.

What are you committed to do?

Connection (Gary)

I walked The Hill this morning alone. Alone is good sometimes. There is that paradox of being alone, and yet never really being alone. I feel the truth is that we are never alone. It just feels that way sometimes. I know I feel freer when I am by myself. That is when there is no one physically present, yet we are always connected to someone. If I have a conversation with anyone, I feel connection.

Connection: interesting word. I feel that there is always a connection going on. People remember you, think about you, or reflect on the things you have said and done. You would have to be pretty isolated to not be connected.

Writing is now more passive than active. I made a commitment to write for two hours a week thinking that meant pen on paper. Now I realize it's more of a revealing, meditative state that precedes the pen moving to paper. I cannot "fix" a book as a man would fix most things.

>Notice not
>the applause you receive
>but rather
>the sound and feel of the footsteps
>beside and behind you.

So, another day of discovery. Have I walked? No. But the motion is set. Walking is more the catalyst, or perhaps the oil that lubricates the imagination and the mechanism of feeling. But of course, it's the endorphins. Another way of being here now. Everything points toward calming. Now every time a car fantasy comes up I ask myself, "How do you feel right now, and is it not good or okay to just be here?" I am finding that I am comfortable and I don't need anything. I pause in this moment and enjoy the truth of that. Can I just be okay the way I am? It feels like I can. Now comes the work to maintain this.

A suggestion might be that I need a vacation, that a time to be quiet with myself could become a choice. A vacation is different from a desire to fill an empty space. I need to schedule vacations, and for the right reasons. Maybe I don't need to keep looking for magic. It seems the world, the universe, my body—even my clients—have conspired to get me to be still. And it's not so bad.

When the Truth Comes Forward (Mark)

I have rarely sought connection. It has been thrust upon me as part of the human experience in the manner of mashed potatoes and meatloaf. It's part of the deal whether I liked it or not. Gary and I share this experience of growing up alone, which for men translates as not having a father. Gary's father died young, and my father's spirit for his son died when he was young, so we both ended up alone.

My father was not good at being a father. It seems he figured that the perfection of his fathering should have worked on me. If it didn't, I must be the one who was defective. That is compatible with a diagnosis of narcissistic personality disorder. Rejection by my father created a deep wound in me that resisted every kind of healing or any anesthesia with risk. The significant loss was not only my father's love. For my personality it laid the groundwork of resistance to connecting with anyone, especially with men.

When I was in my early thirties, I had isolated myself in my apartment with the intention of committing suicide. My therapist at the time was very close to calling the police because I would not take his calls, and he left me a message saying so on my answering machine. He called my father, apprised him of my emotional state, and told him to call me. I had my answering machine on, and I was monitoring my calls, and heard his voice. I answered the phone and attempted to explain that suicide was really difficult, and I was trying to focus. I remember his voice broke, and he said, "Do you know what this is doing to me?" I relented on suicide. I had hurt him enough to wake him up. Days later I realized that my fear of confronting my father was at the core of my drive toward suicide.

We met with my therapist, where I confronted him on being a terrible, abusive father. He genuinely expressed shock at this, and said he did not know the effect his behavior had on me. We met several times during which I related the history of our relationship. I maintained a calm tone of voice and a matter-of-fact attitude. When expressed this way, in the presence of a witness, the pathology of our relationship had greater impact on him than if I had screamed at him. He sincerely apologized. I could see he had great difficulty relating to the effect of his actions and comments on the family. He expressed remorse about the quality of our relationship. Although I felt some vindication for being fully misunderstood throughout my childhood and adolescence, the process felt hollow. At my therapist's suggestion we agreed to spend time together.

During the time that immediately followed these events my father and I developed somewhat of a relationship, but I never trusted him. Looking back on this feeling, I think that I emotionally realized that the true narcissist has limited empathy for others, and has limited concern for what effect his behavior has on others, but at the time I did not have language for this observation, I felt it. I felt empathy for my father, and I also realized I could never get what I needed from him: the supportive teacher and mentor who truly loves and encourages his son. I had modeled his lack of emotional capability as his son, which created deep conflicts for me in relationship, as I felt far more than I let on, and as Gary says, a lack of communication assures the lack of connection.

If you want to talk about a guy being in a tough situation, this is it: my father had to go through life needing attention so badly, and did not have the ability to fully relate to the emotional needs of others, and when he did it was when he could receive admiration, which is why he was so kind to his patients. I realized months later that emotionally emulating my father led me to ending up alone and suicidal. I consciously decided then that being like Dad sucked. Being a narcissist is not for everyone. But without a father to follow, who fills the void?

On one of our walks in Central Park my father told me that when he was a young doctor during World War II he was assigned to the psychiatry service, and he hated it. He could not tolerate hearing men talk about their emotional distress for hours at a time. He begged his commanding officer to be reassigned. His superior told him that the only opening that was available was in surgery, and the only job that was open was in surgical amputations of limbs so mangled they could not be saved. My father said he took that opportunity to "get the hell out of psychiatry."

The thing that has made the work of being a therapist so attractive to me is the connection with another human being. It is an opportunity to intercede in a person's suffering and encourage an active participation in healing. Without empathy this work is impossible.

My father did amputations all day long for four years during World War II. He said it was good experience for orthopedic surgery later on in his career. He also said he drank a quart of whiskey a day, and woke up so drunk one morning that he threw up in his boots. His denial of the emotional effect of cutting off arms and legs all day long was fortified with alcohol, but he did not make that connection, or if he did he set it aside.

The irony of all of this is that the specialty I was drawn to was the treatment of PTSD, the very thing my father could not handle. I did not realize it until I sat down to write these lines. Gary, the deepest friendship I have, has suffered through the symptoms of post-traumatic stress for forty years.

There was some pain in letting go of being like Dad, and relief in deciding to go my own way. It's the kind of relief that comes from pulling a nail out of your foot. It may hurt like hell while you pull on the nail and while it's healing, but soon afterward, walking one's own path gets easier. Thirty years later, The Hill gave me the gift of a father within my own heart.

The reason Gary and I chose this profession is because we can do more with our pain than bitch about it. It becomes a conduit of understanding. My supervised professional experience in behavioral health has taught me the difference between a clinical relationship and one in which I participate as more than an observer. When I review most of my life, from the first moments of memory, I can say I have maintained mostly clinical relationships, where the other person's story was the thing of importance, and I was there as some sort of dark, silent mirror that could "see" them, or reflect who they truly were.

What the New Age woo-woo generation calls "reading a person's aura" is not only an energetic observation. It carries a lot of credibility. The practice may be interpreted as preferentially positive, however, it can be employed as well in transpersonal psychology to see the darkness in a person's being.

Clinically, it can be a highly refined observation of how dangerous a person is to themselves or to others, sometimes consciously, sometimes as an expression of what I prefer to call "The Demon."

The Demon is unconscious of what it does, and takes pleasure in someone else's suffering, which in German is *Schadenfruede*. To me, this is the core content of many violent men's hearts. If this creates a "No, you must be mistaken" response in your head, I suggest that you read newspaper articles on daily violent crime for a week, or track the most recent wars and genocides, and pay close attention to what men are actually emotionally or physically doing to each other, and to women and children.

Bring it down out of the realm of ideas. If you want to get as close as you can to it, recall how many times it has seemed okay to bust another man's balls to see a reaction. If the realization requires violence, you can see The Demon in the shift that causes a man to participate in a hazing that injures or kills someone, to put an axe in his wife's head, to buy a gun and shoot someone for some reason, to set a fire and burn down someone's house, to track a person, capture them, torture them to death, and practice the same action repeatedly with the intent of perfecting it, as in serial murders. Hazing and murder are part of the same reality that is qualified by how far one drifts ethically or morally from behavior that is considered lawful. Also, do not underestimate how attractive the use of violence can be in the human psyche, how literally alluring it can be to almost anyone. Where do you think Hollywood finds the content for its most violent scenes? Violence feeds the industry, as much as it feeds on the innocents who are murdered every day. The Demon can draw anyone into its own lines of force: we not only look—we stare, often with hunger for more.

It takes work to rise above this kind of anger and suffering. It takes work to see the vitality of connection with other men for good purposes in the world. Half the work is not permitting The Demon to enter the picture. Make no mistake about that—The Demon needs permission to be expressed. Its expression does not simply happen, as most of us would prefer to believe. Blame needs to be placed somewhere, if not on someone else, then on madness, or revenge, or a cause that gives The Demon license and engages and enrolls the approval of others, gaining the sanction and therefore sanctity of doing evil. Examples of the Olympic level of this permission can be found in state-sanctioned abuse of people and mass murder, such as the actions of Adolf Hitler, the SS, *die Endlösung* (the Final Solution), and the Holocaust, in which the governing state tacitly or overtly sanctioned torment, torture, and murder, and that made it legally permissible. To bring closer to home the idea of this license to commit evil acts, I offer the nearly complete genocide of the American Indian, and the creation of reservations, which are a less formal design of a concentration camp, where depression, alcoholism, and chemical dependency are the tortures of choice. Another example is Putin's Russia, where any form of political freedom, such as disagreement with actions taken by the state, are met with imprisonment, torture, and death.

Stopping The Demon requires that you *want* to stop it, that you *want* to do some good, that you *want* to help others in every way you can. You have to *want* the emotional and intellectual state of being a good man to be a good man, and hold that as a sacred bond with humanity.

If the rolling energy of men *en masse* is directed into the good work of saving each other from a life of sadness and suffering, we achieve what can be called connection as an authentic outcome of something more than ego acting out. If we can have one minute of this feeling every hour, incredible accomplishments are the outcome. It is a flickering expression, and once we get a glimpse of it we can spend a lifetime encouraging it. That is what Gary has done with the child criminals in juvenile hall and later as a probation officer, and then as a therapist and leader of men's groups for thirty-plus years. He hungers for that moment's glimpse every day, and keeps pursuing it by calling it a hundred different names. The one that sticks is "connection," so he goes with that.

As I work with the men in the practice that I share with my supervisor I keep asking the questions that Gary taught me to ask: "What do you want? What do you really want?" In the same way that I challenge men with this question, I challenge myself. Often, I am afraid of what I will hear myself say, and even more afraid that I will act upon it, as it will stir up a lot of dust in my life. If I don't ask this question, from my heart, with some semblance of authenticity, my life will be a lie and I know it. If I don't feel a little uncomfortable I know I'm avoiding an edge in the quest for what I really want.

As Gary and I walk The Hill we dig into what we want. I feel that Gary has been more conscious in this pursuit for many more years. I struggle with the question of what I want far more than he does because I have completely changed my life in the last eight years. I realize I am moving in a direction that will be changing again and again, taking creative risks that men at this age of sixty-plus years are not supposed to take. The one constant in these recent years has been Gary and me on The Hill. Through every season, through the excitement of preparing for Vision Quest, and in the sharing of the dogged determination that it takes to do this brutal climb two or three or four times each week, Gary and I do our best to be the men we strive to be.

In the other side of my life I am a small-boat sailor, an American Sailing Association certified skipper on San Francisco Bay, known to be one of the most challenging places in the world to sail. With twenty-four feet of deck between me, my crew and water that remains a steady 50° to 60°, that is suckled from the Pacific Ocean beneath the Golden Gate Bridge every day, we go out in any weather with a maximum of thirty-five knots of wind on land. Out on the water the wind speed may be greater.

The other day I went out with two people, a woman who was new to sailing, and a man who had sailed small boats on a lake back east. It was a blustery Wednesday evening sail. The measure of who I was in that moment was entirely in how well I could stay connected to my crew, respecting them every moment for their willingness to risk so much with me, and using kindness as my most important tool on board. The result was that we all learned a little more of what it means to sail this small boat in choppy waters that crash over the deck again and again. I fully understood what it meant to be responsible for these people, and what it meant to be fully connected with them. The results were that we had a very good sail, and I surprised myself with the fact that I had become a skipper, not only from years of sailing experience on the Bay, but also out of a sweet realization.

I had defeated the narcissistic father in my head so completely that I could sail with compassion rather than insult, and could speak commands firmly rather than bark them, encouraging my crew: "If you can handle sails like that it means you can take the tiller in this breeze," and seeing a second's hesitation saying, "You can do this. Try it out. I'll talk you through it." I had developed the ability to connect with people. So much of this came from Gary and me on The Hill, and from my patients. There is a deep reason why the motto of my club, Olympic Circle Sailing Club (OCSC) in Berkeley, is "Inspire Confidence." To be a good skipper is to be a good father.

I can ask myself where the truth lives in who I am, and I can receive a variety of answers from all the parts of my Self with which I am acquainted. I can ask what is going to happen next. I have come to appreciate what it means to be in this moment, to allow the quiet, and the being still with these letters that clatter across the page like the footprints of insects in the dust on The Hill. They remind me of my own footprints in the dust in this unrelenting ascent.

I know what is next when the truth comes forward, and so do you.

Chapter 11

The Tree of Healing

Suspending Judgment (Mark)

A men's group has a condition for its positive, healing effect, and the same holds true for men who are bonded in friendship. A man must take the time and the challenge to discover and speak his truth before he can allow a group of men to help him heal himself. Each man's story may be very different. The theme of healing may be universal. The sense of suspending judgment about himself and his life is a common outcome of a group helping a man to heal himself. The focus is on cultivating space within himself for change, on encouraging growth, on asking for help from the men in the group, and allowing healing to define the elements of this journey that we have observed on The Hill.

The Tree Knows Us (Mark)

A short distance beyond the summit of the Hill of Awareness is where the Tree of Truth stands, and around a very steep S-shaped bend is the Tree of Healing. At this point in the walk up The Hill the elevation of the snaking dusty path has been tempered by the effort of the climb even though it is one of the steepest parts of the trail, and the energy of completion spurs us on. The Tree of Healing is perched on the edge of the fire road in the same manner as the Tree of Truth, and it is an even larger live oak. Its branches cover part of the fire road and are so densely woven that standing under them provides a nearly dry respite in a steady rain.

Every walk up The Hill we marvel at the power of this tree, perhaps because we have projected onto it this theme of healing, and perhaps because the tree actually contains the energy we feel that causes our hearts to go

quiet. Gary and I time our hike up The Hill to the Tree of Truth, and stop our stopwatches as soon as we pass its trunk. We continue up to the Tree of Healing for another reason, deeper than the pride of accomplishment that accompanies a good finish to our hike. At this point in the climb we make our unrelenting ascent around the last bend for this huge live oak, so that we can see the tree, and the tree can see us.

Empathy for My Friend (Gary)

It's August and the leaves are just starting to dry and fall this morning. It's about 9:00 a.m., and the air is very cool and crisp. We begin to see the fog that rolled over a distant mountain range from the coast. It's refreshing, and a reminder that summer is waning: a time of change, another transition.

We are like the environment in which we live. This is why man has survived for so many thousands of years, because we adapt so well. However, as we get older it becomes harder and harder to adapt.

Today we start out fast. Mark is not talking. Usually he talks, and I fill in the blank spots here and there. Today Mark is silent. This is a first.

We make it to The Tree in a great time. A time we haven't hit in a couple years: fifty-six minutes and forty-four seconds. I know my best ever time was fifty-six-something. Today was good. We are cleansed again and we turn back down The Hill.

Last night we went to see his new house, which is a down-size from his more upscale neighborhood, but it's a cute house in a quaint neighborhood. His wife is sick from what I call "executive toxic smelt." The corporate world can begin to smell, and the person affected by it perceives that smell. She melded into it, and it's making her sick. Like putting metal in a forge. I remember that from high school, and the welding of pipe when I worked for the gas utility. There are toxic fumes that come from the intensely heated metal. Spend enough time in the heat and you become one with it, or smelt. Melt and mold into another shape. However, some can't mold; they just burn up or out. The cultural changes that have to be made by the individual have become repulsive.

Mark is also looking for a job now that he has his PhD. He has another obstacle: finding a job to fulfill his hours for licensing. He is preparing one house to sell, buying another house and planning its refurbishment, has a smelted wife, and no job. Add the usual man-woman relationship stuff in your late 50s, and aw shit. It's a truck full. I feel for him. He's my brother and we walk, just walk together. Our pace is not only quick, but also like two men marching. We are a machine: two wheels on a two-wheel tractor, if there was such a thing, climbing The Hill.

Staying Conscious (Mark)

I do not need to wonder what my life would be like if I did not have Gary's friendship and The Hill. Men without friends and simple challenges, which do not require enormous amounts of time and money for embarkation, end up looking at their future in the bottom of a whiskey glass, or the bottom of a glass pipe. When the stress of life is nearly unbearable I find myself fortunate to have a friend with whom I can be silent as we repeatedly face the same challenge that is always difficult no matter how hard we train.

We have learned that we can improve our time on The Hill to what we jokingly call "Olympic-level performance," and we are perfectly clear that it cannot be sustained. The Hill can tear us up very badly if we make a misstep across a root or a rock and blow out an ankle on the way up, or slip and fall on the way down, and blow out a knee on the steeper passages. We stay conscious of how we feel, keeping aware that we are hopeful of coming back another day.

We often joke about being in our 80s: old codgers who just don't know how to give up, wondering who of the two of us will die when we reach The Tree, and who will have to drag the other man's butt all the way down. Figuring the deceased man will be stiff as a board, we will need to carry one wheel and pin it between his ankles. The truth is that I am sick with real estate issues, relationship issues, and profession issues, and The Hill is my reward for not giving up, so I can have one more instance in which I cannot give up, and the reward is in the moment and witnessed by my brother.

Grief/Relief (Gary)

I am by myself again today. It's a warm afternoon, with a light shade of smog over the valley. That means it looks pretty good. I have yet to see the smog so bad this summer that I can't witness the east foothills. Part of me wants to believe that the air quality is actually improving.

I leave from the parking spot that is closer to the trailhead. It just means about ten minutes less of black asphalt and fewer cars on the narrow road. It also means a longer hike on the mountain in order to get in a one-hour hike. I'll end on a steeper grade beyond the Tree of Healing in what Mark describes as "the desert" because it consists of the dry road traversing a portion of the mountainside that is all rock above and below our trail without a trace of green. I like the flavor of that challenge. At the highest point is an overlook with a round, brass marker that identifies the name of The Hill and declares that it is a preserved wilderness.

It is definitely harder to hike when it's hot, and I feel the burden of the hot air hitting my lungs. I persist and the hike is going well. Well, that is, until I get just about to the beginning of the Hill of Cruelty. Deep sighs, more sensitive, cry. Feeling grief at a depth I never felt before. I find myself suddenly feeling emotions, and reflecting on the loss of one of my close friends some years ago.

I find myself choking on my breath, and I keep pushing despite the emotions trying to take away my air. Tears come. It's ancient grief, but it is back to visit today from a very deep place. I go further into the feelings, and find not my grief, but the grief of my friend's wife.

An event a long time ago: my friend, Rick, has died.

My wife and I go to his wake at their home. The bar is open and everyone is having a drink. My friend's wife, now his widow, who is a very pretty woman, pulls me into a side room that is partially curtained off. She sits me down. I am simply following because I am here to honor and respect my friend, and I do what she wants without hesitation or thought. She surprises me by kissing me. Simple me, I think it is just a simple kiss, until I realize she wants to keep kissing me. I feel her lips now. They are not seductive or sexual. They are lips that want connection, and here on the mountain I now feel the grief those lips carried.

My friend and I looked alike in many ways, fair skin, Nordic type I guess you would say. I would also say we had a gentle and happy presentation. People could have thought we were brothers. I am crying now as I let in this ancient memory, and really get the depth of her grief and the depth of her need to reconnect with her man, her lover, her friend.

I stamp forward and eventually catch my breath without ever giving up a moment toward the top. Only then can I let go. I promise myself I will allow relief at the top even though part of me wants to throw up. Ah, the top. I made it in only one second behind my last time. And I found relief from an old grief that I have carried since 1986.

The mountain has done it again. It seems each step is a page, and every climb is a deep process of unwinding and releasing feelings long held. The return is but a re-entry and a release from what I carried up the mountain.

How do you release the tension you carry in your body? How do you process your grief, and does it provide you with relief? You may want to take a moment and put words to it. We all need to grieve to have a tomorrow.

The Great Mystery (Gary)

I reflect back to my deceased friend and me working together at the probation department before Rick eventually went to another job. We shared many ideas spiritually and creatively. We talked about doing workshops and how we might put something together.

We took our sons, both named Chris, to fish at my secret spot on the Stanislaus River. He showed me how to prepare a fish. We promised to repeat the experience or reconnect, but we got too busy with work. I was at El Camino Hospital in Mountain View by then and kept telling myself I should call.

It was almost the end of the summer, as I remember. I was working the evening shift at the Trimble Road and First Street probation office in San Jose. I was sitting at my desk, and I suddenly felt a warm tingling running up my left arm akin to a low voltage electrical charge. I thought it strange and turned to see if I was feeling the setting sun behind me, cast upon my shoulder, but the sunlight on the floor was a distance away. I thought, "I need to tell someone." I wanted a witness to my experience. Maybe this was the sign of a heart attack, but it seemed too electric and without pain. I opened the door and realized that no one was there. It was about 6:20 p.m.

and I was the last person on duty. I took in the feeling, and within three or four minutes it was gone.

I went home and found out that Rick had been badly mangled in an auto accident, his left arm almost torn off, but that he had amazingly lived a short time in emergency care. The accident had occurred about the same time as my experience. My wife told me that a book Rick had loaned me—*Seven Arrows* by Native American writer Hyemeyohsts Storm—had fallen off the bookshelf at home at about the same time. I was stunned, shocked.

I had witnessed my friend in love and dating his wife, I had been at their wedding, we had fished with our sons, and I was at his grave. It was all back, on the mountain today. I relived those moments, and grieved not just for him, but this time, for her as well.

We had a deep connection, deeper than I had been aware of. We had spun dreams together over lunch but we were too busy and too driven to create together what we could have.

What friends have you lost track of because you or they were too busy? Lead, make the call, or wait until . . . what?

The Legacy of Sancho Panza (Mark)

I made my Vision Quest in one of Gary's groups in September of 2002. It was autumn in the Big Sur Forest, within the Ventana, "God's Window" into these mountains. A terrible fire had torn through this forest the previous season. It burned so many trees and the loam beneath the trees so that there was so much black ash everywhere, and the rains washed it into the brown leaves on the forest floor turning them gray. We were dispatched to find our spots on the mountainside and ordered to return and give our location using very clear landmarks—the view of a mountain through a circle of branches, an enormous live oak tree, a shoulder where there are dozens of birch trees, an outcropping of boulders. After thirty years Gary knew every major landmark on this mountain, and had instant recognition of our descriptions, and could add features we had seen but did not remember.

My spot called to me; I heard an internal voice say, "Over here." It was halfway down a hillside of fire-dead oaks. There was one stand of giants, a circle perhaps thirty yards in diameter, and in the center of these leviathans was another circle, without a single animal track, no hint of a route through the forest, and flat in its center. It was as though this inner circle were made sacred by an unknown force. I walked away and returned several times. I felt drawn to be there.

I returned to base camp. After communicating with Gary and staff where I was, I headed out to establish my spot, employing the rituals and processes Gary taught us. We were instructed to leave our tents at base camp. The only reason we would need them would be inclement weather, and we could claim them at that time.

It was not until I had been sitting in my spot for a few hours that I realized I was positioned in the forest so that the transit of the sun and moon were perfect linear arcs over my head. My unobstructed view would give me a box seat for sunrise and moonset, sunset and moonrise.

That was when I realized I had chosen to camp in the center of a living stand of giants whose daughters were all dead. I wanted to cut all the burned ones down, and use their rock hard wood to build, and avoid cutting any new trees, and just take these. It would have been so good to give these sad parents a view of their mountain free of all this death.

In the day the flies were in my eyes and ears and nose from dawn to dusk; their buzzing became a part of my day as normal as playing the radio. But there is no radio on a Vision Quest. They were the voices of all the busying that haunts my every waking moment and distracts me when I think I am centered. No matter how often I attempted to silence them they buzzed and buzzed, determined to steal my peace. Then, at dusk, Nature threw a switch, and all the buzzing stopped at the same time, an eerie experience.

In the night without cover the mosquitoes and their whining wings were circling behind me, approaching my ear simply to let me know they were there in the same way the dentist holds the needle out of view, and says, "Just a little pinch, now . . ." A gratifying moment beyond the view of the bright gold-white harvest moon was the sudden hum of bat wings that signaled the end of flying needles for a little while. My only defense beyond bats was mosquito netting supported by metal rings in the shape of

The Tree of Healing

a lampshade that fit over my head and kept the insects off my face and neck and out of my sleeping bag.

During the day I saw my neighbors at work, making a living: squirrels, birds, insects of every hue and size, a darting mouse. At night I could hear deer walking in the woods, the scamper and cry of a raccoon, and in the light of my headlamp dozens of eyes within the leaves of the surrounding loam reflected the light and identified my mouse neighbors. One night I was awakened by a shape that ran passed my head at high speed, and I wondered if it had been a raccoon or coyote. It did not make a return visit.

After three days out in the forest in my inflatable camp chair the hours pass with furious speed as I sit and stare at standing dead burned oaks that surround my spot. I am certain after three days of flies and sun and heat, and mosquitoes and moon and cold, in the same way I felt I could hear the tone of the universe, and feel it turning, I could hear these enormous trees weeping in their way for their lost children, the moaning of branches rubbing on branches in the evening wind.

On the final day I was unaware that I had not authentically prepared myself for closing the Quest, for rebirthing into the world. There is deep work that must be done, physical work and spiritual work, to prepare, honor, open, and close the Quest. So much of my life had been an "almost" effort, and I was in that pattern and did not know it.

I would be made aware of it. As much as the Quest rewards it also provides the wrath of Nature. As I walked out of the forest I did not know I was the walking dead. My body reacted with so much indignity to the presence of fakery that it tried to die, right there on the trail. This well-conditioned man was reduced to a hobbling old fool by sudden dehydration, demineralization, and demystification of my heroic self.

Even after drinking two gallons of water during the three days in the forest before we started on the trail back, even after consuming a special food bar that Gary provided that contains everything the body needs, and even after the electrolyte drink that restores balance, even after a pint of water in the first half hour on the climb out of the valley, this body started to die. Why?

I imagined that every poison I had ever become cozy with, every drug, legal and illicit, every environmental exposure to some chemical, hormones related to every negative experience I had consciously and willfully taken on, began coming out of my body fat all at once, and fed my blood and muscles a cocktail they could not possibly overcome. And there I was, the sophisticated poetic prick, now reduced to a drooling, pitiful cripple, just able to place one foot in front of the other and breathe. In the throes of dehydration and poisoning, no amount of water or breath could overcome this inner torrent of noxious being that I had been. All of the other men, Gary, and staff, passed me and headed on up. As I was no longer able to carry my pack, one of the staff took it from me and carried it up.

Now stumbling and unable to speak, using walking sticks to pull myself up and up a trail that does not know anything but up I am seeing my own death laughing at me as my heart pounds in my chest and in my ears, and every demon I have ever laughed at is dancing in the open as the sun's heat beats me until I am on my knees, and I get up and keep going because today is the day we march out, and in the blackening edge of an unconsciousness that I refuse to accept I am praying to God, to Shiva, to Ganesh, to Jesus, and I am not seeing that they are answering my prayer each time I go down, and think I cannot get up, and I get up because my Will refuses to believe that I am going to die at age fifty-three on this mountain, die of the internal shutdowns that follow extreme dehydration and heart failure that I can feel are approaching a little closer with every ascending yard that I win, and that winning will kill me, kill me forever, and then I surrender to all of it, to the pain, the poison, the loss of muscular control that is coming and will cause me to shit my pants and die on this trail.

When I surrender, when I am crawling on my hands and knees, looking down to see the drool from my lips forming its little ball in the dusty dirt, and my tears of goodbye are leaving me, and without any voice to speak a word to another human in this last moment I look up to realize I am at the summit, and the trail rolls gracefully down from here; and there, just around the bend are the men who have seen all of this and cheer me as I stand up and hobble to their smiles and encouragements, and sit down in the trailside dirt and welcome the black flies that now mass in my ears and nose without surcease.

Gary had me lead them down the trail to the finish, lead them all, even though my hobbling gate was slower than their powerful march, they had me lead them to the finish of the Quest, to food and drink set for us by our supporters, former Questers, all who knew this journey. I was not content with this ending, this manifestation of all my personal failures revealed in less than a few hours in a climb up rocky, dusty, and unforgiving terrain.

Gary saw that lack of contentment, that sense of personal failure, and took note of it. Days later he chose me to be his assistant for the Quest, which came as a complete surprise. He said, "Now you know how difficult this is and how dangerous. That's why you're the right choice. You will never let that happen to you ever again because other lives will be depending on you just as you depended on other men. That is why you will be co-leader and support the Quest. You have work to do."

I trained in first aid and wilderness rescue, and during the next seven years of Vision Quest in spring and autumn I supported his work. Gary and I trained on The Hill and in the gym, so that were close to peak conditioning throughout most of the year.

In 2004, two years after my own Quest, I was co-leading my third Vision Quest with Gary in Big Sur. The trek into Ventana forest took the day, and we arrived in golden, late afternoon sunlight. I was last man on the way in, and would lead on the way out. So it was my privilege to follow Robert Higginbotham, or "Higgie" as he was known to the group of men we were leading to The Cathedral, the entrance to our sacred ground for the Quest.

Higgie was overweight and a smoker, and on the arduous journey we faced he needed to rest often, and he drank copious amounts of water from the flasks he carried, and sweated profusely until his shirt was soaked. When we rested, we talked. I cannot recall all of the details of what we talked about. I clearly remember the effect it had on me.

I felt I was in an enlightened presence, similar to that of spiritual leaders I have had the good fortune to meet, who were my teachers of Eastern and Western spiritual practices in grad school. So, indeed, I followed this man into the forests and hillsides and along the mountain shoulders on our journey, wanting only to support him in any way I could, as I sensed he was on a sacred mission of his own apart from the Quest.

As we hiked along the uphill trail, Higgie needed brief rests. After several stops he began to say something to me repeatedly that deeply affected me in the moment. I did not realize that the phrase had a spiritual, transpersonal meaning until a few weeks later: he turned to me, looked me in the eye, and then, with a sideways glance over the tops of his glasses, asked me, "Are you ready?" I answered, "Yes," and we continued for a short way, until the elevation and terrain were too much to for him to take in continuous motion with a 50-pound pack on his back. When we stopped, he regarded the unspoiled environment surrounding us, and he leaned on his walking sticks, breathing as if he might die soon. We talked about the richness and value of life, about woodsmanship, and hunting, fishing, and the magnificence of the high country of his youth, when he was a logger in the Great Northwest. And then a moment arrived when I saw his spirit and his pride fuse into steel again, and he turned to me and asked, "Are you ready?"

This particular Quest was to be a unique time for me, as Gary, who enters the role of spiritual teacher when we make this journey, decided he would Quest as well. Gary had invested three years of training in me. He involved me in the six-month preparation he developed for all the men who would quest, helping to train them in meditation, defining their physical training regimens, their spiritual preparations, to be sure they would be in shape for the Quest, and helping them define the question they needed to ask and answer to make their next steps in life. He felt I was ready. I would hold base camp, and see to the safety of all who dispersed into the woods.

The men dropped their gear, and set out to locate the sites where they would Quest. Then they returned to report their locations to us, get their gear, and hike out to settle into their spots, and begin the journey away from everything except a question that burns within without surcease.

One of my tasks was to track each man and locate exactly where he was to ensure his safety, and do so for less than a minute, from a distance, silently and unobserved. Higgie had chosen a high spot in full sun during the morning, and surrounded by tall grass and boulders that offered shade throughout the afternoon. A man needed to understand the transit of the sun in the forest to choose a good spot like that.

Part of our ritual as Quest leaders is to ask each man for a small item that will represent his spiritual presence on the Quest. We have a nearly flat rock, a flake of granite, about one by two feet and an inch or two thick, that we hide under a pile of leaves near a large tree in the center of base camp, which we reveal for the Quest. It has about the same shape as the base of the mountain. On this we place the spiritual totems, laid out in the same pattern as the men spread out over our sacred ground. We hold silence and focus in meditation after we place the totems, passing the image and spiritual tone of each man through our minds. At odd moments, when we need to know the energy of the men on the Quest, we pick up each man's totem and hold it tightly in our right hand. Gary can feel the man's presence, and the tone of his challenge, and how he is faring with it. Gary is far more attuned to this energy, as he has been within this ritual for about thirty years, and his sharing it with me has been a deep learning. Gary taught me to do my best to remember what I felt when I held each totem, a subtle energy that has more of an emotional tone than a thought attached to it.

When the men return from the Quest there is a process engaged for returning to the world. We form a circle when all have arrived. Gary asks each man to recount his experience. Gary and I position ourselves opposite each other in the circle, so we can see eye to eye. During the seven years and 14 Quests that I had the honor to share with Gary and the men I noted the consistent accuracy of Gary's observations when he reported to me what each man was going through during the Quest as he held their totems. What Gary said matched what each man shared, time after time.

In the year that Higgie did his Quest, and Gary decided to Quest along with the men, I went through the ritual of the totems, and witnessed myself having this experience. To this day I believe that it was Gary's presence and his conferring responsibility for the men on me that permitted me this *exceptional human experience* (Palmer, 1999), a glimpse into sacred energy within which I could "see" the challenges of the men. I also attribute my experience to the Ventana wilderness. Ventana is translated as God's Window, and it is regularly visited by spiritual leaders from all over the world who sense this forest's profound energy.

On the return to the trailhead it was Gary who, as last man, followed Higgie, and recounted having the same experience of being in an enlightened presence, and the phrase after each brief rest, "Are you ready?"

Seven weeks later Higgie was a box of ashes on a funeral altar.

I remember what he said in circle, before the men hiked out to their spots, when each man gave the reason for his Quest. Higgie, with a burst of emotion, said, "I need to learn how to pray again." He had pancreatic cancer when he was on the Quest, and had no knowledge of his affliction, but I believe his soul knew what was coming.

Gary and I were invited to visit Higgie in the hospital shortly after the Quest. He had IVs in both arms and his skin was gray. When I approached the bed he looked up at me in a way that suggested my presence was a gift. We clasped hands, and I centered in heart space when I was with him. We had a few moments together and recounted our journey up the mountain. We were back among the pines and live oaks and madrones and high brush, we were on the trail, only three feet wide with a mountain on our left and a one-thousand-foot wooded drop on our right, and he was leaning on his walking sticks and asking me, "Are you ready?"

I could see he was. I looked in his eyes, and he gifted me with some of his spirit. I believe it still rests in my heart, as does the loss of this great man.

At Higgie's funeral every seat and every space in which to stand was taken in the large funeral hall. People were lined up in the aisles, in the entryway, and down the steps out into the street. There were a number of moments when men spoke about Higgie that revealed how valuable he had been to so many people in his work life and personal life. That presence was still apparent, upheld in that gathered throng in the hall. It was shared among what must have been a hundred people within proximity of the grave where his ashes were laid to rest.

I realized after the trek how deeply Higgie had affected me in that one day, and in fact had initiated a transformation in me that I never expected to experience. It led me to wonder if other Quest leaders were as affected as I was by the experience of leading.

Robert Higginbotham was one of the people to whom I dedicated my dissertation, in thanks for his gift. From him I learned that there is more than one hero in the novel *Don Quixote*. One is the main character, and the other is Sancho Panza, the one who follows, who appears comical and the fool, the one who remains loyal in the face of loss of reason, bad weather, risks that have no sensible value, nearly invisible, rarely remembered, and essential to the Quest.

Higgie permitted me that role as a man, for that day, for that Quest, and for the rest of my life, and for all of this I will remember him.

"Are you ready?"

Alone (Gary)

Ah, a walk by myself again. I pass two ladies and wish them a "Good morning, ladies," and get a very pleasant "Good morning" back. I appreciate their warm response but as I get a distance past them I can hear their continued talking and wished they weren't here. I love the feeling of being alone. It is part of me. I spent so much time alone as a child that today I love it. I have done well in other parts of my life to ensure that I never feel alone.

Today I take in how much I owe to Essie and Alan Nichols. They were my caretakers when my mother worked and I would stay with them for a week at a time. They had about four acres, five apple trees, a hammock in the summer, a dog (Skeeter would excitedly run in circles when I came to stay), berry bushes, a small forest, a wood pile to build forts, a place to shoot my BB gun, an awesome swing (you could go so high you could feel the rush in your balls), homemade tapioca pudding and date nut bread, chickens, my toy box, and so on.

I realize now that this memory of Essie and Alan's home has been a power source for me, a reference for me to return to again and again as a source of solace and grounding. I now realize I use the trail on The Hill as a resource for some of those feelings, or maybe have always known this. I am aware today that I need to transfer that power place to something here now, and my little kid is resistant to letting it go. I am getting closer to doing that. I tell the child within, "You need to find your home here, little kid."

Coming Home (Gary)

This is a section I have just added after a period of time away. First it was a trip with my brother to Panama City. Why "Coming Home?" Because all of this, all of my writing, I now truly realize, is part of my journey of coming back home. Coming back to myself. It's not out there. It's in here, as many know. Oh, I knew that too, but only intellectually. You see, the way I learned to survive my dislocation was to look out there. It must be better out there.

For me this journey started almost sixty years ago. Sixty years ago. Sorry I have to look at that twice in print to get it, and I am still not sure I "get it."

I find myself returning to the experience that took place when I was just four or maybe five years old. You may think I am repeating myself, but it is even more significant now. An older boy came up to me on the corner near my home and said there was going to be a fight and we would all need something to help us win. He gave me a Three Musketeers bar and implied we were together in this just like the Three Musketeers. The only thing I understood was that he wanted to be my friend, there was some danger, we were going to be together in this, and he gave me something. That felt good. There was no fight, and I never saw the boy again, but he delivered something to me in that little package. I can still see the illustration on the wrapper, The Three Musketeers.

The symbolic gift, an element of fear, the invitation to join, joining, bonding, feeling safety and power in being part of something bigger than myself set a tone and a mission for my life. I didn't really understand just how powerful that was until our walks and downloading my story with a witness such as Mark.

What part of your story have you buried that might benefit you as valuable lesson and guide for your direction?

An American Cheese Sandwich (Mark)

I have the memory of going to one of my relative's houses when I was small. She was a big, sweet, loving woman with Dutch-Boy blond hair. She gave me a sandwich of American cheese and butter on a hard roll. I remember seeing my mother's face when she saw me with the roll. She looked angry that someone else had given me food that she had not approved. It was not good that I could be experiencing this simple pleasure. It meant she was losing her grip. Yes, my mother loved giving the impression she was powerless, and she was one of the most manipulative people I have ever known.

To this day I cannot forget the kindness in the face and voice of the woman who gave me the sandwich, who spoke to me so sweetly as she made it for me, and looked with excited expectation for my approval after my first bite. I cannot remember her name, as I only met her this one time and so long ago, but I can see her face, I can smell the fresh Kaiser roll and taste the contents, made with far more butter than my mother would ever approve. Perhaps we never went back because of the sandwich, or because of the love it contained. My mother was expert at isolation and cutting off without any further contact.

What I remember of my mother was her sadness, her silent aura of distress and disappointment, her quiet reproach toward my father, and my father's cool distance from her and from me. I suppose my mother showed me the same love that this relative had shown me so many years ago, but it was withheld after I became old enough to reject her control. For many years I did not have anything to reach back into to know what it means to love or to be loved in a way that was anything similar to consistent. I had grown up so ready for rejection that I accepted it as the norm in my family and could not tolerate it for a fraction of a second anywhere else in my life. To this day I cannot tolerate any manipulation of family by family, and will fully reject anyone who engages in bending another person to their will by subterfuge.

When friends, co-workers, and acquaintances tell me I have become softer and more approachable over the years I have a deep sense of weakness and feel very threatened. It is clear that the connection has now reached the point of revealing me for who I am, and no matter how much I accomplish or write or create, I cannot lose this sense of being "less than." This is where my healing needs to live, a little each day, every day, to simply feel that I am enough. It is often on The Hill, when the trail is unrelenting in its ascent, and the challenge is so great I feel my heart will burst, that I get a glimpse of being "enough" with Great Nature as my witness.

Becoming heroic is not required. Even being *special* is not necessary. I want an American cheese sandwich with too much butter on a hard roll and I want to feel loved the way I was loved that day.

Can you think of a day that is filled with memories of events that established your sense of yourself? Can you describe the character of each memory, the thoughts, emotions, and events tied to it? Is there any longing you know of now that is directly related to your awareness of who you are?

When you reach back into your life, you may find moments when you felt unconditional love from someone. Although it can be painful, as that love is often lost, focus on how it felt in your thoughts, your emotions, and your senses. When you are fully within that love, think of a person, now or in the future, to whom you want to gift that love, and then share it with that person at your earliest opportunity.

Chapter 12

The Open Path

Stacking Stones (Mark)

The journey does not end here. The work that men do in support of each other can change communities and organizations. How they choose to use what they have learned is up to them. We know that the work we have done on these mountains has crystallized a perspective that Gary has developed over the last thirty years and I have had the privilege to witness. The idea that men can learn how to support each other in healing themselves will go on. It has been a part of mankind for millennia. We are stacking a few stones on the path. Perhaps they will be remembered, and others will stack theirs near ours.

Time to Stop: Time to Climb the Hills Again (Gary)

I have seen cloud formations that come out of the beauty of a severe storm blowing in, rabbits that come out of hiding to take advantage of a warm morning search for food, coyotes that move when few humans are willing. I love those days when Mark and I have The Hill to ourselves. When the mountain bikers decide to stay home. Then animals roam. I see deer and fox running together. What a treat. My spirit loves it. I feel a connection with their wild spirit. I am one with them.

All the Pieces Fit (Gary)

I am supposed to walk The Hill today. However, I have just come from a recruitment meeting at the California Army National Guard Armory. Now it's fair to spend some time with my wife, so I am home with her.

Friday I had a meeting with Sgt. Mike Frankadakis, who is a real estate broker here in Los Gatos, and we shared old war stories from Vietnam.

I had called in response to a newspaper ad for the National Guard and Homeland Security. The ad said the opportunity was open to people up to age sixty. I was frustrated and disappointed for weeks (I was sixty-three) then decided to call anyway. I was determined to serve. Mike said the limit is extended up to age sixty-three with prior military experience, and so we set up a time at his office.

He said he had a calling to serve after 9/11, but the local recruiter laughed at him. It was three years ago that he learned about the California Guard from another realtor who had recently retired from the Guard at age seventy. I agreed to meet him on Sunday for a further briefing. So a couple hours ago I was inside the California Army National Guard Armory, which incidentally is across the street from the probation department where I worked as a juvenile hall counselor and a probation officer for twelve years.

Mike showed me around until another man came in for recruitment from Sacramento. I could look up to see the window of my old office on the fourth floor (the executive offices) at the Juvenile Probation Department where I was Assistant Coordinator of the Juvenile Court Work Program. I remember looking down and across the street at the Armory and wondering what was in there. Now here I stand looking back. Seems very *déjà vu*. While we were waiting a man came in from the Air National Guard. He is based out of Moffett Field with the 129th Air Rescue Wing. Of course I was interested since I was former Air Force. He supports communication for air rescue of downed airman. Wow to me! My inner kid wants to play! Where's the choppers? Sometimes I wonder, is this life I'm leading already scripted?

Mike gives me a tour of the building, and tells me that this building could be available to me for an event in the future if I wished, and he showed me the kitchen. Oh yes, this would work.

I used to have a men's dinner every year with a guest speaker. I asked Mike if he would speak, and he said he would love to. Now, just now, I called Alain Guichard, who is a top-level chef, and asked him how he was recovering from surgery. He had a cancer removed. He said he was doing well, and would return to work next week. We chatted and updated each other and I had to ask if he was up to cooking for another event and he said, "Yes, anytime I can do something with the men."

It all seems directed sometimes. Like all the pieces fit.

The Sutra (Mark)

Gary and I enjoy seeing a different perspective on life and in the moment of the experience we get the feeling it is related to some spiritual principle that has been established for centuries, and we have stumbled upon it experientially rather than reading about it in a book.

The reason why I saw this happening was because an enlightened teacher such as Dr. Henry Poon handed that very book to me years earlier. Henry Poon established the East-West spiritual psychology program at my grad school, the Institute of Transpersonal Psychology, and because I was his most difficult, argumentative, and resistant student when I first studied his principles—and was stunned by their power by the end of the course—he made me his teaching assistant the following year. What a gift. His vision informs my supervised clinical practice.

There is a Buddhist principle that comes out of *The Sutra of Hui Neng* that Gary and I do not think about—we experience it—when we walk The Hill. Please be clear, we are not Buddhists. Yet there is a natural flow of spiritual meaning that comes from this practice of climbing The Hill that organically parallels a principle (called *subitism*) from the Sudden School: A devotee living a life of repeated prayer and meditation has a sudden catharsis—combined with a sudden vision of the world and all of its life—combined with a shock of consciousness and recognition of universal meaning—that lead to an instantaneous enlightenment.

I don't know if I would call two sometimes spiritually constipated older dudes sweating their nuts off on The Hill a vision of enlightenment. As luck would have it, we have been given a valuable insight that evolved out of the spiritual practice of placing one foot in front of the other at a consistent pace hundreds of thousands of times, in every season, no matter what the conditions. It is this: when encountering any experience in life, any object, any relationship, any powerful or minuscule event, negative or positive, to have one's consciousness naturally seek the place of *not being attracted to it, not being repelled by it, not being attached to it.*

The sense of freedom in this state is limitless. There is a perfect moment without want, without fear or anger, without the desire to hold on to anything. It is a glimpse of what it means to be complete within oneself, free of any implied obligation to any agency, organization, or person.

For us The Hill has become the Sutra, a set of immutable laws about a spiritual encounter, a meditation, a prayer, a chant, a Yoga, a sense of universal consciousness, and a window into the collective unconscious. It was an evolving experience for me, a walk on a sacred labyrinth.

Originally a city kid from Brooklyn, New York, who fell in love with Yosemite, The Hill gave me a nearly daily dose of grandeur and challenge. No matter how many times I walked The Hill I always wondered if I could make it to the top, and I was always surprised that I did. This interplay of doubt and truth expanded the way I took meaning in life. The richness of nature, in all its hues of green and gold and blue relaxed the parts of me that are on guard. Animal sightings, often for only a couple of seconds, helped me envision myself as a part of something much larger than the petty frustrations that can fully occupy the day.

The Hill gave me the gift of my friend, a man who does not share his personal time easily. Gary needed a partner who could keep up, with whom he could share his appreciation of Nature and Her wonders. I did not take that relationship for granted. I still hold it in my soul.

It was after the first couple of years on The Hill that I could perceive an expansion of consciousness in both of us. I don't think we ever figured on the gift of enlightenment, if that is what anyone can call what happened to us. We were released from the fetters we had accumulated during our decades on earth, and experienced a lightness of soul and being we had not known in the past on any of the adventures each of us had pursued. Eventually, I could internally feel myself shift into an altered consciousness for the hours we were joyously struggling along our dusty path. In those moments I was not attracted to any idea or object, not repelled, and not attached. All the parts of me that respond to a demanding world went quiet, any anger or disappointment appeared unimportant. I felt a different freedom in my heart that escapes description, save that it floated on the wind that moves and unites plant and animal, and over time reduces boulder and stone to grains of sand and dust.

To not be attracted to it. To not be repelled by it. To not be attached to it.

Being Here (Gary)

In absence of myself I go somewhere else. Can I not just be here? What is a more compatible way? I see desirable objects now, but I have attained an emotional distance. I am detached and relaxed. There are definite benefits to being without desire, enjoying what I have and where I am, who I am when I have cut out the critic, the evaluator, assessor, comparer. I am enjoying being in a relaxed state. Now I need to let go of money. Approximately $3,000 till the truck is paid off, $10,000 to pay off the Volvo, $2,000 more to pay the Keogh. I need to let that craziness go, too.

I get out of the car at the stable where my daughter keeps her horse. Next to us is a beautiful black Jaguar sedan with an almost perfect front that is creased under the grill. I am distracted by its beauty, but I assess the flaw, and see the deceit of design much like what I discover about the beautiful woman who owns it. I share my impression with my daughter who discloses that all is not well within the woman. Illusion or truth? A friend now deceased used to love to ask, "Do you want the truth, or do you want me to bullshit you?" I love that.

What kind of a bullshitter are you? Most importantly how do you bullshit yourself? It's a common male trait so don't judge yourself for it. Just know it, because the knowing helps preserve your integrity.

I walk through the barn and am greeted by horses' heads. My daughter's horse is beautiful and unflinching as I talk to him and stroke his jaw line. Finally he pulls back just a little and wants my shirt buttons.

I have left my money distractions for the illusions of beauty. Yet beauty quickly shows me its shadow side. Perhaps what is ugly could be the shadow side of beauty. So the comfort comes in not caring, as I move on the dirt floor through the barn, and say hello to more horses. I am in the moment, enjoying myself, and I've forgotten the beauty of the automobile and the woman I just passed. I am free. "Free of what?" you may ask. Free of any attachment other than to the moment.

Now, later in the evening, a more difficult task: can I close my eyes and detach? Tomorrow there will be another hike and a new moment of truth. Awe: the beauty of being in the moment. Time to sleep.

Being Home (Gary)

Now, after a lifetime journey of fantasy I am feeling what it's like to be home. I am going through some withdrawal, and hence some mild depression, but that's okay. The Hill has brought me back to myself.

As Joan Halifax offers a poem by Nancy Wood (1979, p. 107):

> Here on the mountain I am not alone;
> For all the lives I used to be are here with me;
> All the lives tell me now I have come home.

And, typing her in, I write: "Sweet sorrow, I am here."

Soft Focus (Mark)

As therapists Gary and I are not the ones who do the work that needs to be done. We create a space for it, hold space for it, encourage it, and honor the men who own it. They go to dark places that can be very frightening, that invite the desire to fix, to make it all better, to be both mother and father and quickly heal the wound. Yes, make it go away. What a wonderful way to keep the wound festering all the way to a deathbed.

In our culture we hate suffering so much that we miss the balance it provides with joy, and shows its value in the manner that a shard of glass shines in the dust of the trail that we walk on The Hill. A hundred drunken teenagers and a hundred hard working laborers smashed a thousand bottles of beer on this trail, and Gary looks for the glass shards on every hike. We are fully aware of the beauty of the landscape, and fully aware of the surface of the trail, all at once, seeing with soft eyes, allowing the complete picture. This way of seeing is key to spiritual practice, in walking meditation, in Aikido, in the arts, in any pursuit that demands we simultaneously observe the events around us and observe ourselves, to see internally and externally all at once.

Over the years on The Hill, I have applied this shift in vision and have to resist telling Gary where I've seen some of the glass in the dust along the way up that he will invariably search for on the way down, as it is a sin against time to slow down or stop on the way up. Stopping dishonors the effort required, the struggle demanded by the unrelenting verticality of this ascent we have made so many hundreds of times.

Gary is disappointed, sometimes even disgruntled if he cannot find the shiny shards we have seen in the dust on the way up and cannot bring bits of the glass down with him as we descend. It is the collecting of glass that gives additional value to his experience, that gives it a real-world purpose, which is grooming the trail, keeping it pristine. I see this as a gloss over the purposelessness that the experience provides, which to me is far more important. It is important to be without a socially adjudicated purpose for a short time each day. It revises perspective.

We say that we do this walk to train ourselves for Vision Quest, which is true, but not the real reason we do this twice or three times or more each week. We say it is for the physical challenge, and that is not the real reason.

It is in this space where we have chosen to leave all of the unanswered questions that carry the illusion of demanding an answer. We come here to be present to ourselves and each other, and, when we are fortunate, we are present only to The Hill. All the sweat and blood is the price we've paid to be *in* this experience rather than *observing* it. We suffer to be free, and freedom converts suffering to meaning.

Fear (Gary)

My core wound is abandonment. That I knew. I learned how to model that well. I learned how to abandon myself by not being seen. My wife recently complained that when I came home from work I was depleted because I hadn't taken care of myself. I believe that if I sacrifice enough my heroic gesture will be rewarded someday. (One of my mother's words: "Someday.")

I see now that I want to do things for others in a way to get what I need without being seen, more accurately without any need. Just like I had as a child. "Invisible" means to neglect myself as I was neglected. Ignore my needs as my needs were ignored. I can't write a book because then I would be seen. Being seen scares me as much as going back to Vietnam.

I don't know how to be seen except in small venues. I just don't have the experience yet. If I want to make a more significant difference in the world I will have to be seen. In order to do what I want to do, which is write a book, I will have to become visible. It's time that I allowed myself to be seen and not abandon my Self and my dreams to old fears and a role of suffering my abandonment.

Old habits die hard or never do if you medicate yourself. Mark and I chose the pain and pleasure of being awake and we hope this inspires the same in you.

I vaguely remember my parents arguing around me and the job I took on must have been to be invisible or at least quiet. That's it. Now I remember my mother saying that she had to keep me quiet because we lived in a small apartment, and she didn't want to upset our neighbors (and the landlord). That must have included restricting my breathing, thus causing frequent colds and respiratory ailments. It is now easier to breathe. Thanks for another day, different mountain, same spirit. Ah-HO.

It's an interesting shift for me. I am at an age where I will soon qualify for Medicare. There is the confrontation with getter older, but there is also the positive side of being able to save about $300 a month on medical insurance. I was getting to like that idea and what I might do with the money until my wife brought up the fact that I didn't really carry enough life insurance to care for her if something happened to me. The needed increase would be about $300 a month.

I got angry, felt many feelings including feeling cheated, resentful, confused. I ruminated for several days. Then suddenly all those feelings went away. On my walk I asked myself what happened. I unwound the process. I came to a place of feeling wise. The $300 held no energy for me.

I had surrendered to my adult partner's needs. I was in relationship with her. I no longer had to fight for me. I trusted she would be there for me as a partner. I had come a step closer to home. I was no longer in survival from childhood dislocation. I had let go of FEAR of being abandoned. Actually I had let go of FEAR.

I used to think of myself as highly sensitive and some saw me that way. My first wife called me her "baby doll" because of it. There are books written about highly sensitive people. Now I see the deeper truth for me. I was a highly scared person, which made me highly sensitive.

You see, through all this the most important thing that was revealed to me in my miles and years of walking, and trying to come home, was my fear. Only in absence of fear could I come home. Only in absence of fear could I find my home, and claim it by being present to the moment without fear, and old pictures coloring my catalog.

I had to walk away my fears and grieve in order to find my place. Presence is being in a place without the cloud of fear. I visited a lot of pictures on The Hill until they distilled into a common cauldron. Vietnam wasn't the first place I had visited fear. It was only a reminder. It brought me back to where I had come from. From there I had to go back to my first fears. And I knew those fears were about absentee parents and my attempts to control my inner toddler's reality.

What might you be afraid of facing?

The Secret of The Hill (Mark)

A patient came in to see me about his very violent son. Aside from the shaved head, pointed goatee, wallet chain running from his black belt into the back pocket of his greasy jeans, and neck tattoo that read "Fuck Life," I encountered the presence of seething anger. I remember thinking, "So this is the kid's father, huh?" His overall appearance and affect told me a little bit about the father-son relationship and about this father as a role model. I asked myself and my supervisor what it would take to help this parent change himself and save his son. My internal answer was spiritual transformation. But how could he get there? His expectation was that he could put his boy in the hospital, and then a long-term program, and we would repair him, tune him up, and he'd be fine. It was our job. How could I tell him that a possible answer was in sharing an adventure with his son to begin their spiritual journey together without stealing from both father and son the process of finding their own way?

I remembered my own lack of direction in my youth, and my internal hunger for adventure, not understanding what I was really seeking. I was looking for a way to become a man—but more particularly, a good man. I was hungry for a trial by fire, a rite of passage that would be my entry into manhood. This process was as old as mankind and was repeated in cultures throughout the world in any number of rituals and conventions. How could I explain that? Even more, how could I explain that this would be a three-step process known for thousands of years in the East and West? Both father and son would need to know transcendence, transmutation, and transformation within the cauldron of adventure.

To this day the memory of our encounter haunts me. Maybe they are still out there, struggling. Perhaps this is my moment to make amends.

The question that comes to mind around this, so many years later, is, "What am I looking for?" when I consider the pursuit of adventure. I know Gary and I share a process, and we both know what it is. The Hill is a spiritual journey, and it is the undercurrent of adventure that clarifies its explanation.

I want to share with the father who came to see me that adventure can change a person. Most of the time for the better, but how does it do that? I have had seven years on The Hill to think about this process, and the long-term effect of placing one foot in front of the other in a challenging environment. The experience has led to a deep change in the way I see everything in my life.

The effect of adventure that I'm alluding to has its roots in the allegory of turning lead into gold, a process in which the base parts of ourselves can be transformed into positive and valued characteristics. The Hill is like the laboratory of an ancient sage, an alchemist who is able to rise above simple knowledge to achieve great wisdom. Through a long and difficult struggle he discovers how to turn lead into gold.

There is an entire history and lexicon of terms related to medieval alchemy and its mysteries. The most important one here is "transmutation," the reaction that begins with lead and ends with gold. C. G. Jung borrowed this term from alchemy and applied to psychology. He saw this as a process for becoming our true self that he called individuation. From Jung I learned that this was a three-stage process. If you were lucky it gradually proceeded from transcendence to transmutation and eventually to transformation.

As Gary would say, time for some explanations and definitions.

Transcendence

Transcendence is a challenge to the ego, as it involves rising out of the self we think we are. Transcendence literally means to step above and beyond, but it also has a competitive meaning, to outdo or surpass, or achievement of a higher accomplishment than others. It signifies going beyond whatever hinders us, to rise above it. Most of all it can also mean exceeding one's limits with a conscious intention: to better one's self.

Transmutation

Transmutation involves a physical or emotional challenge, a Quest for something of great value, and results in deep change within a person. Transmutation is the term that was used repeatedly by alchemists in the Middle Ages in reference to the change of one substance into another in the presence of energy, usually fire. Jung redefined transmutation as the actual changing process that carries us through each of the steps or turning points in life that make up the transition from lead (base and selfish) into gold (evolved and open) and culminate in our being transformed. It is not a one-step slapdash occurrence similar to hitting "enter" and getting an instant response, as in a game or an application. For Jung it meant a continuous process of individuation that he described as *a personal quest for wholeness.*

Transmutation, for me, has had a real price. I have had to make decisions along the way for which I was willing to pay: It meant giving up what I thought I knew about myself. It meant time, sweat, injuries, and blood. That's what has happened to me in this walk up The Hill, on Vision Quest in the mountains of Big Sur and the forests of Ventana, in the sharp-edged talus fields along the big walls of Yosemite, and sailing small boats from Berkeley to San Francisco.

Transmutation addresses more than adventure. It also involves the white-hot energy of a challenge to our moral core. Our response will be to rise or fall in the presence of this challenge. (These notions of *rise* and *fall* are keys to the meaning of transformation as you will see.) In the process of transmutation we get to turn lead into gold if we have faith that human beings can change. Unfortunately, not all schools of psychotherapy depend on faith. To communicate this idea to the father and son I needed to understand where I could find support for transmutation as something that can actually happen in human psychology.

As therapists encountering transmutation we have a choice of perspective. We can either turn gold into lead, by having the most pessimistic outlook on the impossibility of change in human beings, as is held by psychoanalysis—*or*—from the existential perspective, keep some of the gold, face all the lead, and realize it will always be with us as we overcome our fear of freedom—*or*—from the cognitive perspective, discover the thoughts and emotions that progress toward our actions, and if we can change our thoughts then gold is a possibility (but lead is a waste of time to contemplate)—*or*—from the transpersonal perspective, turn lead into gold by allowing that *human beings can withstand the trial by fire that transmutation demands of them and can consciously experience it.* I prefer to combine the existential and the transpersonal with some thought/emotion/action tools from the cognitive school.

On top of all of this had to be overlaid the notion that changing ourselves has the price of a lot of discomfort. Changing ourselves can be painful whether it is a change for the better (a step into the light) or a change for the worse (a deepening darkness), and either one can be the result. That is the greatest risk of engaging in transmutation, because it can color the next step: transformation and its attendant vision of ourselves. Both the father and son whom I remember seemed to be headed for the depths of The Darkness, which can be one of the outcomes of transmutation and it can lead to an unwanted form of transformation.

Transformation

Transformation is, in my understanding, the accumulation of vision—the ability to see ourselves changed from one set of mental, emotional, and intellectual states to another after transcendence and transmutation have done their work. I am transformed when I can see the change in myself is proceeding or when it becomes apparent, both viewed in a state of self-observation.

Transformation results when we can rise above who we are and when the base metal of ourselves is forever altered into gold by an accumulation of energy far more powerful than that obtained from the everyday accomplishments of life.

Philosophers, psychologists, and spiritual practitioners speak of *progressive* and *regressive* transformation: this energy can have both positive and negative directions. They speak of positive, progressive transformation as spiraling up (rising) and negative, regressive transformation as spiraling down (falling).

The regressive form of transformation is not pleasant. This can

look like a man who gets deep into chemical dependency, starts using more powerful substances, uses more of them more often, and spirals down to addiction. Another regressive transformation is dependence on violence, at first with members of one's family, then with friends, then with strangers, and each incident becomes more physically confrontational and more violent, eventually involving weapons with the intent to harm or kill. When the two are combined, chemical dependency and violence, the results are predictable. Regressive transformation is well documented in current psychological diagnosis as a devolving process, beginning with Oppositional Defiant Disorder in childhood, then Conduct Disorder in adolescence, which after age eighteen spirals down into Antisocial Personality Disorder, which unchecked descends into psychopathy, wherein criminality becomes ritualized, as in serial rape, serial murder, and serial arson. Diagnostic theory does not call this a regressive transformation, yet that is exactly what it is. I was concerned that the son I was seeing was headed in this direction, as it was resident in the behavior and self-image of the father. They were in a crisis.

Gary has taught me that working with men in groups reveals a series of crises. The focus of the work can be on challenges with intimate relationship, or authority figures in business, or a lack of identity, or a sense of being emotionally numb and displaying an absence of feeling that can lead to a crisis.

These men either decide to face these internal crises, understand, live with, and overcome them, or they find ways in which to stay deaf, dumb, and blind to them. In regressive transformation they drift into alcoholism, drug abuse, sexual addiction, addiction to porn, or addiction to anger and the foundation of anger, which is fear. Ever hear of the addiction to "White Power?" Fear is where it lives.

Men may learn in group therapy that they have a choice. They can face their existential crises by exposing them to group discussion, or they can refuse to disclose their inner lives to anyone for fear of being shamed as much as they shame themselves. They can face the struggle between progressive and regressive transformation. Then they can choose to work toward discovering something positive and progressive and flooded with light. In the process they learn to accept what is negative and regressive and fraught with darkness in themselves, and then consciously decide that they have had enough pain and suffering, and move on to a life of creative expression, love, and connection.

I have seen men take on the challenges of self-realization and the leap from personality—the characteristics that make us who we are—to Spirit, a view of ourselves in unity with something greater than ourselves. They seek their original internal unity, preferring that sense of wholeness that they had for moments in childhood. They overcome a state of fragmentation and dividedness that keeps them captive, and develop a sense of internal unity. They see and feel the opportunity to recognize their potential for transformation, an opportunity reflected in the men around them. Within this experience transformation is both an outcome and a process, it is a sense of unity and diversity, it is both creativity and an awareness beyond ourselves.

Our walk on The Hill led me into an opening of consciousness, a heightened awareness, and manifested as a creative process, a spontaneous desire to document the experience. As we climbed The Hill, Gary and I stepped away from our wounds and weaknesses. It put us in touch with a higher self, free of ego, and characterized by an intense vulnerability. The truth of the struggle up The Hill was paralleled with a mutual struggle to become whole, to achieve a state where all parts of self could live without a sense of fragmentation, without a sense of not being enough. The experience contained a conscious intention toward wholeness and a motivation toward internal unity inspired by placing one foot in front of the other in a meditative determination.

We transitioned through a winding and an unwinding. As the fire trail wound its way up the mountain, Gary and I were drawn into a literal upward spiral, and that is the description provided repeatedly by spiritual leaders and philosophers for centuries as a model for progressive transformation. As we unwound the trail we felt everything we had learned embed itself in consciousness, and experienced a sense of being whole. The struggle on The Hill helped to fuse the parts of our selves separated by trauma and loss into a more integrated personality, reinforcing the upward spiral.

For the father and his son, I hoped that they could share a journey together, an adventure large or small, that could lead them into the sense of wholeness. The only suggestion I made was a walk up a hill together, pursued on a regular basis, where they could simply be within each other's company, a brief adventure where they could struggle together within the same experience. Shortly after my encounter with the father the son was discharged from the hospital. I made the suggestion of shared activities with them before they left. Perhaps they could become bonded in something more than anger and rage. At least that is my prayer.

The secret of The Hill echoes in my heart every day. In the simplest way, Gary and I had embarked on what seemed to be nothing more than a hike. About five thousand miles later we learned the meaning of transformation. By going through the experience of transcendence, which took a physical form on The Hill, we rose above who we were in the moment and whatever may have been hindering us. The outcome of the emotional and physical challenges of The Hill, repeated hundreds of times, was transmutation. The cauldron of experience had changed us to the core of who we were. We would never be the same again. When we looked back on the journey, the combined result was transformation.

Gary had been within this process, and was taking men through this process, for more than thirty years as an organic outcome of his work as a therapist. He had tapped into ancient wisdom that is responsible for the continued survival of civilization and had become a conduit for spiritual development. He did his best to appear invisible, to create the ground where men could do personal work. He was doing far more than that. He was all at once a wizard, a priest, a doctor, and a good and loyal friend. He was helping men transform lead into gold, a process that we now express as a simple phrase.

Gary said it best.

Walk 'till you find your way home.

I encourage you to search your world and find a daunting mountain, forest, or ocean challenge to share with a good friend many times, one in which you will literally save each other from time to time. You may see yourself changing in the way you view your life. What I write here now might help you to know the path when it shows up, and it is up to you to trust yourself and your companion enough to take it on more than once, maybe even a thousand times, knowing the risks and facing them with positive spirit again and again.

The Wall (Gary)

I recently visited THE WALL in Washington DC. I found some of the cabbies interesting and would occasionally strike up a conversation. An obviously older gentleman told my wife and me about being wounded in WWII. He was at the Battle of the Bulge. When I told him I was a Vietnam vet he chuckled and said, "That was a junior war." There it was again. I let it go this time, and just decided to respect and honor this elder man for his sacrifices, and accepted that he would never understand my own. Somehow I was okay.

I made my way to the Vietnam Memorial. I placed my hand on THE WALL, cried, and dragged my hand along the length of THE WALL. I found not only tears but my body wanting to touch each person. It was like I was trying to gather all of them and do something with them. I wanted to take all of them with me and touch every one of them. They are with me, and although Vietnam scarred me, it also brought me into consciousness, or better yet my grief has kept me awake. Now much more fully awake, as I am in touch with the depth of my feelings, and give full permission to be where I am.

Home.

What does that really mean? Two stories from my groups come to mind.

In my 4:00 p.m. men's group last Monday a man shared that he visited his friend in the hospital who is dying of a brain tumor. He saw his friend in an oxygen tent with tubes in him just lying there immobilized. He asked his friend how he was doing, and his friend simply said, "I am here." To me that is a partial definition of home. He had surrendered to just being where he was. Sometimes it takes a near death experience to get us here. Something similar to my mother saying, "What does it matter?" You are right, mother, it matters not.

That certainly was true for me when I returned from Vietnam. Like many of us I just wanted to kiss the ground when I returned. I felt I had already faced death, and had a life again when I hit the ground at Travis Air Force Base.

The second story is from the group that followed at 6:30 p.m. We were talking about "home" and a man, just off the cuff, as he was leaving group that evening, happened to share this statement: "Home is just a place. Being there is what matters." Yes, same lesson repeated twice within one evening. Spirit is talking to me once again.

Do you listen? I mean really listen to what is available to you as a teaching? I find I am being informed constantly if I am quiet and listening.

The Great Mystery again: Home is defined by my presence, not by the place. By my kissing the ground, if you will. I need to walk the grounds of my one-third acre and be present to where I am in order to make it "home." The bottom line of course is to be present wherever you are. I knew that, and preached it, but I knew it only on paper.

My childhood fears have kept me wandering, fearful, defensive in some ways and protective in others. It was what made me rip my classmate's drawing to pieces. I became a little animal, nose to the ground, sensing and rejecting, defending, protecting, evaluating and searching for someone or something to provide for me what my parents could not.

It has only been through my walks on The Hill that I have been brought full circle, home to myself, free from fear, fantasy, and to being present. Maybe it brought me back to being an animal, and the assurance of finding my own way, and my own home. The more I sniffed the trail the more I found my own scent, and the more I felt secure, much like an animal claiming his territory.

But wait. There is yet another piece.

I ask my friend Walt at Friday Coffee, which is what I call the men's group that Mark and I started by meeting at 10:00 a.m. every Friday, how his last trip was. He says, "It was completely different this time." I ask him what he means. Walt says that every trip has been an adventure for him but this time he was aware that he was looking for something. What he profoundly realized on this trip (and I can witness the emotion in his eyes) is that he had traveled the world looking to "belong," and that he now knows, "I belong here." "Here?" I ask. "Yes, here in Los Gatos."

I am moved to emotion as I share that mine has been the same journey, and I had just concluded it, but I had used the word "home," yet he has helped me see that it is not home I have sought as much as it is "belonging." I, also, belong here. This is my home, but most importantly I belong, as the dictionary describes: in position, place, group, person. My story is the long journey of longing for belonging. Sigh, "Here."

What does that word "belonging" mean to you?

This has been my impetus in leading men's groups. To provide a safe place (home) where a man can do his work (express his feelings) find acceptance (a place without shame) receive confrontation (direction), and, most importantly, the welcoming hug of belonging (confirmation and validation).

The vital feelings I received from The Hill brought me here. Now, truly now, the cat sits on my lap, I write, I nap, I write: I am home. Peace, love, and "Welcome Home" to me. I write to be free from an old pattern. No longer CONTAINED and invisible. Gary Hal Plep, LOVE the Men, Love Yourself, Be Seen, Acknowledge the Wisdom of the Mountain.

"Walk 'till you find your way home."

The Argument (Gary)

I awoke this morning facing my little kid who is disappointed and always waiting for a better day, and realized how often it happens. I need to negotiate something different or I will forever be in that state of being. I cannot afford to live my life this way any longer. I find my fantasies are less active, but now more in the shadows, yet still very much there. So, what is it? What is my movie?

My movie is my hot wife (Sue, not someone else) greeting me in the early morning wearing a nice wrap. She is lovely with her makeup on and wearing a smile. The backyard is large, and includes quiet, a pool, and my Cedar (dog) and Spunky (the cat). The air is fresh and clean. My Porsche is in the garage, we have two or three million in the bank (investments), our children are happy and engaged in good things in the world, I work two days a week.

Wait, I am starting to feel something is missing.

It's the play. I want to travel to fun places and do fun things with my wife, and adventure travel with my buddies. I want to do road trips, backpack, and roam the planet.

So let's redefine this.

"Are you looking for something beyond fun? Is this longing again for belonging?"

"I know I belong in Nature, and I miss it. I want the cabin at Lake Tahoe, as well as the home in Carmel Valley, and my wife hot and sexy, travel where and when I want, have friends all over the world, serve the Air Rescue Teams, be a hero, serve my country, serve my patients, write books, invest well, be physically fit and attractive, well dressed and groomed. Once a year I would do an adventure trip with my buddies. Sue and I would be traveling for a month in August, my brother and I for ten days in March, Sue and I for two weeks in December/January, I would backpack or road travel for three days a month in July, August, September and October. I would cross-country ski and snowshoe in the months of January through April."

This is what my little kid wants, as well as my adult. (Oh wait, don't forget dancing to rock and roll once a month.)

The problem is my little kid keeps waiting and wanting, and feeling cheated. He is not sitting by the window waiting but resentfully tolerating in his head (room) for it all to come together. That is the truth. So now I am HOME but part of me (my little kid) continues to wait *for something to complete me, to make me whole.*

My wife is tired and frustrated with this "forever unhappy kid." She wants and deserves an adult partner. I need to negotiate a plan based on reality. I don't like that. I don't like the reality. My kid says, "Me and Mark have to make a million dollars on this book!" I will wait, then I will be happy. I can't be happy now. My little kid says he is deprived, cheated, and "Look what everyone else has."

Laugh: How many people do I know have the lifestyle I just described? Hello—no one. Is it possible? Yes, but no. This could happen in a movie (where my kid grew up), but not here. So here is the negotiation:

"I can't give you a replacement for the large happy family that you created in your mind. I can't be in Carmel Valley and here, too. I don't have the wealth you saw and idealized in Playboy. You made life up based on movies, catalogs, comics, and magazines. That is all you had. You picked the best pictures. Only the best. You picked perfection. Those pictures are possibilities, but you cannot have it all."

"So what can I have?"

I have started to feel cheated here. Those were fantasy caricatures of reality that were not reality.

"Get over it. Create a new reality. Let it go. Quit drugging yourself!"

I feel part of me being anxious and resentful.

"Are you telling me I can't ever have all that?"

"That is right. It helped you survive as an emotionally hungry child, a starving (that is a better word) child, but the best was having a lover—my wife, and playing together: Together, fun, friends, the outdoors, sex, and a little money. That was exciting, fun, and happy. That was a reality that was achievable, and low budget."

As soon as I clouded it with the movie background of desire I blew it up. In the movie version I had to have more and more and more and more rather than delivering my passion and playing.

"Does that mean moving back to a small apartment?"

"No, but it means being in relationship. Being present."

"What about having excitement?"

"That can be good or it can mean being addicted to a drug."

So let's put something together here that works so the little kid is off my back and in my lap. No fits of the sullen child please.

"So here is the deal. I will give you fun and excitement in exchange for you giving up your illusions through pictures and movies that were your source of security, safety, and comfort. This won't be a movie or pictures outside of you. It will be real and NOW, and you will feel it emotionally and physically."

I will do it by slowing down, planning, scheduling.

"I will give you a world without illusion where we play every day, explore, feel our freedom, spirit, and creativity. Breathe it in. I will no longer have shoulder, gall bladder, liver, and muscle problems because I will breathe. No longer pursue more perfection of fantasy but the freedom and exploration of a free spirit playing in everything he does. It will require responsibilities, jobs, and work."

I am a little anxious but I know this can be done. Be here; play now. I no longer choose the past; rather I play here and now. The dreams that held me together no longer serve me. I am here. I am home. I am me. Illusions be gone *and* I belong.

"What can I do today that makes this real, to ask this of every day? I have an unyielding need to prove the fantasy is not worth its effort."

"It is an exchange of energy. You are already here. You have manifested most of your desires. Now, to give back, to generate for others, not by giving up the dreams, but by putting the energy out, and trusting that I will get all I desire."

The rules have simply changed.

The Wisdom Hidden in Abandonment (Gary)

My wife and I provided a two-hour therapy session to a couple. Both husband and wife had been abandoned as children. Now they were facing their pain in relationship, and were not able to give each other what they needed. It helped me to see another part of myself. I saw another's sheer terror.

The man was desperately trying to convey to his wife and us how she was not there for him, and how she had broken their agreement by seeking other men. I yelled at him that it was the sex, meaning that he was so focused on the sex in his relationship for his sense of meaning. What I saw was a little kid who was angry that this person, who had so fulfilled his need to be validated, could no longer keep it up. It was never enough. I saw the abandoned child whose mother had left, and he was angry and scared.

Then I saw her reaction to his unwillingness to validate her abandoned child. We couldn't get him to see it. She had been abandoned by her father as a child, and was clearly seeking validation from this older man, and other older men. He had stopped adoring her, and sex had become less important to him after they had married. Instead he became obsessed with work. And when she became pregnant he distanced himself even further. She had become desperate to regain his attention, and acted out by drinking, and getting the attention of other older men.

He simply saw her breaking the agreement he had formulated. What she re-experienced was abandonment. He couldn't see it. She was just wrong for her reactions, and they were two different people. Ironically they were twins in their bond of pain. Divorce became the next subject.

Children who are abandoned by either or both parents become fearful as they have nothing to attach to, no ground, no stability. These children then search for an attachment that will satisfy the need. Often they will make themselves desirable by manifesting traits that they perceive will be attractive to others and deserving of love. They will sacrifice their own internal needs, and often go to extremes in work, sacrifice, and presentation in order to be worthy of the bond they were missing. They will find a similar partner to bond to and complement with the task of achieving the perfection of the imaginary, lovable child. When in relationship they appear to have found the love they so desperately needed. However, when one or the other becomes human, and displays qualities that are not perfect, the relationship starts to unravel. They feel then that this person cannot be the one. Then there is resentment and a realization of an ancient fear, because their partner could not hold up their end of an unspoken agreement, and the anger comes from realizing they are back where they started. The unspoken agreement was that their partner would love and validate them perfectly, and give them the kind of love and validation that only a parent can give to a child. This will not happen. They divorce, and start their search again, but they are more angry and cynical this time.

The longing for belonging was the theme that came home to me from this session. I saw that The Hill gave Mark and me an opportunity to heal the wound of abandonment. The healing that's revealing, the mirror that helps me to see myself, a brother who walks the path with me; I could not have done this alone.

I bring this story up because I see it as an element of our walks. It helps me to see who we are uncovering. I see the abandoned child in each of us who is seeking achievement as a way of ensuring value. Doing nothing is a way of giving up, because the idea of being of value is too daunting. Sooo common.

If you shine enough you will be validated, valued, and never abandoned. Each of us has excelled in many areas seeking some form of security of self that will never ultimately be achieved. I had an attachment disorder of my own. I would attach to anything that I thought could help me feel better. Only by surrendering to our limitations, and accepting ourselves can we be at peace. It is belonging in its deepest meaning.

So what am I saying? I am saying that the child who is abandoned by either or both parents needs at some point to turn to the wisdom of the adult within. It is a disservice to ourselves and our humanity when we avoid facing thousands of years of generational wounding out of fear (epigenetics) and not realize that we could call a time out and stop its effect. NO ONE is coming to save you from your fears. No ego gratifications, addiction, or psychic incantations will do. Only a commitment to a conscious love of yourself can save you.

Fathering yourself is an option. How would a good father "father" you? I find this to be a very helpful tool when stuck. The wisdom is available in most of us.

Instead of judging myself (actually swearing at myself) like I was used to, one day I stopped myself and asked how it was working. I laughed, of course, realizing it was just another way of shaming myself, and it certainly wasn't motivating. I took a couple minutes to simply ask myself, "What would a good father say to me right now?" It brought me to sanity, relief, and gave me a mature direction. I continue to use it as needed. Shame and judgment no longer serve me.

Lessons from Clients (Gary)

Maybe this book should be retitled "Coming Home." My recent reflections and past writing help me to see how much I have been controlled by my little kid who grew up with scattered rewards, and now, today, in my practice I find people very scattered primarily due to the economy, but it makes me a little angry and frustrated, mirroring my own internal anger and frustration. I am realizing there is nothing out there.

I especially witnessed it with two clients. One was raging about giving so much of himself (and his money) and not getting anything back. We talked about his hurt little kid. I could so join with him and laugh. It's about the adult taking charge, and not deferring to his history of being the hurt child.

The other was a seventy-three-year-old man in one of my groups. I have known him for over ten years. He has been presenting more and more of his wisdom as he ages, most especially in the last two years. It started happening as he began to lose his wife to Alzheimer's disease, and he had to manage everything. He is now decompensating rapidly, and is in danger of losing his physical and mental functioning. He has helped me feel the heart-wrenching agony of an adult wise man going away, gradually disappearing.

Therapy at $250 an hour is speeding my recovery along with the mirrors that are reflecting back all of the above.

How much do you resist seeing yourself? What tools or rituals do you have to avoid seeing and feeling?

Lessons from Patients (Mark)

For decades my hurt child believed that his wounds were so great that anyone else's wounds could never match them. Although my sense of wounding had grown an adult gloss, underneath my claimed understanding of pain in human relationship was a hurt child in his room recovering from a beating. When I dug down into my reasons for becoming a doctor so late in life I not only identified a profound need to make a difference in a human life and a deep interest in mental illness and human resilience, but also a desire to truly know who I was and what had meaning for me.

The answer was not in graduate school, which is a really idyllic experience, even with all of the crushing work: it was living in a constant state of reflection. The school of psychology I chose to study, the transpersonal, was devoted to understanding spirit and spiritual development as much as it was to revealing the subtleties within the human psyche and human development. The one dimensional nature of my inner child's emotional life, a view through a lens of childhood trauma, gave way to a broader view that included accomplishment and joy, two notions that a child who is disliked by his parents will rarely remember.

For children like me who get minimal encouragement there is often minimal accomplishment, and where there is a poor source of unconditional love there is very little joy, and the result is an adolescence filled with failure and sadness. I often have the sense that many people have had this experience and have not fully acknowledged it until they are in crisis. The child who is encouraged and loved and reaps the successes that life offers may not understand the experience I have described. If their own children are struck with mental illness they may not have any experience upon which to draw a means for understanding what has happened.

I did not realize while I was in the academic years of my doctoral education that the perspective provided by my history was a gift. During my internships my mentors commented that I had a facility for diagnosis, and I assumed this was said to any intern who worked hard for his patients. It was not until I was working in community mental health and my supervisor loaded me with cases of personality disorder that I realized how much work was required to grasp the criteria and impact of mental illness. When I began working in an acute care mental health facility my director assigned me the opportunity to establish the first therapy group in that hospital for treating PTSD. Perhaps she saw that I'd earned my moments with the Demon PTSD from my own experience with years of childhood trauma.

Before my training in clinical psychology I had never fully understood the PTSD Demon and its power. I grudgingly respected the way the Demon could steal a life, cut wounds as deep as those from a car accident, or a fall from a building, or an encounter with a butcher knife. PTSD wounds are invisible, and can only be revealed by observing behavior, and by listening—most of all by listening. My patients were people having an altered experience of life that was as valid as any other experience, deserving of my respect.

Very often I observed patients' desire to be free of the controls that their illnesses imposed upon them, and the endurance of that desire would determine if they wanted to take that control back. Those who had this desire to be free wanted to own the simplicity of an every day life that was not haunted by traumatic memories.

I knew how hard I had struggled to find my way, going through decades of therapy until Lynn, my last therapist, identified in me the symptoms of PTSD, and helped me heal wounds that had bled for forty years. What saved me throughout those years was resilience.

Without resilience the grinding nature of PTSD sets the stage for self-destructive behavior. In Gary I found someone who had a built-up a reservoir of resilience fed by doing good in the world. Working at the hospital gave me a view of PTSD that is not easily obtained by seeing patients one at a time. At the hospital I saw dozens of patients, and among them were people struggling with the aftermath of torturous, terrifying, shocking, and tragic life experiences, and who developed the symptoms that form a diagnosis of PTSD. In many of them, I saw an ongoing torment. I saw it in veterans and in men and women from every imaginable walk of life, from millionaires to the homeless. On the one hand there was the desire to recover the person they had been, or achieve the person they wanted to be, and on the other hand, alcoholism, chemical dependency, lost hope, and the desire to commit suicide. These patients were in mourning for the life that their trauma had taken from them. They lived in constant pain that they often self-medicated in any way they could. They were willing to endure nearly anything to get their life back, or anesthetize the life they did not want.

It is difficult to understand the level of resilience I am describing without examples. I can recall a few who demonstrated this snatching of control from the claws of the Demon PTSD, and achieved living within an everyday life, or at least began a journey toward mental wellness.

The resilience of human beings is consistently surprising. I have asked myself, "How much can any human being take?" I have found myself consistently rewarded with a deeper understanding of human endurance and the natural tendency of the person to move toward wellness and a full life when there is exposure to encouragement and inspiration toward confidence. I saw our work in the hospital as helping the patients become receptive to encouragement and confidence, and once these forces were in place they could begin to move forward in life.

A powerful experience comes to mind.

In group therapy Ms. B., whose adult daughter committed suicide, met Ms. F., a young woman about her daughter's age who had attempted suicide multiple times. Ms. F.'s parents were both murdered within a year of each other so she was orphaned as a child, and taken in by her extended family. Both women were severely traumatized by their losses and were unable to let go of their anger and depression, and this became their bond in the group. They could not escape the entrapments of memory, temper, nightmares, avoidance of people and places related to the deaths, flashbacks of events related to the deaths, so they could not move through and complete all the stages of grief: denial, anger, bargaining, depression, and acceptance. The anger and depression were left undone.

I offer the following encounter with their experience.

I ask both women if they had ever tried to forgive the people they lost. Both are very resistant to the idea. I explain that their route into the final stage of grief—acceptance—is dependent upon their ability to forgive. They need to forgive themselves, forgive the people in their lives who died, and forgive the situation of their deaths that was out of their control. Psychotherapists call this dispositional forgiveness, literally, actively developing a forgiving disposition.

I explain that there is something else about forgiveness, often ignored or misunderstood, and critical to understanding its effect, that Fred Luskin (2002) talks about it in his book, *Forgive for Good*. Forgiveness does not say that the thing that happened was okay, that we should condone it, or that we need to forget it: not at all. Forgiveness contains the deep, spiritual practice of being at peace in this moment in time, and from that place, accepting the transgression against us, against the ones we love, or the situations out of our control that have harmed us and our loved ones, and from that acceptance move forward with life. I recommend forgiveness to patients as acceptance without resentment.

I ask both women if they are silently holding grudges against the people in their lives who died. Do they resent their deaths? As much as it is a loss—for Ms. B. her daughter, for Ms. F. her parents—are they angry with them for dying? Could they see how their anger is reinforcing their pain? I explain that holding a grudge is like drinking poison, every day, day after day, and expecting the target of the grudge to feel that pain when they are already dead. It makes complete sense that both of them feel sick over their losses. They need to learn how to forgive themselves for holding the grudge, forgive the people who died, and forgive the circumstances of their deaths that were completely out of their control. Without the work of forgiveness, the desire for suicide returns, a soul sickness that prays for death by any means to make the pain stop, to just make it stop.

Both women acquired Luskin's book. Both acknowledged the need to forgive, as well as the challenge they had before them, which was to accept that they deserved to be forgiven.

Working with dozens of suicidal patients at the hospital taught me that suicide is not the desire to die so much as it is the desire to kill the internal process that draws a person into a vertiginous and obsessive pattern of painful review and recrimination, and a tension of opposites between regret and redemption. To a person focused on suicide, regret is a theme of every day life, and redemption, although deeply desired, is perceived as an unachievable dream.

What can we do for these patients? When there isn't a lot of time, as in a brief hospitalization, we encourage patients to change their thoughts, and thereby change their emotions and actions. It is a very effective bandage, and, like many bandages, just about anyone with psychotherapeutic training can apply them, and over time they can fall away.

To me, the most effective tool for the suicidal patient is to fully understand the internal process that leads to suicidal thoughts. Helping the patient discover their process toward suicide helps to separate them from the act itself, and the desire to die becomes a symptom, rather than an action. It amounts to following the red thread that leads down into the labyrinth of painful experience, and then to follow it back out, the way Orpheus used the unraveling of the thread of his red cloak to mark his way down through the maze that led to the lair of a monster called the Minotaur to save his love, Eurydice, and then, following the red thread, guided her up into the light of day. Eurydice in this use of the myth is the love for one's self.

I have come to believe that, for the suicidal patient, the opposite of death is love, and the belief that one is unloved is by far the most painful torment known to mankind.

Freud's theory of a constant tension between Eros and Thanatos, between love (or the conscious lack of it) and death, is one of his most enduring discoveries, and, for many cognitive behavioral therapists, working with suicide this way is seen as a waste of time. Until the tension between

Eros and Thanatos is addressed, the urge toward suicide endures. I saw this in patients who made multiple suicide attempts, who repeatedly returned to the hospital and were repeatedly treated with cognitive therapy and medications. They needed a meaningful answer to the question, "Why do I want to kill myself?" and the cognitive therapist repeatedly told them that "why" questions led to circular thinking and that changing their thoughts was the best direction. I observed that cognitive behavioral therapy (CBT) was easier for the therapist to practice, could be easily apportioned into four-week, eight-week, or twelve-week treatment schedules, could be statistically monitored, was less expensive, and all of these characteristics made CBT more rational to health insurance companies. Those two groups of powerful influencers mutually saw a statistically powerful positive evaluation of short-term patient benefit that made CBT a good mental health care business decision.

In the hospital environment I observed that for some patients, in the long term, the impulse to suicide endured until they had succeeded in killing themselves, or until they sought or were referred to more effective forms of therapy that reached beyond the limited time the hospital inpatient and outpatient programs could rationally provide, and offered greater depth and a greater understanding of the human experience. When CBT was combined with the eclectic therapies that were inclusive of addressing the fear of personal freedom, the presence of archetypal energy, the role of the unconscious, the meaning of dreams, and the importance of loving someone and being loved, the totality seemed to be more effective for some of these patients in the long term. Most of all, the appreciation of forgiveness, for self, for other, and for situations out of one's control provided a long-term healing instead of a short term rationale, repeatedly applied, whose inconvenient failure was repeatedly ignored.

The significance of forgiveness for myself, and that it was to become the linchpin of my future, was not revealed until I was ready to see it. An internal voice speaking from spirit, that had its origin on The Hill, began to focus on a theme that came from my patients in the hospital. I resisted its entry into my conscious mind until I accepted where my own healing needed to progress.

Awakening: The Challenge of Forgiveness (Mark)

Experience with patients who refused to forgive taught me how high the price could be for nursing a grudge in one's life. The effect of developing a forgiving disposition in these patients was stunning in the quality and depth of their recovery that was mediated by allowing forgiveness into their hearts and minds. It shone a light on something I had nursed throughout my adolescence and adult life, something I had avoided.

I was filled with anger at the very mention of my father's name or role in my life, and fed on this dead issue in the manner of carrion protected and devoured by a hyena until its belly is full, and it sleeps by the rotting carcass until it awakens and gorges itself again, day after day, night after night. The one action that could put an end to my grudge and relieve my anger, depression, and isolation was to forgive my father, and I had not fully realized and accepted it until I treated patients who suffered greatly from a lack of forgiveness. I had not even attempted to think about the idea of forgiveness where my father was concerned, yet here it was in my day-to-day work with patients. The measurement of dispositional forgiveness, an idea gently provided by Dr. Fred Luskin, one of my teachers in grad school, was in the very foundation of my research that led to my clinical degree. My dissertation research into what I called "essential PTSD" in the grandchildren of Holocaust Survivors—which I saw as a new type of PTSD that was the response to transgenerational trauma—resulted in one glowing outcome: the participants who had developed dispositional forgiveness did not develop essential PTSD. Everything in my life—my work, my research, my relationships—was directing me toward forgiveness.

I took this to The Hill for a lone walk to the peak of the mountain. I planned to climb beyond the Tree of Truth, and the Tree of Healing, above the tree line, to what I called "The Desert" on the mountain's top. I would carry my mala beads, with the plan of chanting the Ganesha Gayatri mantra one hundred eight times, using the beads to keep count of this prayer to overcome obstacles in life. Halfway up the Hill of Cruelty I was fully feeling fifty years of grief and anger. Everything that Fred Luskin taught me about forgiveness boiled behind my eyes.

Luskin defines forgiveness as the assertive creation of peace within oneself in the present moment in relation to a transgression. He says that resentment about a transgression creates the lack of peace within ourselves, and we are the only ones who can remedy that lack of peace. He explains that an event in life may happen and then we object to life because it did not happen in the way we believed it was supposed to happen, and that objecting to life causes emotional, physical, and spiritual turmoil. He also defines forgiveness as the resolution of our objection to the way our life has happened, or basically, making peace with not getting what we want. He sees resentment toward ourselves, or a person or persons, or a situation over which we do not have control, as a normal response to an event that has caused us great pain. He warns that constantly sharing our resentment with others, and reinforcing our beliefs that someone else is responsible for how we feel, keeps resentment alive and creates a state of being that leads to emotional, physical, and spiritual illness. In Fred's words, "It's like drinking poison and expecting somebody else to die."

How many times had I quoted Fred's line to patients in therapy? How many times had I evinced my resentment toward my father within my mouth as I ate (and bit my tongue), or among friends echoing their anger, or among my family to join their chorus of resentment?

The Ganesha Gayatri is a Hindu prayer for guidance in overcoming obstacles in life. The advantage of this prayer is that it can be applied to anything or all things. I held the goal of forgiving my father in my thoughts as I repeated the chant on The Hill. In the process I saw many childhood traumatic images passing through my mind's eye, and each time I gave forgiveness to the memory and saw it fade, only to have another spring up in its place, and then another, and another. As I reached the brass plate at the very top of The Hill, which announces the name of the mountain (a message that is best obtained by making the climb), I realized that I did not have any more images to remember. I needed to forgive myself for my anger, depression, and isolation, forgive my father for his abusive treatment, and forgive the situation of my being the hyperactive child of an impatient, narcissistic parent that was completely out of my control.

If we are fortunate, as I was in that moment, we can reach back into a positive experience that takes us beyond the negative state of mind that both feeds and starves us at the same time—that feeds us anger and isolation and starves us of love and connection. For me it was a deep learning that came out of the Sterling Men's Weekend. It helped me create an exercise for patients who had been abused by one or both of their parents.

Standing at the top of a mountain I had climbed hundreds of times carrying the weight of this grudge I gently said, "Thank you, father, for beating me, because it taught me compassion and love for others."

"Thank you, father, for casting me aside, because it taught me to be a source of encouragement toward confidence for others."

"Thank you, father, for telling me I was a failure and would amount to nothing, because it drove me to understand the meaning of excellence in human endeavor."

"Thank you, father, for withholding your love, because it taught me to open my heart to others."

I thanked the mountain, and everything that lives and breathes on its breast, and saw, heard, and smelled all of it at once: the ants in the sand, the bees in the flowers, the birds and squirrels nesting in the trees, the wild sage baking in the sun, the bright orange and blue hearts of flowers no larger than a collar button, the giant live oaks, and the one that lives high up on the shoulder of The Hill, The Tree of Healing. I walked down the mountain a little way to that tree, stood under its shade, and saw all the life that has established itself among its leaves and branches and the interstices of its bark, and I was a part of it all, and a breeze allowed the tree to give me a sigh of agreement in reply.

At first I could not characterize the ache I felt in my body in that moment. It was a deep and sudden wave of emotion that ran through my gut and brought in new strength. I sensed that I was given a sign. An inner voice said without words that I could rest. The arduous journey that I thought would never end was done. Within that moment a feeling of completion and of being completed filled me up. I realized I had never felt forgiveness in my heart before, and suddenly I knew where it had taken me. I had walked until I found my way home. Not to a place. I had come home to myself.

The Home That Is and The Home That Was (Gary)

Why am I resisting my good wife? Why am I afraid of partnering with her? She is like the good mom I have never had, and she keeps patiently waiting for me to show up. Well, time is running out.

I did enough therapy around this to finally get that I had to kill my mother. No, she was already dead. I'm not suggesting that anyone actually kill his or her parents. It's about killing the power they have inside of you. That took a lot of work, but I realized that I could not love myself until I had ended the wrath I had for my mistreatment. It became my critic and my shadow. The secondary effect is that no matter how much my wife displayed her love for me, I couldn't fully accept it. No matter what I accomplished in the world, it was not enough. It took remembrance and making note of every little way I felt abused and abandoned by my mother. I had to constantly uncover, reinvigorate, and spit it out over and over until I was able to put it aside. Otherwise I could never be myself or be available for anyone else.

All of this has to do with the pain of the world I created to deal with being alone. I have a home in my mind that no longer exists. It's that little house outside of Coos Bay, Oregon, in the suburb of Englewood. My little kid holds on to it like it is still there when in fact it is not. My dog's not there, my swing is no longer there, and the front yard has been taken over by a large house. Get it, Gary. The only "home" I can now make for myself is here. That creates an internal fight for me to accept.

Finally, I Land at Moffett Field (Gary)

So to speak.

The California Guard has become an important part of my life, and has a new set of responsibilities attached to it.

My Colonel has set me up to be Liaison Officer to the Air National Guard (ANG) at Moffett Field, and I am encouraged by the Vice Commander to drill there. I ask for a transfer, which is up to my Colonel, and I assume he says yes, as I find myself not only trying to make things happen there, but I am introduced everywhere on base by the Wing Commander. Quickly, I find myself as Acting Commander responsible for building a new unit. I am shortly joined by an ex-cop, Chief of Police, and retired ANG noncommissioned officer (NCO). Joint Reception Staging and Onward Movement Integration (JRSOI) is our primary mission, which is to establish an operating area for first responders. This was made clear by the Wing Commander on our tour of the base. They need help on many different fronts to support this little city.

Since I have a great working relationship and friendship with Captain Albright, the A Company Commander, I, of course, want my old company, and a company commander to be in on the action, as well as be a supply of necessary soldiers to accomplish the mission. We set up our first training of twenty-one soldiers. The classroom is the "high bay" where they brought in bodies in body bags from Vietnam. A lot of the classroom is around Air Force Instructions, we used to call them Regulations, but okay. In the field portion of the training the soldiers learn when to use lethal force. I realized in watching that I had no desire to point a gun at anyone. Danger and excitement no longer filled a need the way they used to and there is the reality of pain and dying. Getting shot at meant nothing when I was young. Movies and video games can do that to you.

Just before lunch one of the younger trainers told us about his cross-fit training, and invited the soldiers to come out and participate. He said he was intensely involved in cross-fit, and not weight lifting, because it was the best form of training to allow him to carry a buddy out if he needed to. Somehow that was the contrast to the "body bag" image I had in my mind, and the higher order of why I was there. It was somehow healing to hear. I guess because it was about living and loving your brothers. We have a mission to protect our citizens but also a passion to protect our brothers and sisters in combat. I am all over that. Not enough was or is done to take care of those who are willing to give their life for their country. We are a rescue unit after all.

I am clearly here to Rescue others and My Self. I have landed. I am home.

I am here to cut the cords of others, and honor my wholeness and light and connection to the universe. I am no longer alone. My old way of being was to connect to others' needs, and thus not feel alone. I found a way not to feel alone by identifying with others' needs. I then didn't feel alone but at the same time it cost me a portion of myself, my light, my personal power. From here on I am of a spirit of light connected to the universe and all its power. I don't give up myself to have it. It was a way not to feel alone. But the cost was high.

I no longer need others' needs to not feel alone. I am whole unto myself. I can help myself and others far better as a whole spiritual person than one who needs the injuries of others to not feel alone and in control of my fear.

How much and in what ways do you cover up your needs?

October 2, 2014 (Gary)

The journey continued. Just when you think you have closure, you don't.

Sue convinced me to sign up for VA medical care. I have resisted for a short time, only forty-seven years or so. I didn't want to use something that I didn't feel worthy of. Walking in the door made me nervous, but all was good. Nice facility and nice people. I signed up for a physical and told the doctor about my fatigue. Then I was off on a series of scans and MRIs, treadmill, and such. All good, except I was low in vitamin D, had a large kidney stone (dormant for over ten years) and some deterioration of the lower spine and lungs simply due to age. So basically it was all good. However, I didn't feel any better, and I noticed every time I went to the VA for anything I teared up.

I was on to another chapter. My wife connected me with an Eye Movement Desensitization and Reprocessing (EMDR) practitioner, and I did a 14-hour Intensive. The EMDR cleared most of my trauma from Vietnam. After another individual session the tearing stopped. I walked around the hospital to my spots where I would sit and cry, and I was good. It was now just a hospital. I could breathe.

However, I always seem to find another door to the dark. One of my recent clients turns out to be the daughter of a Marine and a Vietnamese woman from Nha Trang where I was stationed. In other words, she was one of the children left behind during the war, half white and half Vietnamese. She had divorced her American husband and now they were back together working with me in therapy. I disclosed that I had been stationed in Nha Trang. They told me Nha Trang had changed. Later on they emailed me a picture they had taken of the old air base.

The picture triggered emotions for me. They explained that they couldn't get on the base, but the picture taken through the fence around the hanger gripped me. I called the EMDR practitioner for more treatment. I was able to shrink that picture and close the screen so to speak. Then it triggered the images of my office on the base, and the people I worked with. More EMDR.

It was astonishing to me what happened next. I felt this dark energy. I remember feeling somewhat harassed by my sergeant and the first sergeant. They wanted to take me downtown and get me laid. They offered to pay. I was engaged, and always had my girl's picture on my desk. I was studying my catechism, and was baptized at the Cathedral in Nha Trang. I was a good, Catholic boy.

In the process of doing the EMDR I realized that they may have been addicted to alcohol and sex, but I was just as addicted to my fantasy way of being with the woman who was my fiancé. I was probably a pain in the ass with my obsessing about the mail and about her. They were just trying to break the spell, and connect with me. It really wasn't so much about getting laid or drunk. That was a WOW moment. The darkness with which I held them and that office went away. I wanted to thank them for caring or at least attempting to wake me up.

In my work with the couple mentioned above, and hearing about the woman's trauma as an outcast in Vietnam for being half white, I realized that I wanted to do further research on the men I served with. I went back to the journal I kept in Vietnam, and made a list of the names of men I had mentioned. I had looked for the first sergeant and my sergeant in the past without any luck. I had noticed the armorer's name before, and realized he had to be the one who issued me my M16, my pot (helmet), and one hundred rounds the night of the grey alert when we prepared for an attack.

"We" sounds strange as it actually felt like Sam F. and I where the only ones on base, and Sam was in a separate room. Yes, somewhere out there were some guards on the fence a distance apart. But talk about feeling alone and disconnected. More like abandoned. This was my post, and in the military to leave your post is an offense meriting court martial. What was I supposed to do? Turn my desk over and fire from there through a shuttered window? Open the shuttered window and then turn over my desk? Wait in the scant light for directions? WTF big time. All the time, in the NOW, I still live there part-time.

Sam F. seemed more scared than I. All our senior staff and most of the base personnel lived downtown. We were on our own. The last intelligence report I heard said there were 5,000 NVA (North Vietnamese Regular Army) in the mountains preparing to attack us, but we didn't know when.

I smirked and half laughed. It had to be a joke. If we were attacked we had no defensive perimeter. Command had ordered that the sand bag bunkers be dismantled. They were replaced during a base beautification project with little white fences and freshly planted palm tree saplings. My windows were shuttered to keep the heat out but the walls were thin boards with Styrofoam gun boxes inserted between the studs for insulation. We had no firing positions. We were dead if we were attacked. I had put a lot of faith and allegiance into duty, honor and country, my training, the Air Force and my superiors, and it was immediately shattered.

My journal provided no contact information for Sam F. I had to search the Internet. I found his name along with Airman D.'s, and a couple others on a web site, and my first reaction was that they had been killed. I was really upset, to say the least. Then I realized they were listed as the honor guard for someone else who had been killed in Nha Trang.

That brought up the memory before our situation, or after. I can't remember. One of our guys from Security Police was left in the bush while protecting the repair of a downed chopper. Our lieutenant forgot him. Our guys were not trained to fight and survive in the jungle. Shit! Fortunately, he ran into some of our Special Forces and was brought in. Talk about abandoned. No doubt he will have that one to remember. He complained to his Congressman. He and his family were just a tad pissed, and rightly so. I have to call both incidences incompetence and arrogance on the part of command. It somehow feels good to say that. There you go. That is the truth.

I found Sam F. in two different places, but it was obvious the addresses were old. I only had a phone number, so I called. A machine answered. I left a message, and the next day I received a message that just said, "Call me back." I did, and it was Sam F. He said he didn't remember much, but he would try to recall some names. We exchanged email addresses.

He sent me an email, and said he had lived with my sergeant and his girlfriend. I wrote back asking if he had any contact information for Bobby R. S. It turns out they both left a girlfriend and a child behind. Sam said his girlfriend's family was from the north and at the end of the war they probably went back north to join the rest of her family where they would have been killed. So terribly sad. He didn't answer me regarding Sgt. S.

As I come to rest on the subject now I feel like I am bringing home that twenty-two-year-old I had been in Vietnam. It has taken years of work to bring him home. Maybe because there was nothing anyone else could do that would have done it anyway. I realize now that a brass band, or a hero's welcome, or a girlfriend's embrace would probably not have done it. No matter how many "welcome homes" I might receive, I was the only one who could bring that twenty-two-year-old home. I now have a sense of him, that part of me, being here.

I shared this feeling with my psychologist friend, Barry. He said when in his forties, he had burned out in his private practice, became sick, and took some time off in Mexico. On an evening when he was returning to his villa in Yelapa he found himself being followed. Someone was walking on the trail behind him. He felt scared. He said it radically changed his life. He subsequently took five years off from his practice. It was obviously a healing moment for him as well.

I now no longer feel so desperately alone. I went to a former client's wedding reception during this time, and Roberta, a Native American shaman friend of mine I've known for years, was there. We chatted and we took the only two places left at the table. I was then sitting across from another Vietnam vet, and we had a brief conversation about our experiences. He denied any PTSD, but he said maybe it was because he was deployed from Germany where he was having a great time, and returned to Germany. I still thought it was interesting to land there.

I left that party and went to Los Altos for my High School Reunion. I found my old friend Dean and his wife. Dean and I had worked together for PG&E, so it was always great to see him. I mingled and chatted. Somehow Vietnam came up, and I realized several of my classmates had been there. Dave C. was suffering from severe PTSD; he has a one hundred percent disability due to the effects of Agent Orange.

I brought up the name of Robert Burns, and a woman said he was in terrible shape after Nam and would smoke and let the cigarette burn down through his fingers. He had died two years after his return from Nam. That would make him twenty-three years old. That was hard to hear. It left me with a new sense of pain. Why couldn't anyone help him? I had seen him in San Francisco while I was on leave before I had gone to Vietnam. I saw him on Broadway as a buddy and I were going to a Dave Brubeck concert. I had to yell at him. "Hey Burns! It's me man from San Mateo High." He didn't recognize me, and it seemed to take a bit of effort before I could connect with him. He said he was in the Marines. He said he couldn't join us because he was waiting for a friend. That was the last time I ever saw him. I was plagued with the story of Burns. The red-headed kid from San Mateo High who was a good athlete. "Don't mean nothin'" they used to say in Nam. Pain.

Two days later as I am running my trail, trying to put my earphones on, I'm thinking about Robert B., and I almost run two women off the trail. Almost two years later, at almost the same spot on this two-mile trail, whom do I run into? It's Roberta and her sister. We exchange "I love you" and "*déjà vu*," and I go back to running. It's very strange to have this running all together. The trail I now run is relatively flat, and it provides a challenge in weather, but it is *not* The Hill, and I no longer need it.

Not long after I received a call from a Vietnamese woman who wanted to say "thank you" for helping her country. This I was not expecting. As I am on the phone with this stranger a helicopter just happens to whop-whop-whop above my car while I am on my phone. I chuckle about this perfect little test of my usual triggers, and find that it is no longer a trigger. The woman and I agree that the hardships in Vietnam have made both of us wiser and stronger. I appreciate her "thank you" and am taken by the call.

Maybe in a way it's all coming together. My position attached to the Air National Guard as a volunteer may be running its course. The colonel who was supposed to take command changed his mind. He would have been a key player to move our unit forward. Now we are like a three-legged horse, and the new wing commander may not find a need for us. Now my colleague for the last two years, and senior to me, is leaving. I am again left to command alone. A two-legged horse, no, just a two-legged person, how perfect. I am very aware, and believe, that we create or are given exactly what we need to learn or what we need to get over.

Maybe our walk is complete. A necessary walk of healing that we were destined to do. But right now it's time for us to stop all of this writing. Time to climb The Hill again. Time to gear up and gather up my brother. What is next for us I don't know, and we are always grateful for a walk up The Hill to help us find out.

Walking The Hill

Epilogue

Whether we are alive or dead, life goes on. When we are not the focus of everything we are given the gift of seeing everything that surrounds us, the beauty and the ugly and everything in between.

The Gift (Mark)

The journey that Gary and I shared on The Hill continued in crafting our account of two men transformed by a spiritual practice that revealed itself without any conscious intention. That is the gift of The Hill. We climbed, sweated, fell and bled, got up and continued on, and allowed The Hill to teach us whatever it was that our hearts needed to know.

Perhaps the best part, sometimes the hardest, is to listen to the internal voice that develops from a spiritual experience, and follow the path it sets before us. The echo of The Hill clearly tells us that faith is real, the resonance of the universe is real, and, if we are fortunate, we will listen with profound acceptance.

And even at times surrender.

Every Wish Has a Price (Mark)

On The Hill Gary and I saw each other's abandoned kids, and how all the dreams of accumulated things had created a barrier. This barrier was a concrete symbol of a choice we had to make between what was real, possible, and fulfilling in actual life, and the absolute need to pursue a fantasy life built out of men's magazine imagery and catalogues of things that could not be achieved, and did not have a limit. Our inner kids, both Gary's and mine, demanded so much attention that it became almost impossible to be happy in the NOW. I did not know at the time that our journey on The Hill would be preparation for significant change, and the challenge of redefining my life to suit the current reality in which I live.

I mentioned a number of times how I would experience an ache in my left arm and hand when we pushed up the mountain. That was a symptom I chose to ignore at the time. Eventually I could no longer ignore that my heart was beating as if I were climbing the mountain when I was sitting in a chair reading a book.

I had cardiac ablation surgery in 2011 for paroxysmal atrial fibrillation. Dr. Robert Quint, my cardiologist, helped me trade the real possibility of having a stroke at any time, and a few years to live, to a complete remission of symptoms after my heart surgery. Dr. Matt Levy and his electrophysiology team at Good Samaritan Hospital in San Jose saved my life. Afterwards I became acutely aware of unnecessary stressors in my life.

I could no longer willingly subject myself to the accumulating stress of the required onslaught of individually-handwritten paperwork for between fifty and seventy-five patients in each of three to four groups a day in the acute mental health environment (picture 1960s technology in 2014 and writing about three hundred records a day by hand), the pressure of which is far greater than any physical stress a person can endure. Add the additional stress of knowing that the time required for doing paperwork steals energy and depth from patient care and makes the provision of just enough care to enable minimal patient improvement the rule of the day. I fought the good fight for as long as I could, and did my best for the patients. As the wave of paperwork for fulfilling Medicare requirements began to increase and took more of my focus away from patient care, my blood pressure soared to 190/100. Then I had a brief attack of atrial fibrillation and six hours in the ER to return me to my normal heart rhythm.

I sat on a gurney hooked up to an IV line and a cardiac harness and played Scrabble on my iPhone. The cardiologist on duty remarked that I seemed so relaxed. How could I explain that it was the complete acceptance I had acquired on The Hill? In that moment I decided I'd had enough of a system (not the work) that I responded to with this much stress, and retired.

Robyn faced a similar situation. My wife could no longer sustain the amorality and inhumanity of corporate life. She was done with working for companies that encourage a culture of excellence in personal and political vendetta, that enforces mediocrity in performance, grinds away at self-respect, prevents high quality results, and demands a consistent knuckling under for a paycheck. At the middle management level, a woman is expected to become apparently immune to human cruelty for eight to ten hours a day. The international company she worked for was about to be acquired by a US-based corporate behemoth in the northwest, and a big glitch was our relocation to another state. Robyn was given a package and grabbed the money and ran. Once she was gone, her entire team left the company. Powerfully connected incompetents were preferred over people who provided real, measureable success and made the error of holding the company's future in mind. It is no wonder that after the company was fully absorbed by the northwestern behemoth, the entire worldwide executive staff was fired within thirty days. Under the philosophy of the new owner, the now healthful company became successful having cut away the corporate rot that infested its failure and made it vulnerable to acquisition for a fraction of its value.

Both Robyn and I had had enough. Both of us could feel the tick-tock of the clock that measured the time we were not spending in the pursuit of the arts we loved. We did not require massive expenditures for anything. I could set up my writing table in a room with good light and do the thing I had longed to do for the last fifty years. Robyn could pursue her photography.

All I have left is my writing, the very thing I have always wanted, hungered for, during five decades of living an outer life of making a living, or struggling to find work, that was often seen by my inner life as a barrier to my love for the work of writing. I did not think I would have to give up everything that defined my life to have this moment with words on a page. Every wish has a price.

I can say this: It has been decades since I have given myself the opportunity to make the dream of committing art each day a reality. This is a much simpler life. I have a sense of calm in every moment I spend with the craft and art of writing. I have attempted to compare the enjoyment this gives me to working with the mentally ill and the rewards of that effort, and I can safely say that the comparison is a waste of time. The work I was privileged to do with patients, helping them bring themselves back into daily life, had a deep reward that is completely different and gave me a sense of social value that I had not previously experienced.

My writing is an intensely personal journey, and it suffers if I attempt to write for an audience. The craft and art of writing is something I do for myself, and it does the thing that I often feared it would do when I did not allow myself to fully pursue it: writing consumes all of my attention, all of my focus, all of my time in its commitment. When I am in the midst of it I do not need more than this. (Then again I wouldn't turn down a good pastrami sandwich.) When so many hours have gone by and morning has become late afternoon, or the evening becomes early morning, I become aware of being human.

Gary and I see each other on Tuesdays or Wednesdays for a couple hours. That's the way we've completed our account of this walk on The Hill. The visit is a good motivator for both of us to get work done on our book each week. But this is the last chapter. Where do we go from here? I want to maintain the connection, and I think Gary does, too. So, we'll do our best. That is something we have become good at in the face of challenges, big and small.

I carry the expansive horizon of The Hill in my heart now, remembering the crystalline days of summer and the miracle of a winter storm blowing in from the Pacific.

I wonder if the Tree of Healing on The Hill misses us?

My walk on the mountain is complete. I no longer need to be there, save in memory, and on the rare occasion that Gary and I can invest the far greater time it takes us to walk The Hill. What is left to me is a level of confidence, resolve, and discipline that I could not otherwise have gained. I found my spiritual center, my affection for the Quest, and the comfort of forgiveness, and could not have found them without Gary, my good friend, my teacher, and my brother on The Hill.

I wish I could say that I am quiet within my heart. I can say that "home" is no longer *where* I am—it is *who* I am. I've learned to live in my own skin to the extent that I can forgive most of my errors in life. I adventure not for the risks, but for the gifts. When I ask myself if it is time to stop, as I am in my sixty-eighth year, I can hear a soft, compassionate voice within saying, "You may be gray, and you may be wrinkled, but you are not weak, you are not old, and you are not done."

Whenever I hold The Hill in my heart the echo tells me that I can do the thing I lost in childhood, the simple lesson my father was too selfish to share, that adventuring has given back to me: have confidence, believe in myself seeing something greater than myself, and not take any circumstance in Great Nature for granted. I am thankful for the grace of having a good friend, a companion on this journey, in whom I can see the reflection of what we have done, where we have been, and what we have accomplished.

I want to share with you a piece by Mary Oliver, a great poet who is an impassioned walker, especially in the woods and along the shores of New England. The winner of the Pulitzer Prize and the National Book Award for poetry, she has said many times that walking in Nature is her greatest inspiration. That is not what is important about this poem. It is the moment this poem captures along a windy shore on an overcast day within a full heart.

Wild Geese

You do not have to be good.
You do not have to walk on your knees
for a hundred miles through the desert, repenting.
You only have to let the soft animal of your body
love what it loves.
Tell me about despair, yours, and I will tell you mine.
Meanwhile the world goes on.
Meanwhile the sun and the clear pebbles of the rain
are moving across the landscapes,
over the prairies and the deepest trees,
the mountains and the rivers.
Meanwhile the wild geese, high in the clean blue air,
are heading home again.
Whoever you are, no matter how lonely,

the world offers itself to your imagination,
calls to you like the wild geese, harsh and exciting—
over and over announcing your place
in the family of things.
Mary Oliver, 1986, p. 14.

We all need to believe in something, and, if we are fortunate, it will be about something larger than ourselves.

Although I may not know you, our readers, I am thankful for your interest in what we have written over these seven odd years. I hope you will pursue adventures of your own that will take you places you need to know, bring you and your companions home safe when the journey is done, and transform your heart with wonder.

The Journey (Gary)

I never had a home. It seems a little strange to look back on the seven years of writing this journey, walking The Hill. It has been an unwinding that has taken me through my whole life.

For a while I thought it was about loss, grief, and gratitude. Then I thought it was about abandonment. Then I thought it was about Vietnam. Now I realize it was all about finding a home for my neglected three-year-old who had to deny the depth of his aloneness, and fear. He was a scared little boy, and I didn't know that till now. He was so scared he shut down all his feelings so he could take care of people so maybe they would take care of him. The little old man had a little kid inside. Well, he is now out and looking for his toys. I have to father him in such a way that he values feelings more than pictures. That was all I had then, but now I can fully feel—*vitality*—our human capacity to grow or develop physical or intellectual vigor and energy.

My realizations had come together one early morning shortly after waking. The image is like that of a dark helium balloon bouncing around amongst other dark helium balloons way up in the sky. But the gas that had filled them is not helium but fear fed by absence of human contact. Fantasy balloons. Now the gas has seeped out and my balloon has fallen to earth and my feet now touch the ground. It's more than an Aha! moment. I feel I have let go of something big. In absence of fear I find myself.

It's funny to me how answers or perhaps tips come to me from the Universe. I am realizing so much of my life's void has been filled up with fantasy because of an absence of touch and feelings. As I begin to realize this and write about it, I notice that one of my wife's clients dropped off a book and left it on our desk at the office. I couldn't help but notice it even before I reached this place within myself in the last couple weeks. Then, when I understood the subtle message I grabbed it, and now can't put it down: *Feelings, Buried Alive Never Die* by Karol Truman (2003). I don't know if it will address my new reality, but it certainly seems like another helper from the other side giving me a hot tip. I again remember my mother's typical response to any negative feelings I had: "Oh Gary, don't feel that way." In other words, don't feel. Also, don't hug. I don't remember ever getting hugs or kisses from my mother. I do remember asking her to tuck me in. She would do that. That I liked. There was no affection or soothing in my family unless there was drinking. The only time I remember my relatives fawning over me was when they had been drinking. It felt, as a child would say, "icky."

Epilogue

I recently discovered the word *vitality* as though for the first time. I thought it captured what I was looking for. I wanted a vital life and relationships. Now the word was just a stopover to the core need for *feeling*. I feel a different harmony in my body, and today, Valentine's Day, I woke with a feeling of enthusiasm for this new world of feeling. I no longer need to go further than my own back yard, as I feel the joy of watching my dog chase his ball, and I watch his big blond ears go up and down. I used to feel my feelings for others. Now I can have what I need for myself.

I believe I have put it all together now for this journey. My wanderings on The Hill have taken me on a circuitous path of unwinding, not just my life but my ability to feel. Being with myself and my friend for four to six hours a week on the mountain has taken me through a whole range of feelings. It has only been through these feelings that I now understand my life-long hunger for connection, my fantasy life, my loneliness, my need for excitement, and my grief.

Vietnam highlighted my wound. The search for home was to find a home in me, a place where I could be at home with my feelings. It wasn't because of an ex-wife or a war. It was that I couldn't be at home while all that was stirring on the inside. Yet I had been taught that it was all about the world outside of myself. Six months of a daily grief meditation (thanks for that, Roberta) brought me closer to it, but it hadn't been enough. Eighteen years of therapy off and on had not been enough. Fantasy and material things have been a life-long substitution for feelings, touch, and love. I startle at this a bit now when I think about how much of our world believes that life is about how much excitement something can bring to you rather than just being where you are. The simplest sport gets amped to its highest potential of technology. The unspoken message is that you and yours are not enough.

I am tired of wandering and looking outside myself. I am happy, even a little blissful to realize that I have it all right here. Oh, I might get distracted from time to time, everyone does. But I know that when I stop a moment and go inside, I'm good. My long journey is done. My hands and nose are no longer pressed on the glass window. There will be other places that also have meaning for me, but I now have a sense of peace I have never had before. Big sigh here.

In the book I just mentioned, *Feelings Buried Alive Never Die*, Karol Truman says it well:

> Many people have a difficult time identifying their feelings and their thoughts. This was my problem, also. Too many of us have been taught—or perhaps not allowed—to be cognizant of what's going on inside our mind or our body. Perhaps, due to overwhelming pain or abuse, our early conditioning kept us from being consciously aware of our feelings and thoughts. Consequently, it's impossible for us to be sensitive or mindful of them today. Or, we could simply be so accustomed to turning our pain and hurt over to something (i.e., drugs/food) or someone else to *fix*, that our ability to be consciously aware of what is taking place inside ourselves has turned off. It's usually for these reasons we haven't been schooled in how to resolve our feelings for ourselves. Sadly, the majority of the human family's consciousness is either fragmented or missing entirely. You may be asking, "So what do I do about it?" Your first challenge will be to get in touch with your external and internal dialogue. That is, what you are saying out loud and what you are saying to yourself. What you say—out loud and silently—leads you to what you are thinking inside your head. This then leads you to what you are feeling inside. One way to help yourself become more aware is be sensitive to what is happening around you. Take yourself outside any situations and just be an observer . . . .

Great sex doesn't come from having the coolest car. Nor from connecting with images and symbols of things instead of what is real. Nor from creating fantasies, or ritualizing things rather than substance and sustenance. Great sex involves touching and making it real.

Emotional markers, that's what this is all about.

I think when we started these walks we were two disappointed, adult, abandoned children who tried desperately to be good enough to be validated by the world, a world that will never give our inner child the validation and love we have so desperately been seeking. Whether it is through physical fitness or the presentation of the well-intended therapist, we carry an edge. It is an edge of disappointment. The blame, if you will, belongs to our parents who could not give it to us, and not to the world or our relationships. However, blame could actually be placed back many generations, so what purpose does it serve? None. It would be a waste of energy to blame anyone.

What I am certain of now is that my need to come home to something, to belong after Vietnam, is only part of the deeper wound of abandonment. The walks have helped me unwind it all, and Mark and I are twins in grief who were not given the validation we needed from our childhood gods. The love we have been so desperately seeking is here in Nature, and here within us. It has been a circular walk that unwound our histories, our wounds, our struggles, and anxieties. It took us away from ourselves for the purpose of the telling. It gave us a mirror to see ourselves, and a witness for validation. In essence it has cleansed and re-birthed us. Mother Earth has nurtured and guided us into becoming adult men who are deep, full, and present. The journey has been a long one but worth every step.

Thank you Great Spirit that moves in all of us.

Endnote

The Gift (Gary)

We had completed the account of our journeys. We were satisfied with the work. And then something happened that broke me open once again.

I lost my dog. My Cedar.

Sue gave Cedar to me as a fiftieth birthday present. Sue picked him out of his litter and thus chose one of the loves of my life. My own puppy: It was like being handed a sacred gift of love.

Cedar was a lab-retriever mix. He was my little brother. I took him to play ball and walked him every day. He was ninety-six pounds of blond fur. My spirit animal, I guess. At fourteen years of age Cedar was struggling to walk and I knew I couldn't ask any more of him.

We had a family gathering and put him to sleep on the back deck on an Indian blanket. He was my bear, my friend, my loyal companion. Cedar was safe to open my heart to. I became very depressed. Sue pushed me to go to the VA for help.

I had a PTSD assessment in Oakland in 2015. I asked Sue to go with me. It was what seemed like a long drive to an isolated area I had never been to before. It ended at a funky old building on the baylands not far from Oakland. It was a long wait to see the psychologist that was doing the assessments. While waiting for the psychologist to do my assessment I chatted with other waiting vets and it was just like being back in the military.

I was anxious about the interview but felt a sense of relief and support when I found out Sue could join me. My anxiety increased as we waited over an hour and a half but was relieved when I was finally greeted by a woman psychologist who was a seasoned Navy veteran.

She questioned me for an hour and a half about my experience in Vietnam and when our time was almost up she asked how I felt about what I had shared. I told her I didn't know. I was frozen on the spot. I couldn't talk but my chest hurt. I thought I might be having a heart attack. She asked me again. I couldn't answer. I just knew my chest hurt. She finally asked Sue, "What do you think he is feeling?"

She volunteered, "Heartbroken." I lost it and broke down sobbing. She nailed it.

It wasn't fear it was heartbreak. I wasn't scared, I was horribly disappointed and humiliated that I was left alone, abandoned to die in a pathetic, isolated situation with nowhere to go. Needless to say it was a horribly painful experience, but a therapeutic breakthrough to a depth of feeling I had never felt before.

It brought me home to all I have written but hadn't felt before—MY HEART.

The Gift (Gary)

Acknowledgments

It all started with our first walk up a mountain to talk about Gary's private practice, the five groups he was running, and the possibility of documenting his methods in a book. Our walks over the course of seven years became an unexpected spiritual journey into what it means to be a man, and the book became an account of our thoughts and our conversations while walking up and down the same mountain nearly 800 times. During the years that followed, we did our best to clarify what the mountain taught us and motivated in us. We were influenced by key people who became companions on our journey as a result of the effect they had on us, individually and collectively, as we both crossed paths with some of them over the years. Some were aware of our work and supported us in the process. Many had no idea how much their influence contributed to our awakening and speaking to what it means to be a man in the world.

Gary is not a theoretician about men's work in the traditional sense. His perspective is built out of lived experience, so we made the natural choice to pursue that perspective rather than theory. The editorial challenge became the creation of an experiential guide that embodies Gary's theoretical vision for men's group work. We sought a "how to" rather than a "why to" explication of the experiences that can and will support spiritual and emotional transformation in men's lives. A major theme of this perspective is that our connections to others define us, so we acknowledge them here.

After many drafts, we reached out to a trustworthy friend who has no truck with indirect opinion, and it was our good fortune that Michael Gurian was willing to help. He carefully read our work, and then spoke directly to our weaknesses and our strengths. He made it very clear that we had a lot of work in front of us. I thank the good Lord for inventing rum at moments like this, as a shot can help ease what smarts. After a few days of exercise, healthful food, and some time in Nature, the work got organized and eventually it got done. Michael, you are a brilliant guide and a gem of a man.

No matter how good you think you are at assessing your own writing, you need someone to edit the work with vision you do not have. After researching and interviewing people to help with this task, we found someone who had the background and experience we needed to guide us in cleaning up our act, and that is Judith Larson, PhD. Judith is a clinician in private practice who is also an editor, and a fine one at that. She asked dozens of questions and suggested thousands of corrections that increased the quality and the clarity of our work, and exercised her determination and dedication through every draft to the finished book. She is a joy to work with.

Both of us have the good fortune of being married to women who invested their positive energy in us with love and respect. Robyn Gomes-Yoslow and Sue Amende-Plep, MFT, were always there for us. When a husband retreats weekly at odd hours for months that become years, time is given up for reasons that are not always obvious. As Gary's partner in this work, and his editor, Mark's incremental commitment was not always convenient for Robyn, and she fully understood his perseverance. Sue was patient and supportive but wondered what was so important about our commitment to our walks. Then she read a draft and comprehended our personal work: we were walking a path that was made of more than earth and stone.

We extend our appreciation and heartfelt thanks to The Flying Yahoos, the men's team that we founded that has been meeting for twenty years, including Barry Hayes, PhD, Walter Jesson, PhD (now deceased), Robert Land, PsyD, Stacy Smith, MA, LMFT, Kirk Watson, and the men who have passed through our men's group as members or visitors, including Adam Dorsay, PhD, and Rev. Jeff Munnis, MA, Div. This team grew out of the spiritual commitment to "holding the ground" that lives in Gary's work with men's groups and organizations, and his commitment to sharing the experience of Vision Quest with men on a spiritual journey of discovery.

In addition, we honor those who have deeply affected our perspective regarding life's challenges, gifts, and joys, including: Ken and Maria

Acknowledgments

Amende; Yosi Amram, PhD; Willie Bento, PhD; Dr. Michael Berenbaum; Ann Bernhardt, PhD; Airman Basic Michael Borzon; Tim Corcoran, Headwaters Outdoor School; Cielo Black Crow; Susan Cunningham and family; Ed de Deo, DC; Russ Davis, Gray Dog Press, guide, mentor, and friend; Rabbi Yitzchok Feldman; Maria Flaherty, PhD; Rick Gordon, LCSW; Rabbi Dov Greenburg; Michael Gurian, MFT, PhD, The Gurian Institute; Dennis Hayesly, CADC; Mildred and Ray Jacobson; Dr. Matt Levy; Brad Leslie; Brian Lippincott, PhD; Fred Luskin, PhD; John and Katie Martin; Men of Fire; Robert Morgan, PhD; Tommy Little Bear Nason; The Nation of Men/Momentum; Essie and Alan Nichols; Chris, Heather, and Sarah Plep; Dennis R. Plep and family; Olga and Helmut Plep; Henry Poon, PhD; Neal Province; Patrick Purcell, MFT; Dr. Robert Quint; Sue Richards; CMSgt Roberts; Dick Robertson and family; Mark Ruskell, DC; Mr. Russell, Brentano's Bookstore packing and shipping department; Lisa Shields, PhD; Dr. Thomas Singer of the Jung Institute, San Francisco, CA; Dr. Patricia Sohl of the Jung Institute Archive for Research in Archetypal Symbolism (ARIAS), San Francisco, CA; Justin Sterling, The Sterling Men's Weekend; Ed Sustrick; Six Man Press; team BUF; George Wettach; Morgan Yamanaka, MSW, SFSU; Miriam Schreiberg Yoslow, Ed.D. and Wilfred Littauer Yoslow, MD, FACS; AIC Chuck Brotherton, VN; LTC Ted Albright; Brigadier General Steve Butow; Members of the 129th California State Guard, most especially Colonel Roger Higby, MSG Michael Frangadakis, MSgt Nilo Cataluna, SMSgt John Clark, MSgt Ralph Bumgarner, TSgt David Dooley, LT Vadim Rotberg; AND—especially—that kid who gave Gary a Three Musketeer's Bar and changed the trajectory of his life.

References

Assagioli, R. (1965). *Psychosynthesis: A manual of principles and techniques* (2nd ed.). New York: Hobbs Dorman.

Boorstein, S. (Ed.) (1980). *Transpersonal psychotherapy*. Palo Alto: Science and Behavior Books.

Boorstein, S. (2000). Transpersonal psychotherapy. *American Journal of Psychotherapy, 54*(3), 408-423.

Bradshaw, J. (2005). *Healing the shame that binds you*. Florida: Health Communications, Inc.

Brookes, C. E. (1980). A Jungian view of transpersonal events in psychotherapy. In S. Boorstein (Ed.), *Transpersonal psychotherapy* (pp. 57-78). Palo Alto: Science & Behavior Books.

Brown, S. V. (2000). The exceptional human experience process: A preliminary model with exploratory map. *International Journal of Parapsychology, 11*(1), 69-111.

Burns, D. D. (1999). *Feeling good: The new mood therapy*. New American Library. New York. (Original work published 1980)

Childe, V. G. (1951). *Man makes himself*. New American Library. New York. (Original work published 1939)

Deida, D. (2004). *The way of the superior man*. Boulder: Sounds True. (Original work published 1997)

Dispenza, Dr. J. (2107). *Becoming supernatural: How common people are doing the uncommon.* Carlsbad, CA: Hay House.

Edinger, E. F. (1999). *Archetype of the Apocalypse: Divine vengeance, terrorism, and the end of the world.* Peru, IL: Open Court.

Ellenberger, H. (1970). *The discovery of the unconscious: The history and evolution of dynamic psychiatry.* New York: Basic Books.

Feldman, H. (2008). MCI and Alzheimer's Disease. Eighteenth meeting of the European Neurological Society 7-11 June 2008, Nice, France. *Journal of Neurology, 255*(27) (Suppl. 2).

Firman, J., & Gila, A. (1997). *The primal wound: A transpersonal view of trauma, addiction, and growth.* New York: State University of New York.

Firman, J., & Gila, A. (2002). *Psychosynthesis: A psychology of the spirit.* New York: State University of New York.

Foa, E. B., Hembree, E. A., Riggs, D., Rauch, S., & Franklin, M. (2005). *Common reactions to trauma: A National Center for PTSD fact sheet.* Philadelphia: Center for the Treatment and Study of Anxiety, Department of Psychiatry, University of Pennsylvania. Retrieved March 15, 2005 from http://www.ncptsd.va.gov/facts/disasters/fs_foa_handout.html

Foster, A. D. & Lucas, G. (1976). *Star Wars: The Adventures of Luke Skywalker.* New York: Ballentine.

Glover, R. (2003). *No more Mr. Nice Guy.* Philadelphia: Running Press.

Gurian, M. (1993). *The prince and the king: Healing the father-son wound (a guided journey of initiation).* New York: Penguin Publishing Group.

Gurian, M. (1994). *Mothers, sons, and lovers: How a man's relationship with his mother affects the rest of his life.* Boston: Shambhala.

Gurian, M. & Ballew, A. C. (2003). *Boys and girls learn differently: Action guide for teachers.* New York: John Wiley & Sons.

Gurian, M. (2006). *The wonder of boys: What parents, mentors, and educators can do to shape boys into exceptional men.* New York:

TarcherPerigee.

Gurian, M. (2010) *The invisible presence: How a man's relationship with his mother affects all his relationships with women.* Boston: Shambhala.

Hart, Tobin (2000). Transformation as process and paradox. *Journal of Transpersonal Psychology, 32* (1), 157-164.

Hui-Neng. (1990). *The diamond sutra and the sutra of Hui-Neng* (A. F. Price & M. Wong, Trans.). Boston: Shambhala.

Jones, K. B. (2003). *Addiction to hurry: Spiritual strategies for slowing down.* Valley Forge: Judson Press.

Jung, C. G. (1976b). The concept of the collective unconscious (R. F. C. Hull, Trans.). In J. Campbell (Ed.), *The portable Jung* (pp. 59-69). New York: Penguin Books.

Jung, C. G. (1976c). The relations between the ego and the unconscious (R. F. C. Hull, Trans.). In J. Campbell (Ed.), *The portable Jung* (pp. 70-138). New York: Penguin Books.

Jung, C. G. (1976d). The stages of life (R. F. C. Hull, Trans.). In J. Campbell (Ed.) *The portable Jung* (pp. 3-22). New York: Penguin Books.

Jung, C. G. (1976e). Symbols of transformation (R. F. C. Hull, Trans.). In H. Read, M. Fordham, G. Adler, & W. McGuire (Eds.), *The Collected works of C. G. Jung* (Vol. 5, pp. 121-440). Princeton, NJ: Princeton University Press. (Original work published 1956)

Jung, C. G. (1977a). The practice of psychotherapy: Essays on the psychology of the transference and other subjects (R. F. C. Hull, Trans.). In H. Read, M. Fordham, G. Adler, & W. McGuire (Eds.), *The Collected works of C. G. Jung.* (Vol. 16, pp. 163-210). Princeton, NJ: Princeton University Press. (Original work published 1954)

Jung, C. G. (1977b). Two essays on analytical psychology (R. F. C. Hull, Trans.). In H. Read, M. Fordham, G. Adler, & W. McGuire (Eds.), *The Collected works of C. G. Jung.* (Vol. 7, pp. 64-79, 90-113, 127-

138). Princeton, NJ: Princeton University Press. (Original work published 1953)

Jung, C. G. (1978). The Shadow. In R. F. C. Hull (Trans.) *Aion: Researches into the phenomenology of the self.* In H. Read, M. Fordham, G. Adler, & W. McGuire (Eds.), *The Collected works of C. G. Jung.* (Vol. 9, Pt. II, pp. 3-8). Princeton, NJ: Princeton University Press. (Original work published 1959)

Jung, C. G. (1978). The structure and dynamics of the self. In R. F. C. Hull (Trans.) *Aion: Researches into the phenomenology of the self.* In H. Read, M. Fordham, G. Adler, & W. McGuire (Eds.), *The Collected works of C. G. Jung.* (Vol. 9, Pt. II, pp. 222-265). Princeton, NJ: Princeton University Press. (Original work published 1959)

Jung, C. G. (1981). The structure and dynamics of the psyche (R. F. C. Hull, Trans.). In H. Read, M. Fordham, G. Adler, & W. McGuire (Eds.), *The Collected works of C. G. Jung.* (Vol. 8, 2nd ed., pp. 92-104, 129-138, 167-173, 200-216). Princeton, NJ: Princeton University Press. (Original work published 1960)

Jung, C. G. (1990). The archetypes and the collective unconscious (R. F. C. Hull, Trans.). In H. Read, M. Fordham, G. Adler, & W. McGuire (Eds.), *The Collected works of C. G. Jung.* (Vol. 9, Pt. I, 2nd ed., pp. 3-74). Princeton, NJ: Princeton University Press. (Original work published 1959)

Jung, C. G. (1997). Confrontation with the unconscious (R. F. C. Hull, Trans.). In J. Chodorow (Ed.), *Jung on active imagination* (pp. 21-41). Princeton, NJ: Princeton University Press.

Kalsched, D. (1996). *The inner world of trauma: Archetypal defenses of the personal spirit.* New York: Routledge.

Karasu, T. B. (1999). Spiritual psychotherapy. *American Journal of Psychotherapy, 53*(2), 143-162.

Kipnis, A. R. (1991). *Knights without armor: A practical guide for men in quest of masculine soul.* New York: Tarcher/Putnam.

Kopp, S. (1972). *If you meet the Buddha on the road, kill him.* New York: Bantam. (Pages 8-9.)

Lawrence, T. E. (1991). *Seven Pillars of Wisdom.* New York: Doubleday. (Original work published 1922)

Levine, S. (1997). *Waking the tiger: Healing trauma.* Berkeley: North Atlantic.

Long, B. (1940). *Memo from Assistant Secretary of State Breckinridge Long, to State Department officials dated June 26, 1940, outlining effective ways to obstruct the granting of U.S. visas.* Retrieved August 25, 2005, from http://www.pbs.org/ wgbh/amex/holocaust/filmmore/reference/primary/barmemo.html

Luskin, F. (2002). *Forgive for good: A proven prescription for health and happiness.* New York: HarperCollins.

Maugham, S. (2003). *The Razor's Edge.* New York: Vintage. (Original work published 1944)

Melville, H. (1950). *Moby Dick; or, the whale.* New York: Random House. (Original work published 1851)

Metzner, R. (1986). *Opening to inner light: The transformation of human nature and consciousness.* Los Angeles: Jeremy Tarcher.

Moore, R. (2013). *King, warrior, magician, lover: Rediscovering the archetypes of the mature masculine.* New York: Harper Collins.

Niederland, W. G. (1964). The problem of the survivor. *Journal of Hillside Hospital, 10*, 233-247.

Neumann, E. (1990). *Depth psychology and a new ethic* (E. Rolfe, Trans.). Boston: Shambhala. (Original work published 1969)

Oliver, M. (1986). *Dream work.* New York: Atlantic Monthly.

Ortony, A. (1988). *The cognitive structure of emotions.* New York: Cambridge University.

Palmer, G. T. (1999). *Disclosure and assimilation of exceptional human experiences: Meaningful, transformative, and spiritual aspects.* Unpublished doctoral dissertation. Institute of Transpersonal Psychology, Palo Alto, CA.

Polanyi, M. (1964). *Science, faith and society.* Chicago: University of Chicago.

Polanyi, M. (1969). *Knowing and being: Essays by Michael Polanyi* (M. Grene, Ed.). Chicago: University of Chicago.

Polanyi, M. (1983). *The tacit dimension.* Chicago: University of Chicago.

Schmitt, B. D. (1975). The Minimal Brain Dysfunction Myth. *The American Journal of Diseases of Children, 129* (11), 1313-1318.

Sprinkle, P. (2002). *Women who do too much: How to stop doing it all and start enjoying your life.* Grand Rapids: Zondervan.

Storm, H. (1972). *Seven arrows.* New York: Ballentine.

Tolle, E. (1999). *The power of now: A guide to spiritual enlightenment.* Novato: New World Library.

Truman, K. (2003). *Feelings buried alive never die.* St. George: Olympus.

Van Sant, G. (Director). (1997). *Good Will Hunting.* Los Angeles: Miramax.

Walsh, R., & Vaughn, F. (1993). The art of transcendence: An introduction to the common elements of transpersonal practices. *Journal of Transpersonal Psychology, 25*(1), 1-9.

Wilber, K. (2000). *The collected works of Ken Wilber: A brief history of everything: The eye of spirit.* Boston: Shambhala. (Original works published 1996 and 1997.)

Wood, N. (1979). *War cry on a prayer feather.* Garden City, New York: Doubleday

Yoslow, Mark. (1992) *Drugs in the body: Effects of Abuse.* New York: Franklin Watts.

References

Yoslow, M. (2007). *The pride and price of remembrance: An empirical view of post-Holocaust trauma and associated transpersonal elements in the third generation.* Unpublished Dissertation. Institute of Transpersonal Psychology.

About the Authors

Mark Yoslow, PhD

Mark has worked as a book packer in Brentano's Bookstore mailroom, a laboratory technician in cancer research, a library runner, wheel potter, advertising copywriter, ditch digger, concrete mason and brick layer, firewood supplier, cook, fitness and strength trainer, science writer, undergraduate and graduate level instructor in behavioral sciences, and a supervised psychotherapist, group therapist, and educator for patients with acute mental illness.

For 30 years, before pursuing his PhD in clinical psychology at the Institute of Transpersonal Psychology (now Sophia University), Mark wrote about brilliant minds in psychiatry, biomedical research, dermatology, orthopedics, cardiology, oncology, and microbiology for international corporations. He also writes narrative poetry, flash fiction, short stories, and novellas, pursuits that have held his attention for 56 years. His most recent work is *The Town*, a flash fiction novella about a young woman's shift in life path after being saved during a mass shooting.

Born and raised in Brooklyn, New York, Mark moved to central California and lived there for 25 years. He recently returned to New York, and now lives in the Hamptons on Long Island with his wife, Robyn, and Maru the deaf cat. After surviving heart disease and lung cancer, he invests his time in writing, long-distance cycling, swimming, and trying new recipes.

To learn more about the availability of his written work you can contact Dr. Mark Yoslow at walking.the.hill@gmail.com.

Gary H. Plep, LCSW

Gary lost his father at age three, was raised by an emotionally distant mother, and his early neglect and isolation led him to a spiritual journey in the dense forests of rainy, grey, Coos Bay Oregon. The wilderness and mother nature became his safe place. At the age of 14 Gary and his mother moved to California where his undiagnosed ADHD inhibited his success in school leading to his working in construction.

After volunteering for four years in the Air Force, including traumatic service in Vietnam, Gary experienced PTSD and yet he developed a new-found sense of self-discipline and purpose. His military service and family experiences motivated him to get an education and be of service.

He returned to construction to support himself and his family while attending college in the evenings. After completing his undergraduate degree, he worked as both a juvenile hall counselor and probation officer. Upon completion of his graduate degree and becoming a Licensed Clinical Social Worker, he practiced psychotherapy for a local hospital and transitioned into his private practice.

A deep regard for the personal knowledge gathered from childhood isolation and contemplation in nature, combined with teaching from Native American elders in the traditions of Vision Quest, inspired Gary to lead wilderness quests for over 40 years.

The events of 9-11 prompted Gary to volunteer for 13 years as a Behavioral Health Officer with the California State Guard where he was instrumental in supporting the Air National Guard.

In practice for over 40 years as a guide, mentor, and leader in men's work, he has led as many as five men's groups a week. He provides therapy for individuals and couples, and is an EMDR Trauma Specialist.

He is co-founder of Plep Psychosocial Consultants where he practices with both his wife and daughter.

Gary lives in Los Gatos California with his wife Sue of 44 years where he continues to hike, walk Levi, explore, plant trees and spend time with his three children and grandchildren. Contact: camensctr@aol.com.

www.ingramcontent.com/pod-product-compliance
Lightning Source LLC
Chambersburg PA
CBHW062031290426
44109CB00026B/2598